HOUSING AND URBAN SPATIAL STRUCTURE; A CASE STUDY

Housing and Urban Spatial Structure; A Case Study

HARRY W. RICHARDSON
University of Southern California

JOAN VIPOND
University of New South Wales

ROBERT FURBEY
Sheffield Polytechnic

SAXON **H** HOUSE | LEXINGTON BOOKS

Published by

SAXON HOUSE, D. C. Heath Ltd.
Westmead, Farnborough, Hants., England.

Jointly with

LEXINGTON BOOKS, D. C. Heath & Co.
Lexington, Mass. USA.

ISBN 0 347 01108 X

Printed in Great Britain
by Unwin Brothers Limited
The Gresham Press, Old Woking, Surrey
A member of the Staples Printing Group

Contents

List of tables

List of figures

Preface

This book is the major product of a research project on 'Property Values since 1905: Analysis of Data from the Register of Sasines' conducted at the Centre for Research in the Social Sciences at the University of Kent at Canterbury. The project has received generous financial support from the Social Science Research Council since 1970. Without this support it would have been impossible to undertake this research and we are very grateful indeed to the Council for its help.

We should also like to thank: Mr G. Black, Keeper of the Register of Sasines, for his encouragement; Mr R.C. Fulton, who supervised the research assistants and solved many tricky problems arising during the project; the team of research assistants: Mrs A. Black, Mr C. Finlayson, Mrs A.C. Fulton, Mrs C.F.K. Lorimer, Mrs I. Martin, Miss L. Matheson, Mrs L. Skea and Mrs S. Swift in Edinburgh, and Mrs Z. Voisey-Youlden in Canterbury; the computer programmers: Miss J. Dobby, Mrs P. Sales and Miss P. Jones; the punch operators: Mrs M. Double and Mrs S. Gates; and the secretaries: Mrs S. Sharples and Miss B. Phelps. Professor T.C. Barker was very helpful, particularly when we were getting the project under way, Mr I.R. Gordon and Mr P.S. Taylor gave us the benefit of their advice on technical points, and Mr D. McCrone and Mr B. Elliot of the University of Edinburgh were kind enough to make available to us some results of their study of landlordism in Edinburgh.

We are grateful to the editors of the *Scottish Journal of Political Economy, Urban Studies* and *Town Planning Review* for permission to use material in Chapters 4–6 and 8 of this book derived from papers first published in these journals.

Harry W. Richardson
Joan Vipond
Robert Furbey
April 1974

1 Historical Background

Introduction

The comprehensiveness and legal reliability of the Register of Sasines over a period spanning most of the twentieth century[1] offers a great opportunity to test empirically some of the models of urban spatial structure developed in the social sciences. However, it is first only fair to acknowledge the limitations of urban models intended as general theories. For example, Briggs (1968, pp. 33–4) argues: 'However much the historian talks of common urban problems, he will find that one of his most interesting tasks is to show in what respect cities differed from each other ... nineteenth-century cities not only had markedly different topography, different economic and social structures, and quite different degrees of interest in their surrounding regions, but they responded differently to the urban problems which they shared in common'. Hence, it is not surprising to find that the elegance and internal consistency of general models of the city, such as the concentric zone theory (Burgess, 1925; Haig, 1926) depend crucially on unrealistic assumptions and the models have to be modified drastically to accommodate the specifics and local distortions of each case. More recent writers, particularly sociologists, have been less willing to leave local factors in the sidelines and have instead stressed the importance of the interaction between local and more general processes (for example, Plowman, Minchinton and Stacey, 1962; Foster, 1968). They have also been able to take account of the role of the individual and social groups in the creation of a city, and show that the city is not entirely the product of impersonal economic and social forces.

If nineteenth-century cities are so varied it is possible that no 'model city' exists. Thus, even if Edinburgh is used as a case study for testing general theories, it is also necessary to give some attention to the effects of the city's long and eventful history, its physical geography and its distinctive socio-economic structure on the development of its present day spatial structure. This may not only improve interpretation of the empirical results and their relation to urban theory but also, by drawing attention to the importance of local factors in Edinburgh, may suggest lines of inquiry for other local case studies.

1

Site and situation

The evidence suggesting human settlement for over 4,000 years in the Edinburgh area indicates the suitability of the site for development (Watson, 1967). However, the area by no means corresponds to the featureless plain of urban theory (Losch, 1954). Instead, the tectonic movements, glacial erosion and deposition, and igneous activity which together produced Edinburgh's distinctive topography, have exerted a major influence on both the nature and extent of the city's development. The most obvious of these land-forming processes is the igneous eruption which penetrated the softer carboniferous sandstones and shales of the area to form massive outcrops of rock which are highly resistant to erosion. Not only did these volcanic outcrops withstand erosion by the retreating ice of the glacial period, they also provided protection to the softer material in their wake.

It is upon the most distinct 'crag and tail' of this kind that Edinburgh first developed from the Castle Rock, a military strong-point, down what is now the Royal Mile to Holyrood Palace. The largest crag, however, is Arthur's Seat, composed of a huge basalt core which has served to consolidate the surrounding rocks in the face of various forms of erosion (R. Richardson, 1902, p. 339). Rising to 823 feet and lying within two miles of the Castle Rock, Arthur's Seat and the nearby Salisbury Crags are a formidable obstacle to urban development and today form the nucleus of the large Holyrood Park. Still closer to the city centre, though much smaller, is Calton Hill, consisting largely of volcanic ash but reinforced by layers of solid lava (R. Richardson, 1902, p. 347). Further igneous activity produced more high ground in areas now in suburban Edinburgh. In the south the Blackford, Braid and Craiglockhart Hills rise to 539, 675 and 575 feet respectively and in the west Corstorphine Hill is 529 feet high.

The glacial period was an important phase in the creation of Edinburgh's topography in two respects. First, in the course of its retreat the ice deposited a thick, undulating layer of boulder clay over a large part of the region and contributed to the formation of the higher land of the Lauriston, George Street and Grange ridges. Second, the undulating nature of the land was accentuated by the erosive quality of the ice. The scouring effect which produced the examples of crag-and-tail formation also produced the deepened channel of Edinburgh's main river, the Water of Leith, and the steep depressions flanking the Castle Rock of the Nor' Loch, Holyrood Loch and the Cowgate which, prior to artificial drainage, severely limited the burgh's expansion. Indeed, lakes were a prominent feature in the early Edinburgh landscape, many being contained in the lower areas of boulder clay, notably one of a mile's length stretching from Gogar to Corstorphine and another two miles long from Corstorphine to the Haymarket. Only Duddingston Loch survives of these lakes. Smith (1964) notes that the level ground created by both natural and artificial drainage has been most important for urban development.

To the south of the carboniferous sedimentary rock which lies under most of Edinburgh City are the older igneous rocks of the Pentland Hills. This range of hills is composed of harder rock as well as being the product of tectonic faulting and the up-turning of strata; it provides a strict constraint on the southward expansion of the city (Smith, 1964).

Not all the region is marked by such dramatic land-forming processes. Large parts of the northern and northeastern areas of the city are situated on a series of low and relatively level raised beaches produced by marine deposits. From Leith, built largely upon the lowest, nearest beach, the land slopes gently upwards toward central Edinburgh, the highest areas of raised beach exceeding 100 feet (R. Richardson, 1902, pp. 339–40). In addition, the mere existence of the sea has also influenced the course of the city's development for its expansion has absorbed several old-established settlements such as Leith, Granton and Newhaven based upon fishing and shipbuilding, and Portobello, once fashionable for its sea-bathing. The northeastern constraint on expansion due to the sea has also resulted in the relative displacement of the Castle Rock away from the geometric centre of the city as development has been forced to concentrate to the south and west.

Finally, the geology of the area exerted a number of more indirect effects upon the twentieth-century spatial structure of Edinburgh. For example, the fine building stone available locally permitted elegant and solid construction in the older areas which has influenced the history of Edinburgh's 'inner city', while the existence of soft water and of coal measures in the limestones of the southeast has had great significance for the industrial life of the city.

If the site of Edinburgh itself was very suitable for the growth of human settlement, the same is also true of the *regional* location of the city. Edinburgh developed in 'a gap within a gap' (Watson, 1967), being situated in a strategic position between the Pentland Hills and the Firth of Forth, which in turn are found between the Highlands and the Southern Uplands of Scotland. It is not surprising therefore, to find Edinburgh at the intersection of several important routes including those from England via Berwick and Dunbar; Aberdeen and Dundee via Queensferry; Stirling; Glasgow; and England via Carlisle and Biggar. The proximity of Leith and

Granton harbours, particularly in modern times, has encouraged commerce and industry in the city by providing convenient trading links with London and overseas, particularly Scandinavia.

Early history

Although the discovery of Roman bricks in the foundations of St. Margaret's Chapel in Edinburgh Castle suggests that the Castle Rock was fortified and settled at least by the late pre-Christian era (Russell, 1922, p. 19), little of Edinburgh's earliest history is known. One of the first recorded incidents is the grant by David I to the Abbey of Holyrood out of his rents accruing from the burgh of Edinburgh, indicating Edinburgh's established status as a king's burgh by the twelfth century. In view of the later expansion of the city it is interesting to learn of a second grant by the King to the Abbot of the land on which the separate burgh of Canongate developed between the Castle and the Abbey, a mile away from the latter (Macrae, 1949, p. 6). This indicates how small was the area occupied by the burgh in the early medieval period.

To the modern observer, what is now called the 'Old Town' of Edinburgh, with its tall, densely packed buildings, stands in sharp contrast to the expansive, orderly boulevards of the 'New Town' across the valley. However, Macrae (1949, p. 6) detects a definite plan in the spatial structure of medieval Edinburgh when houses lined what are now called the Lawnmarket and the High Street which together formed a broad thoroughfare extending down the tail of the Castle Rock towards Holyrood. In these early centuries land use on the ridge was not intensive and the plots on which the houses stood extended down the steep north and south slopes of the ridge. As the population grew, however, and as the burgh became constricted by the defensive city wall reconstructed between the fourteenth and early sixteenth centuries, so the density of settlement increased and the long strips of land which had hitherto been gardens began to be occupied by buildings. These additional dwellings were gradually separated only by the steep and narrow 'wynds' which Youngson (1966) likens to 'ribs' extending from the backbone of the main street.

Particularly interesting in view of this book's central concern with spatial structure is the observation that, although few individual medieval buildings have survived 'the whole medieval pattern and plan of the Old Town is still unchanged' (Macrae, 1949, p. 8). In addition to this general influence of the period prior to the mid-sixteenth century, the city's early history influenced later spatial structure in at least two other important respects.

First, with the Reformation and the disestablishment of the Roman Catholic Church, a large area of land to the south of the burgh became available for a change in land use. Mary Queen of Scots granted these lands to the town council for educational and other social purposes, a decree which led to the construction of buildings such as the High School (1578), the College (1581), the Surgeon's Hall (1697) and the Royal Infirmary (1738) (Macrae, 1949, pp. 9–10). Modern maps of the city show that this social and cultural use of the relatively central area south of the Cowgate and the Grassmarket has persisted.

Second, study of the early relationship between Edinburgh and its local port of Leith helps in understanding the modern structure of the city which, of course, incorporates Leith within its boundaries. In his history of Leith, Russell observes that 'a good deal of more or less unfriendly feeling has always existed between Edinburgh and Leith' (Russell, 1922, p. 70), and traces this rivalry from roots in the social, economic and political arrangements of the Middle Ages (ibid., pp. 70–134). Although it is probably an older settlement than Edinburgh, Leith undoubtedly owed its prominence as a port to the development of Edinburgh and the latter's importance as a royal burgh. However, the relationship between the two burghs in the Middle Ages was in many respects exploitative.

By being resident upon the royal demesne, the people of Edinburgh had as their feudal lord the supreme landowner in the kingdom. Hence, in addition to the rights of protection and landholding generally held by subjects within their lord's estate during the medieval period, they enjoyed privileges which extended beyond the boundaries of their burgh. Most significant of these privileges when discussing the relationship between Edinburgh and Leith were the right to trade anywhere in the country without paying toll, the right to inherit capital or goods, and the sole monopoly of conducting foreign trade. These concessions were important as a stimulus to the growth of a merchant class and to the associated development of Edinburgh as a trading centre with Leith as its port. Since Edinburgh's privileges were bought by its people at high cost in terms of labour and military service and since the limited returns from overseas trade made commercial competition undesirable it is not surprising that Edinburgh was vigilant in maintaining its rights over Leith.

In addition to its control over trade, during the late fourteenth century Edinburgh began to secure a still more direct form of power over Leith, for by purchasing the feudal rights of the traditional land superiors of Leith she gradually acquired the complete authority over the lives of the

Leithers characteristic of the feudal overlord. The relationship between the two towns came to be that of master to serf and Leith was governed according to the interests of the Merchant Guild of Edinburgh, members of which had the monopoly of membership of the town council of the city. Leith's subordinate position was maintained long after the social, economic and political conditions in which it developed had changed. It was not until the harbour and docks came under the control of the Dock Commission in 1826, the town elected its own Member of Parliament under the Burgh Reform Act of 1833, and was made a municipal burgh with the right of electing its own town council in the same year that the last legal remains of the feudal relationship were rescinded. During the preceding centuries Leith had no form of political representation, either national or local. The effects of this on the twentieth-century spatial structure of Edinburgh are not quantifiable but the low class residential areas and the environmental impoverishment of Leith compared with Edinburgh may be traced, at least in part, to this historical rivalry and specialization between the two towns.

The period from the late Middle Ages to the mid-eighteenth century contained many obstacles to the growth in size and wealth of Edinburgh. Early in the period the burgh lived under the constant threat of invasion from England, a threat that was realised in 1513, culminating in the disastrous battle at Flodden, and in 1544 with the actual devastation of Edinburgh by the Earl of Hertford. With the Union of Crowns in 1603 a state of war between Scotland and England was impossible, but it was not until the suppression of the 1745 Jacobite rebellion that the turmoil associated with the decay of medieval society, the Reformation, and the struggle for the monarchy was ended. Even the developments connected with peace were of uncertain benefit to Edinburgh. For instance, several writers have remarked upon the great loss in prosperity and prestige of the burgh with the departure of the Court and Parliament to London in 1603 and 1707 respectively (Gilbert, 1901, pp. 7–10; Adams, 1910, p. 311; Youngson, 1966, p. 8).

The stagnation associated with these events helps to explain why Edinburgh remained, with a few minor exceptions such as the milling settlements on the Water of Leith, inside its city walls for much longer than required by purely military considerations. Nevertheless, the population continued to grow and the inevitable result was increasing overcrowding in the burgh. Gilbert (1901, pp. 7–8) stated that the inhabitants of seventeenth and early eighteenth-century Edinburgh 'had learned the art of building into the air in the days when it was necessary that houses should be crowded together within the walls for mutual protection'. Macrae suggests that it was during this chapter in the city's history that 'The tenement of several storeys became a fixed feature of life in the Old Town and gave a set in this direction when two centuries later the rapid growth of population in the Industrial Age had to be housed' (Macrae, 1949, p. 9). Inside these tall tenements there developed a kind of vertical class segregation with the rich, the learned, and the titled occupying the middle floors and the middle classes the adjacent storeys. This spatial proximity of classes is seen by Young (1967, pp. 8–11) as an ideal setting for 'a unique cross-fertilization' of ideas and customs and important in endowing the subsequent so-called Scottish Enlightenment with its characteristic versatility and practicality.

The late eighteenth and nineteenth centuries

In the middle of the eighteenth century a social revolution in the life of Edinburgh completely overshadowed the preceding moribund period. The coming of the Enlightenment had a direct and dramatic effect upon the spatial structure of the city and confirmed it as the administrative, cultural and commercial centre it has since remained.

The conditions promoting the intense activity of eighteenth-century Edinburgh were as complex as those surrounding the age of the Enlightenment during which it took place. The intellectual climate of the period was characterised by the growing challenge of reason to the traditional religious world-view and by optimism in the potential for human progress. Scotland could boast a major contribution to this movement in the work of such scholars and scientists as Adam Smith, Adam Ferguson, David Hume, James Watt and James Nasmyth. However, in eighteenth-century Scotland intellectual change was also paralleled by technological advances, notably in printing, agriculture and the use of water power for manufacturing, which were both a cause and a consequence of a reorganization of economic arrangements and social relations. In this period of unprecedented economic expansion it was the new middle classes of merchants and manufacturers who acquired a disproportionate share of the growing total wealth (Youngson, 1966, p. 40). The interests and ambitions of the merchant and professional middle class of Edinburgh were in the vanguard of the city's eighteenth-century advance. In their 'Proposals for carrying on certain Public Works in the City of Edinburgh', Sir Gilbert Elliott and George Drummond stressed the need to stem the drift of the wealthy towards London by a programme of planned construction which would make Edinburgh a more attractive city in which to live and encourage the commercial expansion which its exceptional situation and proximity to the port of Leith warranted.

Despite Edinburgh's gradual decline in relation to London, its capital city role as a source of winter society for the Scottish landowning class, and as a centre of education and for the professions with their associated industries of papermaking, bookbinding, and the service trades, ensured that these plans received a positive response. The guaranteed peace which followed the abortive 1745 Jacobite rebellion was a further factor encouraging investment in the development of Edinburgh and, in 1767, a major barrier to the implementation of the plans was removed when the Royalty, the area within which the privileges of a royal burgh were enjoyed (Youngson, 1966, p. 297), was extended.

The story of the construction of the 'New Town' is well documented and requires little elaboration in this study. The construction of the North Bridge and the Mound across the Nor Loch served to link the Old City with the New Town, the first stage of which was designed by James Craig. The buildings and the street plan of the area immediately north of the loch reflect the classical heritage of the Enlightenment and the rationality and optimism of the period with the broad boulevards of Princes Street, George Street and Queen Street and the geometric regularity of the street pattern. The South Bridge across the Cowgate was opened in 1788 and paved the way for extensive development south of the city, including the new university buildings.

The expansion of the New Town continued to the north with Reid's Heriot Row extension, to the west with James Gillespie's development on the Earl of Moray's land, and to the east with Playfair's redesigning of the Calton Hill area. The many public buildings constructed before the great expansion in the 1830s included Register House, the Royal High School, the Exchange, the City Observatory and the Post Office.

'Edinburgh is one of the few cities in the world which have been definitely planned on a large scale' (Adams, 1910, p. 311). Macrae (1949, p. 13) commented on the unprecedented involvement of local government as the planning authority, a local government which was as yet unreformed by the Act of 1835 and described by Youngson (1966, pp. 49–50) as 'an oligarchy of a few tradesmen and merchants, supported by "men of taste" and guided in some degree by the legal profession'. Certainly, in physical appearance, geographical area, and spatial structure, there was a marked difference between the Edinburgh of the early Victorian period and the medieval burgh of the early eighteenth century. Those initiating the changes would have taken great satisfaction in the success of modern Edinburgh as a centre of tourism, the arts and entertainment, for one of their aims was to make the city comparable with London in such amenities. Their aim of stimulating the commercial life of the city also seems to have succeeded. Evidence for this is seen in the extension to Leith docks completed in 1806 (Gilbert, 1901, pp. 33–4) and in the dramatic increase in population from 66,000 in 1801 to 136,000 in 1831, an increase in line with the general urbanization trends of the period but not possible within the limits of the Old Town.

By removing some of the wealthier inhabitants from the crowded Old Town to the strictly residential and cultural world of the New Town on the other side of Princes Street Gardens, spatial segregation of social classes in Edinburgh was inevitably increased. However, apart from the need for domestic servants resident in the huge new Georgian houses, there was some low class housing nearby. 'Within a stone's throw of the elegant mansions of Charlotte Square are the mean flats of Rose Street, occupied by the poor' (Adams, 1910, p. 314). Nevertheless, Adams also records that in the New Town 'there is no unpleasant *(sic)* contact between the classes'. With the coming of the New Town, though there was still considerable residential intermingling, the housing of one class literally above another was reduced.

Impressive though it seemed at the time, the spatial growth of Edinburgh during the Georgian period was by modern standards quite limited. Virtually the entire city was still within a one-mile radius of the Castle Rock. However, although Edinburgh could by no means be described primarily as an industrial city (see pp. 40–2), it shared in the general increase in prosperity associated with Britain's nineteenth-century advance in manufacturing and trade. The major change from the point of view of Edinburgh's modern spatial structure was the introduction of steam power as a transport technology.

The coming of railway transport had a considerable effect on the subsequent development of Edinburgh and continues to exert a powerful influence on the city's modern spatial structure. National rail links with Glasgow, London and northwest England via Carlisle were opened in 1842, 1846 and 1848 respectively and provided an important means of expansion for local commerce and industry. In addition, stimulated by intense competition between the North British and Caledonian railway companies, a fairly extensive suburban rail complex had developed by the end of the century, providing for the carriage of both freight and passengers (Hunter, 1964).

Although the railways had to compete within the actual boundaries of Edinburgh and Leith with the tramways, at first horse drawn and then at the end of the century the steam-powered cable variety, there are several reasons why the railway was a more important nineteenth-century determinant of Edinburgh's subsequent spatial structure. First, several settlements such as Corstorphine, Slateford, Joppa, and Barnton which lay outside the city and therefore also outside the tramway system were nevertheless either situated on or linked with main railway lines into central Edinburgh. As a national rather than a municipal transport system, the railways provided the first rapid transport link for future suburbs with their city centre. Second, the circuitous route of some of the suburban lines, notably the southern Edinburgh loop which passed through the growing fashionable suburbs of Morningside and Newington, in addition to linking these districts with one another by cutting across the radial tram routes, also offered a means of transport to the city centre for people living between these routes in areas such as Blackford. Third, the railways in Edinburgh, as in other cities, determined future land use directly by devouring large areas of what is today relatively central land, the most prominent example being Waverley Station itself.

Finally, the railways influenced modern land use and spatial structure in a more indirect manner. Historically, the limited manufacturing industry of Edinburgh and district tended to concentrate near the water power afforded by the Water of Leith, particularly in Leith where the sea port also attracted manufacturing firms. Briggs' generalization that the railways received their 'first impetus' from 'groups of active businessmen' (1968, p. 13) appears to be applicable to Edinburgh. The city's new railways satisfied the interests of factory owners by supplying the transport facilities to promote industrial expansion.[2] Thus, the railways, being cheaper to construct on level ground, reinforced industrial concentration on low ground, a tendency which persists in modern Edinburgh. The environmental disamenity created by both the industry and the railways and the need for working-class housing in the last quarter of the nineteenth century led to the first areas of uniformly working-class housing such as Dalry, Gorgie, Abbeyhill, Easter Road, Bonnington and Leith on the adjacent low-lying land. At the same time, the growing Victorian middle-class suburbs developed on the well-segregated, more attractive, and usually higher land of Merchiston, Morningside, Grange and Newington in the south and Trinity in the north.

Hence, if the new technologies and commercial organization of the Victorian period induced rapid population growth and higher population densities in Edinburgh as elsewhere, these same innovations, and especially the introduction of rail transport, moulded the spatial structure and expansion paths of the city. Although the railways, particularly the suburban lines, have now become relatively unimportant in the social and economic life of Edinburgh, their impact on the city's modern spatial structure remains.

This analysis of the history of Edinburgh to the beginning of the present century, though necessarily brief, has provided several examples of the importance of local topography and history in the formation of the city's modern spatial structure. The feudal relationship with Leith, the constraints placed upon expansion by the city wall, the threat of war, the limited area of the Royalty and the early introduction of town planning in the eighteenth century are particular to the Edinburgh case and rule out an explanation of twentieth-century land use in the city *solely* in terms of abstract theory. Even where these local factors reflect a more widely experienced phenomenon, such as the effects of Victorian economic expansion or the growth of the railways, their impacts have been influenced by the unique physical environment and social class and economic structure of Edinburgh itself. Allowing for even more specific factors, such as the power of feuars[3] to control land use[4] or the effects on the spatial structure of Greater Edinburgh of the absorption of old settlements such as Portobello into its periphery in 1896, adds further complications to any attempt to rely on a general analysis.

Notes

[1] The Register itself is, of course, much older going back as far as 1617. A new Register was started in 1871, but the virtue of the second modern Register begun in 1905 is that comprehensive price data were included for the first time.

[2] Youngson's account of the conflict over the siting of Waverley Station reveals that, though there was much powerful opposition to the railways, the growing commercial interests of the shop proprietors and hoteliers were an important factor in the eventual acceptance of the railway route through Princes Street Gardens (Youngson, 1966, pp. 276–8).

[3] See the description of the Scottish land tenure system in chapter 3, pp. 49–69.

[4] As for example when the George Heriot Trust, as feuar, prevented the erection of working-class housing on a site at Pilrig (Gordon, 1971, pp. 237–8).

2   The Social and Economic Development of Edinburgh

Edinburgh at the beginning of the twentieth century

This section presents a backcloth for the analysis which follows via a description of the social and economic structure of Edinburgh at the beginning of the century, based on the 1901 census. Figure 2.1 illustrates the area of the city at this time compared with its extent today. Leith retained its separate burgh status until its inclusion within Edinburgh in 1920, although the two burghs were spatially contiguous long before 1900.

Since the 1901 census statistics were collected for the county of Edinburgh, for the combined burghs within the county of Edinburgh, and for the burgh of Edinburgh itself, care must be taken to specify the unit of analysis in the following discussion. Although the burgh accounted for 304,000 of the total county population of 489,000 in 1901, the importance of mining, agriculture and other industrial sectors will exaggerate the importance of some sources of employment if the county data are equated too readily with those referring to the burgh. More important, statistics in 1901 were not published at the enumeration district level adopted in more modern censuses so that this census is of limited value in building up a picture of the internal spatial structure of the city at that time. However, census returns were aggregated at the level of the larger registration district unit so that it is possible to make some observations on population movements within Edinburgh.

Tables 2.1 and 2.2 show that, in the sixty years prior to 1901, the county of Edinburgh expanded its population much faster than Scotland as a whole. However, the county data for Lanark, Renfrew and Dumbarton show that Glasgow and the other industrial towns of the Western Lowlands grew still faster, and maintained their higher rate relative to Scotland up to the end of the nineteenth century, whereas the rate of population growth in Edinburgh converged towards the overall Scottish rate. Part of the urban expansion could be explained by rural depopulation, as suggested by the negative growth rates of Perth and Argyll.

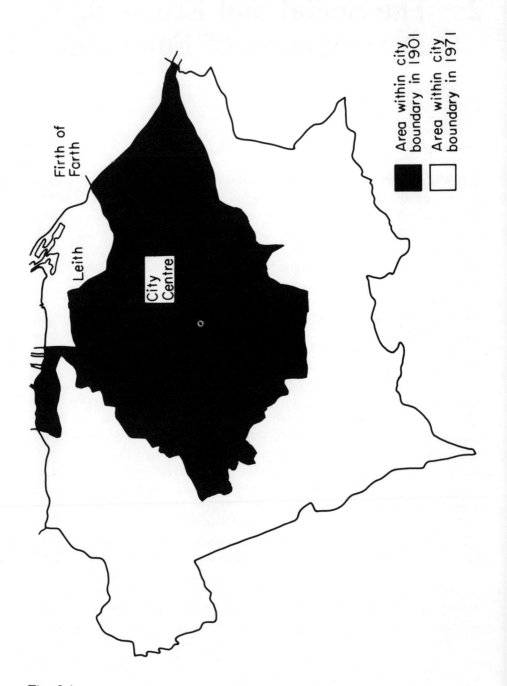

Fig. 2.1

14

Table 2.1

Total population of Scotland, the County of Edinburgh, and other selected counties, 1841–1901

	Total population						
	1841	1851	1861	1871	1881	1891	1901
Scotland	2,260,184	2,888,742	3,062,294	3,360,018	3,735,573	4,025,647	4,472,103
Edinburgh	225,454	259,435	273,997	328,379	389,164	434,276	488,796
Lanark	426,972	530,169	631,566	765,339	904,412	1,105,899	1,339,327
Renfrew	155,072	161,091	177,561	216,947	263,374	230,812	268,980
Dumbarton	44,296	45,103	52,034	58,857	75,333	98,014	113,865
Perth	137,457	138,660	133,500	127,768	129,007	122,185	123,283
Argyll	97,371	89,298	79,724	75,679	76,468	74,085	73,642

Source: Abstracted from Registrar General for Scotland (1902); *Census for Scotland, 1901;* vol. 1, table XIX.

Table 2.2

Rates of increase of the population of Scotland, the County of Edinburgh, and other selected counties, 1841–1901

	Percentage increase or decrease in population					
	1841–51	1851–61	1861–71	1871–81	1881–91	1891–1901
Scotland	27·8	6·0	9·72	11·18	7·77	11·09
Edinburgh	15·1	5·6	19·85	18·51	11·59	12·55
Lanark	24·2	19·1	21·18	18·17	22·28	21·11
Renfrew	3·9	10·2	22·18	21·40	−12·36	16·54
Dumbarton	1·8	15·4	13·11	27·99	30·11	16·17
Perth	0·9	− 3·7	− 4·29	0·97	− 5·29	0·90
Argyll	− 8·3	−10·7	− 5·07	1·04	− 3·11	− 0·60

Source: Abstracted from Registrar General for Scotland (1902); *Census for Scotland, 1901;* vol. 1, table XXI.

Although Edinburgh acquired considerable numbers from rural Scotland (table 2.3), the city did not experience the same degree of immigration from Ireland as the Glasgow area. Table 2.3 also shows that, although the county contained relatively more immigrants from England, the Empire and foreign countries than Scotland as a whole, reflecting its more cosmopolitan character and its role as a capital city, the proportion of its population born in Ireland was only about one-half of the Scottish share and one-quarter of that in the western counties of Lanark, Renfrew and Dumbarton. The absence of large-scale immigration from Ireland to work in local industry is important both as a determinant of the different social structure of Edinburgh from that of Glasgow and district and as a component in their differential population growth.

The age structure of Edinburgh's population (both male and female) had a bias in 1901 in favour of the intermediate age groups relative to the whole of Scotland (table 2.4). While the statistics for the male population of Glasgow and the female population of Dundee exhibit a similar pattern, this tendency for a higher proportion of the population to be in the main working age groups is more marked in Edinburgh than in any of the other large burghs. In Aberdeen (both sexes), Dundee (males) and Glasgow (females) there are signs of an opposite trend. This age structure characteristic of Edinburgh's population, not common to other Scottish burghs, is in part a consequence of the city's role as an employment centre. Since it had a larger proportion of young people of both sexes than Edinburgh and a much lower proportion of people aged over sixty years, the inclusion of Leith within Edinburgh raises the proportion of young people nearer to the Scottish average but reduces still further the relative proportion of old people.

Table 2.5 throws light on the socio-economic structure of Edinburgh in 1901 relative to that of other burghs. Occupational data were arranged rather differently in 1901 from the classifications employed in more recent censuses. Economically active members of the population were arranged into 23 orders corresponding to sectors within the employment market (i.e. industries) rather than to levels of skill or status. The orders were grouped into 6 broad 'classes' to permit comparison with the socio-economic data of the 1891 census, and these are used in table 2.5. Although there is no 'vertical' classification comparable with that adopted for the 1966 census, the 'horizontal' scheme used in 1901 nevertheless illuminates the socio-economic structure of the city reasonably well. For example, a large professional and administrative class or a large industrial class would be suggestive of the type of city and of the relative size of its middle or working classes.

First, looking at males, compared with the other Scottish cities of Glasgow and Dundee, Edinburgh had in 1901 a much larger professional and administrative class and a significantly smaller industrial class. In addition, Edinburgh had a larger proportion classified as 'unoccupied and non-productive' (class VI). These differences primarily reflect Edinburgh's role as a capital city, and its associated functions as a governmental, administrative, financial, legal, academic, cultural, educational and

16

Table 2.3

Birthplaces, 1901

	Percentage of persons born in											
	United Kingdom							Abroad				
	Scotland			England	Wales	Ireland	Isle of Man or Channel Islands	British colonies or dependencies	British subjects by birth	British subjects by naturalisation	Born at sea (British subjects)	Foreign
	Within county	Outside county	Total for Scotland									
Scotland	–		91·36	2·94	0·06	4·59	0·02	0·36	0·24	0·03	0·01	0·40
Edinburgh	65·28	34·72	90·94	4·83	0·08	2·45	0·04	0·73	0·27	0·07	0·01	0·58
Lanark	73·87	26·13	85·99	3·41	0·08	9·05	0·03	0·35	0·30	0·04	0·01	0·75
Renfrew	69·41	30·59	87·21	2·52	0·05	9·42	0·02	0·28	0·28	0·03	0·01	0·19
Dumbarton	55·17	44·83	87·64	2·64	0·05	8·66	0·03	0·33	0·30	0·02	0·01	0·32

Source: Abstracted from Registrar General for Scotland (1903); *Census for Scotland, 1901*: vol. 2, table XLV.

Table 2.4

Age distribution of population, 1901

	Percentage of males at each age					Percentage of females at each age				
	Total under 15	Total under 20	20–40	40–60	60+	Total under 15	Total under 20	20–40	40–60	60+
Scotland	34·77	45·37	31·07	16·95	6·61	32·19	41·98	31·77	17·62	8·63
Edinburgh	31·26	41·71	34·30	17·96	6·01	25·98	36·16	36·44	18·93	8·42
Leith	34·00	44·25	33·38	17·29	5·08	32·94	42·87	32·76	17·61	6·70
Glasgow	32·51	42·87	35·32	17·22	4·59	34·57	41·63	35·01	17·14	6·21
Dundee	35·79	47·11	29·78	17·02	6·09	29·55	38·86	33·91	19·35	7·88
Aberdeen	36·96	48·00	29·91	15·85	6·24	31·54	41·94	32·06	17·30	8·68

Source: Abstracted from Registrar General for Scotland (1903); *Census for Scotland, 1901*: vol. 2, tables XIX, XX, XXV and XXVI.

Table 2.5

Occupational classes of Edinburgh, Leith, Glasgow, Dundee, 1901
(male and female)

	Total occupied and unoccupied		Total engaged in occupations classes I–V		Professional class I		Domestic class II		Commercial class III		Agriculture and fishing class IV		Industrial class V		Unoccupied and non-productive class VI	
	M	F	M	F	M	F	M	F	M	F	M	F	M	F	M	F
Edinburgh	100·00	100·00	82·11	37·73	9·10	3·02	1·55	16·05	18·68	2·56	1·06	0·11	51·72	15·99	17·89	62·27
Edinburgh & Leith	100·00	100·00	82·73	36·50	8·20	2·81	1·37	14·83	20·95	2·48	1·14	0·10	51·03	16·28	17·26	63·49
Leith	100·00	100·00	85·13	30·69	4·94	1·83	0·68	9·03	29·70	2·12	1·47	0·08	48·34	17·63	14·87	69·31
Glasgow	100·00	100·00	86·95	36·77	3·97	1·95	0·64	7·95	20·73	2·81	0·32	0·06	61·29	24·00	13·05	63·23
Dundee	100·00	100·00	86·64	51·66	3·49	1·50	0·67	4·14	16·10	1·11	0·71	0·03	65·67	44·88	13·36	48·34

Source: Calculated on the basis of Registrar General for Scotland (1903); *Census of Scotland, 1901*; vol. 3, table XII.

medical centre. The large 'non-productive' male component is due to the substantial proportion of the population attending educational institutions, bolstered by the high value attached to education in Scotland in general and Edinburgh in particular. The relatively small industrial class underlines the limited importance of manufacturing industry in the history of Edinburgh as compared with Glasgow, Dundee and other Victorian cities. The larger male domestic sector in Edinburgh is indicative of the very different social class structure from that in Glasgow and Dundee.

The female employment statistics tend to confirm these observations. The domestic female class in Edinburgh in 1901 was proportionately twice the size of that in Glasgow and four times that in Dundee, though far fewer women were employed in industry. As shown in tables 2.6 and 2.7, the sex ratio in Edinburgh favoured females far more than elsewhere in Scotland, and the proportion of spinsters was much higher, both facts

Table 2.6

Sex ratios, 1901

Area	Scotland	Edinburgh	Lanark	Renfrew	Dumbarton
Proportion of females to 100 males	105·73	112·10	98·67	106·26	101·18

Source: Abstracted from Registrar General for Scotland (1902); *Census for Scotland, 1901;* vol. 1, table VI.

Table 2.7

Marital status of females, 1901

	Percentage to total females aged 15 years and over		
	Spinsters	Wives	Widows
Scotland	44·47	44·28	11·25
Edinburgh	47·40	41·21	11·39
Lanark	40·05	49·06	10·90
Renfrew	44·54	44·26	11·20
Dumbarton	43·90	45·43	10·67

Source: Abstracted from Registrar General for Scotland (1903); *Census for Scotland, 1901;* vol. 2, table XXVIII.

supporting the hypothesis that Edinburgh, with its unusually large upper and middle class, provided large outlets for employment of women in domestic service. Table 2.5 also shows that a much larger proportion of women was to be found in professional or administrative occupations in Edinburgh than in Glasgow and Dundee. The census shows that most of these were employed in schools and other educational institutions.[1] Although the female activity rate in Edinburgh was about equal to Glasgow's, it lagged very far behind that in Dundee, where the jute industry offered considerable manufacturing opportunities for women.

Leith had a very distinct socio-economic structure from that of Edinburgh despite its geographical proximity and imminent integration. For both sexes its professional class and its female domestic class, while larger than in Glasgow and Dundee, were much smaller than in Edinburgh itself. Surprisingly, in view of the concentration of Edinburgh's industries in Leith, its male industrial class was even smaller than that of Edinburgh. The explanation of this paradox is a very large commercial class, much larger even than that of Glasgow. Clerks and accountants for shipping companies, dockworkers, warehousemen, porters and railway workers in Leith, were all classified as belonging to the commercial class in the 1901 census. Combining Edinburgh and Leith reduces the average status largely because the professional class suffers at the expense of the commercial class (table 2.5). The more detailed census statistics for occupational orders shows that most of the commercial workers were in semi-skilled, unskilled manual or lower non-manual occupations.[2] The amalgamation of Leith with Edinburgh in 1920, therefore, increased the city's working-class population share.

Finally, population statistics for some selected registration districts in Edinburgh in 1901 are shown in table 2.8. Registration districts were the areas within which births, marriages and deaths were registered, beginning in Scotland in 1855. As table 2.8 shows, not surprisingly in view of late nineteenth-century urban growth, population increased in virtually all districts including those in the burgh itself. However, the St. Andrews district experienced a below average rise while St. Giles actually declined. Already by 1901 Edinburgh was beginning its outward expansion, with relative stagnation in some central districts balanced by rapid population growth in districts still outside the city boundary but served by the recently completed railways, such as Colinton, Corstorphine and Duddingston.

The 1901–11 decade experienced an accentuation of these trends with population increasing faster in the outlying wards and either not at all or actually declining in the central wards. Edinburgh City itself expanded by

Table 2.8

Population increase or decrease in selected registration districts
in the County of Edinburgh, 1891–1901

Registration districts	Population 1891 ('000)	Population 1901 ('000)	Percentage increase or decrease
Colinton*	4·65	5·50	18·26
Corstorphine†	2·23	2·73	22·03
Duddingston*	1·57	2·02	28·53
Edinburgh:			
St George	72·51	90·17	24·36
St Andrews	56·36	61·70	9·47
Canongate	38·25	44·97	17·56
St Giles	31·78	29·46	− 7·29
Newington	65·69	77·41	17·84
Portobello	8·18	9·18	12·20
Leith:			
North Leith	25·96	29·83	14·92
South Leith†	43·93	49·07	11·70
Liberton†	4·91	5·30	7·96
Total for Edinburgh County	433·55	488·06	12·57

*Land added between censuses
†Land subtracted between censuses

Source: Calculated from Registrar General for Scotland (1902); *Census for Scotland, 1901;* vol. 2, pp. 85–6.

only 0·9 per cent in that decade while the parishes of Cramond, Corstorphine, Colinton, Liberton, Inveresk, and the Burgh of Leith combined increased their population by 12·1 per cent. It is interesting that contemporaries reacted to these trends in the same way as some observers of cities today. Thus, a report by the Company of Merchants of the City of Edinburgh pointed out (Company of Merchants, 1919, p. 23):

It will thus be seen that the people are steadily migrating outwards and this movement would undoubtedly be accelerated by rapid mechanical transport. These districts are thriving at the expense of the city and they may be expected to thrive still more whenever attractive and hygienic localities are linked up. They are draining the people away who make a diurnal journey between schools and city to earn their living and are thus depleting and restricting Edinburgh's rate-producing power.

Several conclusions may be drawn from this examination of the 1901 census data. First, Edinburgh's position as the capital of Scotland and as a centre for administration, education, science, culture and leisure led to an exceptional middle-class bias in its socio-economic structure, reflected *inter alia* in the large professional and domestic sectors. Second, although not primarily an industrial city, Edinburgh was more industrial than is sometimes realised, and examination of the numbers employed in the various industrial 'orders' in the 1901 census shows a highly diversified industrial mix. The occupational structure becomes even more varied when the commercial activity of the port of Leith is included. Third, although Edinburgh gained as many migrants as other Scottish cities from the rural areas in the nineteenth century, its population did not increase as rapidly or as continuously as in the Western Lowlands. This reflects that it is not a typical Victorian city, based primarily upon manufacturing. In fact, many of its immigrants from rural Scotland were probably single women, seeking jobs in domestic service. For similar reasons, plus the longer distance, the city received few immigrants from Ireland. Although Edinburgh was more cosmopolitan than Glasgow, probably a larger proportion of its working class was native to the city, and as a result was more adapted to the local socio-economic structure.

Spatial expansion of residential areas[3]

Figure 2.2 illustrates the extent of Edinburgh's residential districts in 1918. In the early years of the century many central areas of Edinburgh and Leith (the hatched areas on fig. 2.2) were still residential, even though movement of population away from the inner city had already begun. Housing conditions in the Old Town had long given cause for concern (Edinburgh Trades and Labour Council, 1921) and, although many working-class dwellings had been displaced by non-residential land use or vacated by order of the town council under the Housing Act of 1890, this area remained the location of the most overcrowded and inadequate working-class housing in the city. A major problem was the relatively poor return from investment in housing for letting to working-class families.

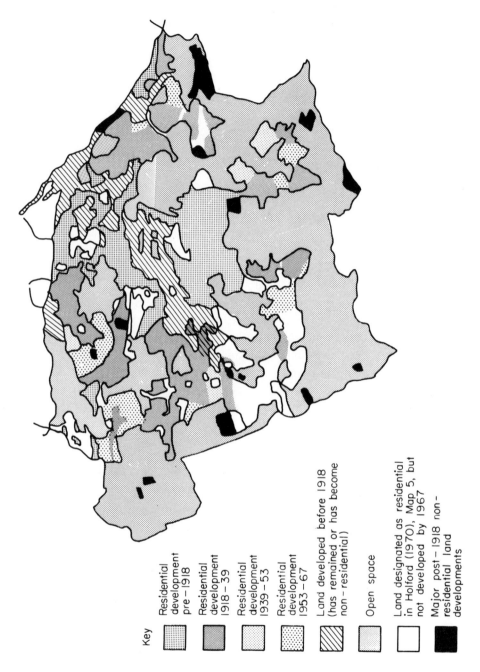

Key

Residential development pre-1918

Residential development 1918–39

Residential development 1939–53

Residential development 1953–67

Land developed before 1918 (has remained or has become non-residential)

Open space

Land designated as residential in Holford (1970), Map 5, but not developed by 1967

Major post-1918 non-residential land developments

Fig. 2.2

With urban growth and the general rise in population, increased building costs and more stringent construction standards, private enterprise could not supply enough houses which poorer families might afford (Cramond, 1965). In addition to these national problems, a further limitation was placed upon the expansion of lower-class residential areas by the Scottish system of feuing as operated in Edinburgh. The supply of land in Edinburgh in the early twentieth century was controlled by 'a comparatively limited number of superiors, all of whom were concerned to secure the maximum long-term income which their properties would yield' (Smith, 1964, p. 287). Not only did this limit the amount of new and relatively cheap housing becoming available outside the Old Town, but it also exercised a powerful constraint on the character of new working class areas: '. . . feu duties . . . ranged from £150 to more than £600 per acre: the implications for density of development are obvious when it is realised that £1.10s per house per annum was considered a reasonable duty for working class occupants' (Smith, 1964, p. 288). Consequently, the new areas of working-class housing which had been built by 1918 in districts such as Abbeyhill, Greenside, Meadowbank, Gorgie, Dalry, Fountainbridge, St. Leonard's, Bonnington, Easter Road, and areas north of the New Town, continued to be of the closely arranged tenement type and were located on low value land. Hence, the tendency for working-class housing to be located near industrial workplaces and the rail links and water supply so necessary for manufacturing industry was reinforced by the land tenure system. This additional spatial determinant must be regarded as an important factor in the unusually high degree of segregation in social classes and property prices in Edinburgh (see pp. 127–34 and 156–79).

The Edinburgh Valuation Roll of 1914 shows that the New Town and its extensions were subject to invasion by non-residential land use, notably commercial offices, to the point where status classification of Georgian Edinburgh was made 'almost impossible' (Gordon, 1971, p. 170). However, the large domestic class in the city, according to the 1901 census, suggests that many of the huge and magnificent terraced dwellings in the streets, crescents and squares of the New Town were still used for their original purpose as homes for the wealthy. Indeed, Gordon himself stresses the continuing importance of the Moray development, Heriot Row, Abercromby Place, the Royal Circus, and the Calton Hill area as nuclei of high status housing. On the other hand, by the early twentieth century the New Town was declining in its attraction as a residential area and land use in this district was becoming increasingly heterogeneous. Against the background of Victorian industrial and commercial expansion the possibility of preserving the New Town as the aesthetic and cultural

24

haven envisaged by its architects receded, and the increased smoke and noise from the relatively nearby industrial areas, the railways, and the street traffic associated with the general growth in population and mobility gradually eroded its suitability as a residential area. The rising value of central land, increasingly in demand for non-residential use, also helped to push wealthier families out of the New Town.

In addition to producing the environmental and social changes which made the central areas less attractive residentially, Victorian technology also provided the means of escape in the form of the suburban railway system constructed mainly during the 1890s and virtually complete by 1914, and the tramway network, converted almost entirely to steam-driven cable traction by 1902 (Hunter, 1964, p. 92). The movement of the higher social classes was largely to the south, a direction which was determined partly by a repulsion from the industrial belt which ran from Leith in a southwesterly direction around the north of the New Town and along the steep river valley and low ground to Dalry and Gorgie, and partly by the attraction of the area itself with its open prospect and relative tranquility.

This southward expansion took place at the same time as the construction of the working-class tenement areas and, as shown in fig. 2.2, was considerable in extent. The dwellings in the new suburban areas varied in size and specification. In the Merchiston, Morningside, Churchill, Grange and Mayfield districts there was an innovation in Edinburgh housing in the form of large detached houses built in spacious grounds (Macrae, 1949, p. 15). However, the feu system again imposed a constraint by limiting the degree to which low-density housing of the usual suburban style was economically feasible. Hence, in the middle-class areas adjacent to these highest-class districts, areas such as Comiston, Bruntsfield, Newington and Marchmont, the tenement or the terraced house continued to prevail. There were high quality detached dwellings at Trinity and Inverleith north of the New Town which served to house the wealthier citizens of increasingly industrial Leith to the east. A district of high quality housing also developed at Ravelston on the Queensferry Road and became bordered by the middle-class tenement areas of Comely Bank and Saughtonhall.

New means of transport were important in fostering this suburban development, and fig. 2.3 of the tramway system in 1906[4] mirrors the geographical extent of the city at this period. Of particular interest is the route linking Morningside Road with Newington Road, the only orbital departure from an otherwise radial network which, together with the southern suburban loop railway to which it ran parallel, emphasizes the

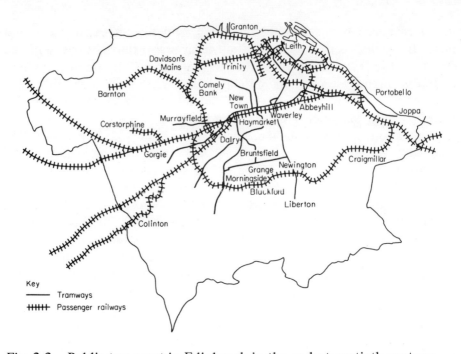

Fig. 2.3   Public transport in Edinburgh in the early twentieth century

Source: Edinburgh Tramways (with connections in Leith), Edinburgh Public Libraries, 1906. Hunter (1964), appended map.

southward bias of suburban expansion to Edinburgh in the early twentieth century. Figure 2.2 shows that by 1917 the villages of Barnton, Corstorphine and Colinton had all expanded, and this development was also stimulated by the extension of the suburban railway (see fig. 2.3). A large proportion of the highest class detached accommodation erected prior to the First World War was to be found in these suburban communities, partly due to the presence of railway links with central Edinburgh, and partly due to the high feu duties inside the city boundary forcing such developments outside into the adjacent countryside (Smith, 1964, pp. 288–9).

Edinburgh had thus expanded substantially by the late nineteenth century, and the city in 1918 extended far beyond the boundaries of the ancient burghs of Edinburgh and Leith and the New Town. It was not until after the 1914–18 war, however, that there was any appreciable twentieth-century growth. Further examination of fig. 2.2 provides a guide to the residential expansion of Edinburgh during the inter-war period. The major innovation of the period was undoubtedly the growth of public sector housing. Of 43,471 new dwellings approved for construction between 1918 and 1939, 15,142 were built by the corporation, and about 6,000 of these were for families from slum clearance areas (Edinburgh Town Council, 1949, p. 18).

The distinction between local authority houses built to meet general housing requirements produced by immigration into the city, population increase, rising minimum standards, and housing obsolescence and those built to rehouse families from overcrowded inner city areas is important for understanding the nature of residential expansion during the inter-war years. During the early years of local authority housing provision the quality of accommodation provided was correlated very highly with the income of the residents. Families from dwellings in central housing areas condemned under the various improvement schemes of the period, therefore, were rehoused in areas surrounded by industry and railways at very high densities. Development occurred invariably on low, level ground and so presented few problems of construction or conflict with other proposed land uses (Smith, 1964, p. 297). In addition, rehousing areas such as Lochend, Prestonfield, Gorgie, Quarryholes, Piershill, Granton and Pilton were all on or near existing tramways and relatively close to the old tenement districts. An exception to this was the large area of corporation tenements built at Craigmillar in the early 1930s for, although built on flat land adjacent to the breweries on the Braid Burn, this site was 2½ miles from the city centre. A partial explanation is the increasing scarcity of more central land. However, sites closer to existing residential areas in the southeastern sector of the city, apart from being liable to flooding were 'too easily overlooked by areas of high-cost housing' (Smith, 1964, p. 305).

With few exceptions, such as the small pockets in the Gorgie–Dalry industrial area, the cheap council housing of the inter-war period was concentrated in the northern and eastern districts of Edinburgh. In terms of area, however, most of the land acquired by the corporation was in the western and northwestern sectors in areas such as Pilton, Stenhouse, Saughton Mains, Chesser and Hutchinson (both to the southwest of Gorgie), Saughtonhall and Sighthill. Later in the 1930s more land was acquired east of Cramond on the coast and at Drylaw. Most of these districts were reserved for a higher quality council housing for working-class and lower-middle (non-manual) class families who could afford to pay higher rents and higher fares on the public transport system. The limited amount of superior council housing east of the city centre was confined largely to the early development at Willowbrae, adjacent to the fine amenity of Holyrood Park.

The second half of the inter-war period was marked by a boom in private house construction. Many of the new dwellings were bungalows, large numbers of which were built on the area between the Firth and the main railway around the Craigentinny golf course east of Leith, adjacent to the Queensferry Road at Blackhall and Craigleith in the northwest, and at Craiglockhart and Kingsknowe to the southwest of the existing high-class suburb of Merchiston and relatively close to the environmental amenities of the Craiglockhart Hills and Colinton Dell. Other developments were at Southfield, Bingham, Liberton, Buckstone, Colinton, Corstorphine, Drylaw and Barnton. Gordon (1971, p. 179) emphasises the importance of the builder in determining the character of these new housing areas. Districts of outstanding environmental quality such as Corstorphine, the land above Colinton Dell, and the belt of land adjacent to Braid Hills were reserved for the finest housing while the intermediate areas, often devoted to bungalows, were directed towards a more middle-class market. These districts were often close to the areas of superior inter-war council housing. Finally, there was housing subsidized by the council but built privately. These usually consisted of terraced houses adjacent to existing or future council housing since the ground was bought from the corporation. This type of housing was primarily confined to the western areas of the city.

It is clear from fig. 2.2 that, after the almost complete standstill in building during the Second World War, postwar development has been much more limited in spatial extent than during the inter-war period. As in other large cities, most housing completions in Edinburgh since 1945 have been in the public sector. This has been due largely to the greater responsibility placed on local authorities for housing by the central government, but in Edinburgh an additional factor has been the shortage of land for private development. This shortage is the result of the natural constraints imposed by the Firth of Forth and the Pentland Hills and the danger of subsidence due to mining in the south east, and the artificial constraints of land zoning and the preservation of green wedges around environmental amenities such as Corstorphine Hill, Braid Hills and Arthur's Seat. With the local authority already controlling large areas of land by 1945 and, being committed to providing housing for the large numbers of people in need, active in its negotiations for new sites, the land available for new private houses was severely limited. The little building that occurred before 1953 was virtually all by the local authority and, apart from the completion of schemes begun before the war, most of this was concentrated in the south east at Southhouse, Ferniehill, and Liberton which were now served by main drainage and sewers (Smith, 1964, p. 352).[5]

The major expansion in postwar local authority housing in Edinburgh, however, took place after the acquisition of new sites in the early 1950s. The shortage of land relative to housing needs, the greater ability of people to pay public transport fares, and the increased transport flexibility provided by the bus and later the motor car, were all factors determining the peripheral location of these sites. Hence, the typical location of the postwar council housing estate in Edinburgh was on the outskirts of the city often in the spaces between earlier developments which had usually been located on main radial routes (e.g. Colinton Mains, Hyvot's Bank, Muirhouse and Silverknowes). Although council estates, because of their scale, continued to occupy distinct areas the rigid inter-war spatial segregation between private and council housing could not be maintained. The most conspicuous example of these changed conditions was the new estate at Clermiston which was sandwiched between the high status areas of Corstorphine and Barnton. Not surprisingly, the private residents in the area reacted against certain aspects of the council's plans and succeeded in forcing several important modifications (Smith, 1964, p. 356).

The distinction between council housing for general housing needs and for rehousing was not made as explicit as in the inter-war years. However, different council housing areas were perceived as varying in status, and there was a confidential ranking of estates compiled by the Assessor's Department in existence (Gordon, 1971, p. 221). For instance, high-density flats built in areas such as Muirhouse to combat the shortage of building land are a postwar modern counterpart to the inter-war rehousing schemes.

Postwar private development hardly re-started in Edinburgh until 1954–5[6] and the main periods of postwar construction were 1959–64 and 1971. The largest developments in the 1950s were at Southfield and Mountcastle in the east, Inverleith in the north, the Corstorphine district in the west, and sites of 265 and 162 houses at Oxgangs and Colinton in the south built by George Wimpey and Co. In the late 1950s and early 1960s, further substantial areas of housing were completed at Mountcastle (55 dwellings), Clermiston (82), Liberton (129) and at a number of sites in Corstorphine (notably the development of 111 houses on the periphery of the city at Wester Broom) and Craigleith (105). Although public and private housing were now more likely to be adjacent, the inter-war tendency for housing in the eastern sectors to be of lower cost has continued (see p. 116), while new houses in other parts of the city have varied widely in price. The western and southern sectors of Edinburgh are characterized by a more irregular topography and this makes for more variation in the environmental quality of building sites. The historical pattern of high ground and areas of considerable environmental attractiveness being used for the finest housing has been maintained with the construction of expensive dwellings at Buckstone, Mortonhall and Craighouse near the public open space of the Braid Hills, at Bonaly and Colinton on the southwestern periphery near the Pentland Hills, at Corstorphine and Barnton, and in the pleasant village of Cramond. Several of these sites were developed over a period of ten years or more.

Figure 2.2 confirms that the most extensive areas of later postwar building have been in the northwestern sector of the city. Although most housing activity has been in the public sector, there have also been significant private developments at Barnton, Clermiston, Craigleith and Cramond.[7] This twentieth-century growth in the residential areas of Edinburgh towards the northwest has significantly altered the geometric shape of the city. The city boundary of 1901 (see fig. 2.1) reflects the earlier northeast to southwest axis of the city from the port of Leith through the Old and New Towns and along the low ground and river valley of the southwest to Gorgie and Dalry. The tramway system developed to serve the population living broadly on this axis and on its suburban extensions to the south and north. During this century, in addition to the increase in population, the greater responsibility placed on local authorities for large-scale public housing provision, and the greater ability of the population to afford transportation, there has also occurred a greater flexibility in transport facilities with the motor bus and car replacing the tram. With the extension of the drainage and sewerage systems to meet housing demands, this has permitted urban expansion into new areas even within the city boundary. Hence, modern Edinburgh has filled out to a more circular shape, particularly as a result of the northwest expansion.

Several factors have combined to limit central redevelopment in Edinburgh compared with other cities. These include postwar concentration by the local authority on peripheral housing schemes, the fine quality, sound construction, and historical value of many of the buildings in the Old and New Towns, and the absence of war damgage. However, many buildings have changed their function and have been subdivided into smaller dwellings or commercial offices (see p. 55). The invasion of the New Town has continued and districts adjacent to the central area, such as Newington and Polwarth, have become attractive as sources of accommodation for schools, hotels and other institutions. Nevertheless, although by the 1960s the New Town could no longer be regarded as the main fashionable area, the appearance of its dwellings, their spaciousness, elegance and centrality, questions this conclusion. The continued high socio-economic class of individual buyers in the New Town confirms that some households preferred the attributes of a flat in Moray Place to those of a suburban villa at Barnton (see pp. 174–7). Moreover, areas such as Morningside, Churchill and Grange, which stand close to the city centre and contain housing of the type expected in potential 'zones of transition', have remained relatively high status areas. This may be the result of, *inter alia,* the high quality of the buildings, the good physical environment with relatively easy access both to open space and the city centre, the close proximity of Edinburgh and Heriot Watt Universities and other major institutions employing the large professional class of the city, and the postwar shortage of private residential sites for high status housing within the city boundary.

Households and the housing stock

Table 2.9 assembles some relevant census data that shed light on population and housing stock relationships in Edinburgh over the study period. The population of the city (including the contiguous areas which were not incorporated until 1920) increased moderately up to 1921, rather more rapidly between 1921 and 1951, remained stable in the 1950s

Table 2.9

Households and housing in Edinburgh*, 1901–71

	1901	1911	1921	1931	1951	1961	1971
Population ('000)	413·0	423·5	420·3	439·0	466·8	468·4	453·6
Households ('000)	88·5	92·5	101·6	114·1	141·4	156·3	157·8
Persons per household	4·45	4·14	3·91	3·66	3·11	2·85	2·72
Occupied houses ('000)	81·8	87·1	95·1	105·7	134·0	151·8	159·2
No. of one- and			41·0	40·7	36·4	33·4	27·8
two-roomed houses (%)	–	–	(43·2)	(38·5)	(27·2)	(22·0)	(17·4)
No. of three- and			34·9	42·6	72·8	89·5	89·8
four-roomed houses (%)	–	–	(36·7)	(40·3)	(54·3)	(59·0)	(56·4)
Average number of							
persons per room	1·28	1·26	1·18	1·11	0·94	0·85	0·71
Tenure distribution:							
owner occupiers (%)	–	–	–	–	–	44·4	46·9
council, SSHA (%)	–	–	–	–	–	25·2	31·6
private rented (%)	–	–	–	–	–	30·4	21·5

*The data include Leith and other districts which were not incorporated into Edinburgh until 1920.

and declined in the 1960s. The overall moderate rate of population growth, however, did not depress housing demand very much because of the trend towards a much smaller household size. By 1971 the typical Edinburgh household was only three-fifths of the average size at the beginning of the century. Despite the decline in household size, the proportion of very small dwellings (one and two rooms) in the housing stock has persistently fallen. Before 1914, almost one-half of the housing stock was of this type, primarily because of the huge segment of the stock consisting of tenement buildings. Since then, higher incomes, changing tastes and upgrading of housing standards have resulted in a marked change in composition of the stock. Up to 1961 the decline in the share of one- and two-roomed dwellings was almost exactly offset by an increase in the share of three- and four-roomed dwellings. Between 1961 and 1971, however, the proportion of the latter size group fell as a further upward shift in tastes and standards called for more houses of five rooms or more. The net effect of a larger average house size and a smaller household size was, of course, a fall in overcrowding and in net residential densities as measured by persons per room. The improvement here has been very marked, especially since 1931.

The changes in the size distribution of the housing stock have been paralleled by related changes in tenure distribution. These changes have taken the form of a decline in the role of the privately rented sector but expansion in the shares of both owner-occupiers and council tenants. As implied in the discussion of housebuilding (see below), since the end of the Second World War the council tenant share has increased faster than that of owner occupiers within the city. Although the fall in the privately rented stock has been sharp, especially in the last decade, its contribution remains relatively large compared with other British cities, still accounting for more than one-fifth of the housing stock.

Housebuilding in Edinburgh

Prior to 1914 virtually all the housebuilding in Edinburgh was by the private sector, although a fair proportion of this was for letting rather than owner-occupation. In the inter-war period the local authority became a major supplier of houses, though its contribution varied widely from year to year, particularly between the 1920s and the 1930s. Of 44,000 houses built between 1920 and 1945, about 35 per cent were built by the corporation. It was not until after 1945, however, that the local authority became the dominant housing supplier within the city, mainly because the corporation was able to dominate the land market which was characterised by an extreme shortage of land. Of more than 38,600 houses built between 1945 and the end of 1966 almost 26,000 were provided by the local authority, only 11,000 by the private sector and the balance was made up by the SSHA (Scottish Special Housing Association) and other agencies. In recent years the level of housebuilding has fluctuated around an average of 2,000 houses per annum; the local authority contribution has varied but has always been the major supplier particularly in 1969 and 1970. It is interesting to note that of the four major Scottish cities, Edinburgh's total housebuilding performance in per capita terms has been the least satisfactory in the postwar period. This reflects both the more serious land shortage and the less active local authority sector. On the other hand, despite the land supply obstacles, private housebuilders in Edinburgh have performed rather better than in the other cities.

Private residential development in the postwar period

Some information on postwar private residential developments in Edinburgh was obtained from the private land purchase survey analysed on pp. 145–9. This does not give a complete picture of postwar private housebuilding since it deals only with sites purchased *after 1945,* and many Edinburgh builders and property companies had held land on a substantial scale since the inter-war period. However, the data on new house sales in table 2.10 are broadly representative of the fluctuations in private housebuilding activity: its non-existence in the immediate postwar period because of the tight building controls, the slow start in the early 1950s, the improvement in the late 1950s and the new housing boom between 1959 and 1964, followed by a much more subdued period with only 1971 as a year of substantial activity. Even in the peak years, the level of sales was low for a city of almost half a million population. But this reflected the severe land shortage. Another consequence of the land scarcity was that most of the residential developments were very small in scale. As shown in table 2.11, of 171 estates 140 contained less than 50 properties and of these 111 were of less than 25 properties. At the other end of the scale, only 3 of the estates contained more than 250 houses.

Despite the small size of the typical estate, its development and sales were frequently spread over a long period. As the distribution in table 2.12 shows, properties on 40 estates took more than three years to sell, and on 18 of these estates the sales period extended beyond five years (the maximum period was almost fourteen years). Conversely, on one-half

33

Table 2.10

New house sales on postwar sites, 1945–72

Year	No. of houses	Year	No. of houses
1945–49	0	1961	357
1950	1	1962	423
1951	1	1963	357
1952	11	1964	554
1953	41	1965	286
1954	61	1966	258
1955	162	1967	220
1956	304	1968	147
1957	265	1969	274
1958	326	1970	229
1959	390	1971	478
1960	503	1972	217

Table 2.11

Size distribution of postwar private housing estates

Size class	No. in class
0–4	26
5–9	31
10–24	54
25–49	29
50–74	8
75–99	7
100–249	13
250+	3
Total	171

Table 2.12

Phasing of private housing developments

Period between first and last sale*	No. of estates
Less than 1 year	85
1 year – 1 year 11 months	31
2 years – 2 years 11 months	15
3 years – 3 years 11 months	15
4 years – 4 years 11 months	7
5 years – 9 years 11 months	13
> 10 years	5
Total	171

*Average period between first and last sale = 2 years 1 month of the estates all the properties were sold within one year, some indication of Edinburgh's chronic housing shortage over this period. The price data for these new estates are reported in chapter 3, table 3.3. They show that the prices of new properties built on expensive postwar sites were considerably higher than the mean price level for all Edinburgh residential properties (from the late 1950s almost 50 per cent higher). Also, the year-to-year fluctuations were not necessarily in line with the average city price, but varied according to the costliness of sites developed in particular years. Site cost changes with location, so that a relatively large estate built on expensively located land could, given the absolutely small scale of total private residential development, easily distort the property price level prevailing in a particular year out of its trend pattern (1957 and 1967 are good examples of this phenomenon).

The structure of ownership of rented property

This book concentrates on the phenomenon of residential property ownership without making a clear distinction between investment property for letting and owner-occupation. Implicitly, much of the analysis, particularly in regard to empirical testing of theories, refers to owner-occupation. It is rather important, therefore, that a little attention should be given to landlordism. A summary of the present distribution of rented properties by type of landlord is given in table 2.13.[8]

The typical landlord in Edinburgh is an individual, and the typical number of properties owned is one − mainly though not exclusively by individuals. If 70 per cent of landlords are individuals and these own 35 per cent of the properties, the converse is that there is a heavy concentration of properties in few hands. This is shown in table 2.14. Eight landlords own 16·3 per cent of the 30,000 plus properties; one landlord (the local building firm MacTaggart and Mickel, Ltd.) alone owns 6·9 per cent of the total rented properties.[9] Ownership remains concentrated over the top 5 per cent of landlords, after which the distribution becomes more equal. Of the 7,654 landlords 418 own more than ten properties, 92 own more than forty and only 33 own more than one hundred.

However, table 2.13 shows that the distribution of ownership varies widely among types of landlord. At one extreme, there is the individual landlord; at the other, property companies, although less than 2½ per cent of the number of landlords own almost one-quarter of the total properties. Institutions (e.g. hospitals, the University of Edinburgh,

Table 2.13

Landlords in Edinburgh, 1972

	Landlords		Holdings		Mean size of holding	Distribution of landlords by size of holding				
	No.	%	No.	%		1	2–10	11–40	41–80	80+
Individual	5,332	69·6	10,534	34·3	1·9	4,109	1,093	119	7	4
Trust	1,401	18·3	5,854	19·1	3·9	922	361	100	11	7
Property company	180	2·4	7,435	24·2	41·1	43	69	36	15	17
Firm	502	6·6	3,539	11·6	6·5	261	183	46	7	5
Institution	78	1·0	1,737	5·7	21·4	25	26	19	5	3
Welfare organization	161	2·1	1,577	5·1	9·3	94	50	6	5	6
Other			3	0·0						
Total	7,654	100·0	30,679	100·0	3·2	5,454 (71·2%)	1,782 (23·3%)	326 (4·3%)	50 (0·7%)	42 (0·5%)

Table 2.14

Concentration of ownership of rented property

Landlords (%)	Properties (%)
0·1	16
1	39
5	61
10	70

churches) also own relatively large holdings with the mean size of holding 21·4 compared to 41·1 in property companies. Trusts tend to be small landlords, and probably hold property in that form rather than as individuals for tax avoidance purposes. Middle-size landlords are more typical of firms and welfare organizations. However, as the size distribution data in table 2.13 suggests, most of the landlords in all six categories are small (i.e. owning less than ten properties), yet each type contains a few large landlords. Four individuals own 90–100 properties each, and there are five major trusts (owning 122–212 properties), some dominant concerns such as the National Coal Board, the Co-operative Societies and the banks, and a few sizeable welfare organizations. But only in the case of property companies is there a large block of major landlords, with 17 companies in the 80-plus property size class.

Although the privately rented sector has declined in Edinburgh as elsewhere, [10] the 1971 census showed that privately rented households still accounted for 21·5 per cent of all households in the city. Of these, 7 out of 10 were flats and a similar proportion was unfurnished. Privately rented properties were heavily concentrated in inner city areas, especially those containing many tenement blocks. For instance, 26·4 per cent of the city's privately rented stock were located in three wards (Gorgie–Dalry, St. Giles and Central Leith) and almost 56 per cent in nine inner city wards. [11] However, there is also a smaller but significant sector of suburban privately rented housing mainly in Colinton, Sighthill, Corstorphine and Pilton. The major landlord in these areas is the building firm Mactaggart and Mickel who built properties for rent, typically four-flat blocks, with the aid of State subsidy schemes in the 1920s and 1930s. In terms of landlord type, this category of housing explains why in Sighthill and Pilton property companies own 90–95 per cent of all privately rented properties. Property companies were less important than individual landlords in the inner city working-class wards [12] and least important of all in the inner city mixed [13] and middle-class [14] wards.

Finally, over two-thirds of the properties are administered not by the landlords themselves but by house factors (estate agents and, to a lesser extent, lawyers). Control is heavily concentrated on a few factors, since nine of them (out of a total of 1,098) control 42 per cent of all privately rented housing.

Recent decentralization trends

As pointed out earlier (see pp. 20–2), there were already signs of a centrifrugal movement in population in Edinburgh City at the beginning of the century. More recently, decentralization has proceeded at a faster rate under the influence of transportation changes, rising incomes and the associated shift in tastes in favour of new houses that could be provided only in suburban and satellite locations. Population growth has also been a factor, but a much less significant one than in other cities in developed countries. Between 1901 and 1931 the population of Midlothian (excluding Edinburgh) increased at double the rate of Edinburgh itself, and since 1951 the population of Edinburgh City has actually declined (see table 2.9).

Table 2.15 shows the population changes in the 1960s in the wards of the city. In 17 of the 23 wards population fell. The declines tended to be steeper in the high density areas which are invariably also the inner areas. The declines were greater in Holyrood, St. Andrews and St. Giles, i.e. the most central areas of all, and this reflects the pace of central area redevelopment. The other main areas of population decrease were George Square, Central and Southern Leith and Calton, again very centrally located wards.

In several wards of the city, Newington, Morningside, Craigentinny, Portobello and Craigmillar, the population remained more or less stable, as in the city as a whole. The six areas experiencing population growth were all located on the periphery of the city and were contiguous spreading from Pilton in the northwest, via Murrayfield–Cramond, Corstorphine, Sighthill, and Colinton to Liberton in the southeast. With the exception of Pilton, an important site for relatively high density council housing, these expanding wards had the lowest population densities within the city.

There is other evidence consistent with the negative population changes of the 1960s in most city wards and the faster (though still modest) employment growth than population growth. For instance, commuting data whether from the census or from the Ministry of Labour (now the Department of Employment) show that commuting into the city has

38

Table 2.15

Population changes 1961–71 and densities in the city wards

	Population ('000)		Percentage change 1961–71	Density 1971 (persons per ha.)
	1961	1971		
St Giles	17·69	10·85	−38·7	67·8
Holyrood	13·95	7·98	−42·8	22·0
George Square	16·33	13·10	−19·8	102·3
Newington	22·96	22·55	− 1·8	61·8
Liberton	34·61	37·76	+ 9·1	19·2
Morningside	17·21	16·42	− 4·6	58·9
Merchiston	16·07	15·40	− 4·2	50·8
Colinton	26·87	35·61	+32·5	14·4
Sighthill	23·82	26·07	+ 9·4	39·6
Gorgie–Dalry	18·61	16·09	−13·5	94·7
Corstorphine	21·51	23·99	+11·5	17·1
Murrayfield–Cramond	22·19	30·36	+36·8	22·6
Pilton	28·17	30·67	+ 8·9	69·4
St Bernards	25·82	23·38	− 9·5	41·4
St Andrews	14·50	8·74	−39·7	57·5
Broughton	16·81	14·96	−11·0	71·6
Calton	15·39	12·46	−19·0	97·3
West Leith	16·02	14·63	− 8·7	55·8
Central Leith	17·16	13·89	−19·1	116·8
South Leith	18·21	15·31	−15·9	60·8
Craigentinny	20·26	19·51	− 3·7	61·3
Portobello	19·32	18·89	− 2·2	41·2
Craigmillar	24·91	24·60	− 1·2	25·8
Edinburgh City	468·36	453·22	− 3·3	33·7

consistently exceeded out-commuting, usually by a ratio of three to one. However, the scale of commuting has been rather small, in *net* terms only between 2 and 4 per cent of the labour force. To the extent that all this evidence indicates decentralization, and generally increasing decentralization, it supports the view that changes in the spatial structure of the Edinburgh district have tended to relieve pressure on the city housing market. This is not to say, of course, that the relief was sufficiently strong to have much impact on the high rate of house price inflation in the 1960s and early 1970s. It does help to explain the higher prices on the periphery of the city. On the other hand, the rate of price increase in recent years has been as high in the better areas of the inner city as in the outer suburbs. Since central city depopulation has not slowed down, the explanation is in terms of composition of demand rather than its aggregate level (i.e. more middle-class competition for housing in the western end of the central city) and, to a lesser extent, of an increased demand for inner city dwellings for conversion to non-residential use.

Employment structure

The sectoral distribution of employment in Edinburgh and changes over time in that distribution as recorded in the decennial census are shown in table 2.16. The main feature is the dominance of the service industries and, at least since the end of World War I, the under-representation of manufacturing. The agricultural share was not unexpectedly small for a city of half a million. The decline was particularly sharp after 1931, partly as market gardens in the beach areas from Portobello to Cramond, on the limey soils of Stenhouse and Gilmerton and within the lee of Corstorphine Hill were gobbled up as land for housing, partly because of a secular fall in fishing employment in the Newhaven and Leith areas. Employment in mining increased substantially between 1901 and 1921, fell in the 1920s but then remained more or less stable. There are fluctuations in the construction share, but these should not be taken too seriously. The labour force in construction adjusts rapidly to changes in the levels of activity in the building industry so that the census data reflect the state of the building industry in the year of the census rather than any secular changes in the share of building employment.

There were major shifts within the manufacturing and service sectors. Most manufacturing industries shed labour over the study period, but textiles declined the most. The only manufacturing sector with a significantly larger labour force at the end compared with the beginning of the period was metals and engineering. This was largely due to growth in electrical engineering, particularly as a result of the establishment of the Ferranti works and the continued growth of other firms such as Bruce Peebles and Co.

From the point of view of impact on the housing market the changes within the service sector are more significant. Service industries contain a wide range of labour in terms of skill and pay, including substantial numbers of very low-paid workers. However, in Edinburgh's case the marked increase in the service industries' share was concentrated in sectors with labour forces skewed towards high class workers such as commerce and finance, professional services and public administration and defence.

40

Table 2.16

Employment distribution in Edinburgh, 1901–61

	1901*		1921		1931		1951		1961	
	'000	%	'000	%	'000	%	'000	%	'000	%
Primary:	2·68	1·5	7·79	3·9	6·49	3·0	4·51	2·1	3·81	1·6
Agriculture, forestry and fishing	1·82	1·0	4·06	2·0	3·85	1·8	2·30	1·1	1·20	0·5
Mining and quarrying	0·86	0·5	3·73	1·9	2·64	1·2	2·21	1·0	2·61	1·1
Manufacturing:	83·67	45·9	64·78	32·2	60·30	28·3	68·81	31·3	58·94	25·2
Food, drink and tobacco	19·46	10·7	10·58	5·3	14·35	6·7	17·59	8·0	16·93	7·3
Chemicals	4·28	2·3	2·15	1·1	1·95	0·9	3·12	1·4	2·81	1·2
Metals and engineering	14·31	7·8	19·40	9·6	13·38	6·3	21·54	9·8	18·20	7·8
Textiles, leather and clothing	19·72	10·8	9·71	4·8	7·30	3·4	6·01	2·7	3·50	1·5
Bricks, pottery, glass	1·22	0·7	1·31	0·6	1·09	0·5	1·79	0·8	1·26	0·5
Timber, furniture	5·10	2·8	4·16	2·1	4·59	2·2	3·80	1·7	2·48	1·1
Paper, printing and publishing	11·33	6·2	11·29	5·6	11·20	5·3	10·19	4·6	11·02	4·7
Other manufacturing	8·25	4·5	6·18	3·1	6·44	3·0	4·77	2·2	2·74	1·2
Construction	16·14	8·9	7·98	4·0	11·83	5·5	15·81	7·2	17·95	7·7
Services:	79·82	43·8	120·48	59·9	134·47	63·2	130·58	59·4	152·07	65·2
Gas, water and electricity	1·30	0·7	1·81	0·9	2·26	1·1	3·58	1·6	3·73	1·6
Transport and communication	21·19	11·6	19·43	9·7	18·71	8·8	22·03	10·0	22·14	9·5
Commerce and finance	13·17	7·2	39·65	19·7	47·36	22·2	38·61	17·6	49·11	21·0
Professional services	12·07	6·6	16·06	8·0	17·01	8·0	24·70	11·2	31·06	13·3
Miscellaneous services	27·49	15·1	23·53	11·7	30·60	14·4	22·20	10·1	28·50	12·2
Public administration and defence	4·60	2·5	20·00	9·9	18·53	8·7	19·46	8·9	17·53	7·5
Unclassified	–	–	–	–	–	–	–	–	0·56	0·2
Total	182·30	100·0	201·04	100·0	213·10	100·0	219·73	100·0	233·33	100·0

*1901 data include Leith

Source: *Census of Scotland*, 1901–61, General Registry Office, Edinburgh.

This suggests that Edinburgh has become more middle class during this century, and given the association between social class and owner-occupation rates, employment shifts have had repercussions on housing demand and on the spatial residential structure. These repercussions are examined in more detail in chapter 9 (see pp. 173–4).

Another point of interest is that employment increased over the period at a rate rather faster than population as a whole. In part, this reflects the fact that the decentralization of homes has been more extensive than that of jobs. In part, it is explained by a secular rise in activity rates.

A partial consequence of the employment structure with its absence of heavy industries, apart from some firms in metals and engineering, is the lower unemployment rates in Edinburgh relative to the rest of Scotland. Over a long period of time Edinburgh's unemployment rate has been only one-half of the Scottish rate, and frequently less. For many years Edinburgh was the only place in Scotland not scheduled as a development area and eligible for regional development assistance. Not only were unemployment rates lower, but the amplitude in their fluctuations was much narrower. The marked stability of the Edinburgh economy coupled with the high status service-dominated economic structure helps to explain why owner-occupation is more prevalent in Edinburgh than in other Scottish cities. This is particularly because, given the trend towards building society mortgages as the main source of finance, building societies tended to take the type of employment and stability of earnings into account in decisions to grant mortgages.

Location of industry

The major impact of non-residential development, particularly of industry, on residential property values and on the residential spatial structure is, of course, the locational impact. Given the importance of environmental amenity and neighbourhood attractiveness as determinants of house prices, the presence of an industrial plant in a residential area can set up a chain of adverse price repercussions and locational moves that may severely disturb that area's stability. This is the central argument for zoning, and the compelling force of this argument explains why in most cities there is a high degree of segregation between residential and industrial land use. In the case of Edinburgh, this is particularly noticeable because residents, the local authority and other public and semi-public agencies have been very amenity-conscious. At the same time, the long history of the city as an administrative, cultural and service centre combined with the limited availability of local raw materials have tended to repel heavy industry so that the risks of residential districts being blighted by visual disamenity, pollution and industrial traffic congestion have been lower than in many other British cities.

These facts have important implications for the spatial structure of the city housing market. First, good quality private housing is not restricted to a small area in or near the city, but may be found in a wide variety of districts, both close to the city centre and in suburban areas. Second, because industrial development is fairly localized, there are significant house price differentials between the east and the west. These area differentials are accentuated by the fact that between the wars, though not after 1945, industrial sites and council housing estates tended to be located close to each other because of the importance of accessibility to the workplace as an influence on local authority housing site selection. Third, in a city which has traditionally attached a high value to amenity and a pleasant environment, and where there is a large and relatively prosperous professional and managerial class, houses in areas which offer especially attractive surroundings command a premium. This helps to explain the existence of a few very high price zones.

Fourth, the modest rates of both industrial and population growth in Edinburgh over this century, and the preponderance of service activity in the economic growth that has occurred, have resulted in a situation where the industrial areas of the city have remained very stable over time. The only new industrial area of any size has been the Sighthill Industrial Estate established by the city corporation in the west after the 1939—45 war. One aspect of this locational stability has been the severe shortage of urban land for all purposes. Green belt and public open space requirements, housing land needs and other constraints have meant that the only sizeable prospective new sites in the city in recent decades have been on land reclaimed from the foreshore. Indeed, many sites zoned for non-residential use between the wars have been subject to the pressures of housing, and public space demands, and have subsequently been re-zoned. The shortage of sites has led to most major new industrial developments in Central East Scotland being located outside Edinburgh in smaller places such as Broxburn, Dalkeith, Bathgate, Livingston and Glenrothes.

The main industrial areas in Edinburgh are confined to the parts of the city shaded on fig. 2.4. As the map shows, the main industrial area is based upon the port of Leith but has spread over time across the city centre to Gorgie and Dalry in the southwest and there is also a southern finger in the St. Leonard's and Newington area. The other pockets of industrial development are found at Granton on the river estuary,

43

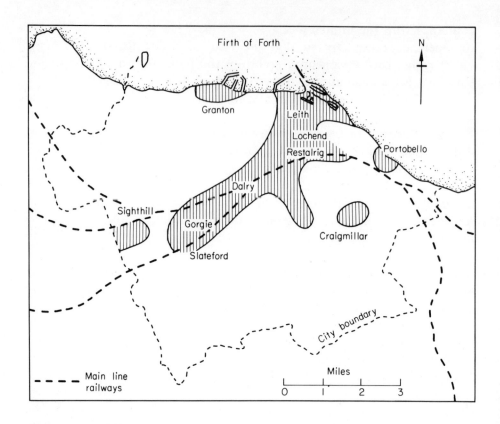

Fig. 2.4   Location of industry in Edinburgh.

Portobello on the seashore, and Craigmillar to the southeast, plus the
more recent concentration at Sighthill. The rest of the city is virtually free
of industry, apart from isolated plants. The industrial belt and pockets
conform quite closely to maps of low-class residential areas and to cheap
housing zones (see fig. 9.1, p. 161 and pp. 127–34). These findings are clear
evidence of the influence of industrial location on the social class and
house price elements of the urban spatial structure.[15]

   All the industrial locations shown on fig. 2.4 are influenced by access to
the transportation network, either the railway and the Water of Leith or
the ports and the sea. Many of the early industrial establishments in
Edinburgh were located next to the Water of Leith because they used
water power, while in the nineteenth century the railways were a major
locational attraction. Although these locational forces are obsolete, they
have nevertheless continued to exert a locational pull. This is explained by
several factors: the cumulative effect of interdependent industrial location

44

decisions; the survival of old-established industries; the fact that, given the scarcity of industrial sites, the most easily obtainable sites for new plants were frequently those abandoned when old firms closed down; the journey-to-work transportation system and the location of basic services were spatially biased towards the traditional industrial areas; and, most important of all, the new major road arteries (the A8, A71 and A70) reinforced the north—east to west—south—west axis on which industrial Edinburgh had developed. The strengthening and extension of this axis over the study period (e.g. the filling-up in the Gorgie area in the 1920s, and the postwar development on the Sighthill estate) reflects, *inter alia,* the market orientation of industrial location decisions, i.e. the benefits of accessibility to the west in order to be closer to the concentrated market of the Scottish industrial belt. Most of the industrial development has taken place on level land. How far flat sites have been necessary because of factory layout or whether this fact merely reflects the pull of the railways and water is unclear.

Industrial structure varies between districts. Industrial development in Leith, for instance, largely reflects port-related industries such as ship-building and marine engineering and export and import industries such as whisky blending, grain milling, fertiliser works and saw milling. More recently, newer industries such as some types of engineering and paint manufacture have developed. In the 1950s and 1960s residential decline in Leith has taken place alongside industrial growth, and this has had direct repercussions on the house price structure. In the Gorgie—Dalry area the main industries are the drink industries (brewing, malting and distilling) originally located there because of the availability of water. Other industries are rubber, food (including the slaughterhouse, cattle and corn markets) and general engineering. Dalry was the original location for the paper industry (1675), but in this century this industry has dispersed not only within Edinburgh but also to nearby towns. Holyrood and Craigmillar were major locations for brewing (water being easily obtained from artesian wells and the Niddrie Burn) while engineering predominated at Abbeyhill. Development in the Granton area tended to be related to its port functions (e.g. wood pulp factories; exporting facilities for coal, coke and machinery), although the gasworks constituted an important activity. The major employer in this area towards the latter part of the period, however, has been the Ferranti electronic engineering works at Crewe Toll, Pilton located to the south of Granton itself. Only at Sighthill was there a highly diversified industrial structure including light engineering, precast concrete and other building materials establishments and food processing plants. This diversification is fairly typical of postwar industrial

45

estates. Most of the commercial, financial and major distribution establishments remain in the city centre, since decentralization of offices and shops has not proceeded very far in Edinburgh. The main impact of service sector growth on the housing market has been the invasion of the New Town by non-residential establishments.

Industrial specialization by local area has an influence on the downgrading of nearby residential areas because the disamenities arising from proximity to industry vary according to type of industry. For instance, industries associated with the ports tend to have strongly adverse effects on nearby residential neighbourhoods, and this is consistent with the relatively very low house price levels prevailing in recent decades in Leith, Portobello and Granton. At the other extreme, the influence of the invasion of offices, especially where conservation orders prevent the destruction of historical structure as in the New Town, is not inimical to continued residential use apart from the fact that when properties come on to the market private housebuyers may find it difficult to compete with business establishments. Finally, the impact of industrial development on residential amenity is a function of the size of the development. Apart from the industrial estate and the port areas, there was a sufficient scatter of establishments within the industrial axis to moderate this impact. As for the size of individual industrial plants, there were few large factories in the Edinburgh area, [16] probably not more than half a dozen plants employing more than 1,000 workers, mainly in the engineering sector.

Notes

[1] Registrar General for Scotland (1903); *Census of Scotland, 1901,* vol. 3, p. 620.

[2] Ibid., p. 621.

[3] This section has benefited greatly from the earlier detailed studies of land use and residential areas in Edinburgh by Smith (1964) and Gordon (1971).

[4] *Edinburgh Tramways (with connections in Leith),* Edinburgh Public Libraries, 1906.

[5] There were also some large areas of temporary houses erected, but most of these sites have now been redeveloped by the corporation.

[6] In discussing postwar private development, use has been made of Sasines data on private land purchase and construction, examined in greater detail on pp. 145–9.

⁷ The largest estate was a site developed by Wimpeys at Clermiston involving the construction of 355 dwellings.

[7] The largest estate was a site developed by Wimpeys at Clermiston involving the construction of 355 dwellings.

[8] We are indebted to David McCrone and Brian Elliott of the University of Edinburgh for this information. It is derived from the valuation roll not from the Sasines Register. Their research project, 'The property owners: the sociological significance of landlordism', is sponsored by the SSRC.

[9] The other leading property owners were Joint Properties Ltd, The University of Edinburgh, Stewarts (Holdings) Ltd, the National Coal Board, Caledonian Heritable Estates, and the Secretary of State for Scotland.

[10] Abercrombie's estimate for 1946 was that privately rented properties accounted for 52 per cent of the housing stock.

[11] The six others were St. Andrew's, George Square, Holyrood, Calton, South Leith and Broughton.

[12] Gorgie–Dalry, St. Giles, Central Leith, Holyrood and South Leith.

[13] Calton, Broughton, St. Andrew's and George Square.

[14] Merchiston, Newington, Morningside and St. Bernard's.

[15] For additional evidence of the impact of the presence of industry in an area on the level of property values see pp. 130–1.

[16] Indeed, some of the largest employers are in the service sector, such as the Scottish Office and the University of Edinburgh.

3 Description of the Sasines Data

The Scottish land tenure system

Scotland has a distinctive land tenure system very different from that operating in the rest of the United Kingdom. Basically, the system is a form of feudal tenure, a residual of the feudal landholding system developed in the eleventh and twelfth centuries. Originally, with a few minor exceptions, only the Crown could own land absolutely. A limited number of other persons, vassals-in-chief, held their lands in return for services and payments to the Crown. They could, in turn, make grants of land to *vassals* of their own, in which cases they were in the position of *superiors*. This process could be repeated several times creating a superior—vassal feudal chain. Via this process it was possible for simultaneous interests to be developed in a single piece of land. At a minimum, these rights were those of the Crown, those of at least one other superior, and those of the vassal occupant.

Over the course of time, there were major modifications in this system. First, the grant of land by a superior to a vassal, originally only for the vassal's lifetime, became perpetual and heritable. By the late eighteenth century, the lowest vassal in the feudal chain (the occupant) had for most practical purposes become the owner of the land provided he observed the terms of his feudal charter. Second, a variety of distinct forms of tenure were gradually replaced by one, originally called feu-farm, now simply described as feudal tenure. Third, the services (as distinct from the payments) which a vassal might owe to his superior, together with the superior's rights over the vassal's land or person, were either abolished or commuted into monetary payments. This process was a gradual one, completed only in 1914 when the Feudal Casualties (Scotland) Act finally abolished all feudal casualties, i.e. additional payments due to a superior on specified occasions such as the death of a vassal.

The main remaining features of the feudal tenure system are obligations on the vassals, first, to pay in perpetuity an annual sum (feuduty) to their superiors and, second, to observe conditions and limitations on the use of land ('land conditions') that can be enforced by the superior alone.[1]

Some comment is required on these two remaining obligations. Since, historically, no initial payment, apart perhaps from a nominal sum, was made for the land, the feuduty served as a kind of perpetual ground rent. Even today land is occasionally conveyed without any initial price or other capital payment, though this is no longer the general practice and land is transferred at a price similar to that which would prevail under a non-feudal system. Indeed, it is very doubtful that, say, a house buyer pays a price that is lower by an amount equivalent to the capitalised value of the feuduty. Like most other feudal provisions, the amount of feuduty cannot be altered except by agreement between the parties. At the same time, there has been an increase in the level of *new* feuduties in recent years. As a result, there are considerable inequities among proprietors in the amount of feuduty they pay for land conferring equivalent services.

Some of the land conditions may be unreasonable, such as specifying the materials which have to be used for the upkeep of properties or prohibiting a reasonable use of the property. Also, enforcement of land conditions is a serious problem. Sometimes, the superior will prevent a proprietor from carrying out reasonable development by refusing to waive a land condition. In other circumstances, the superior may waive a condition readily, though it may be against the interests of neighbouring proprietors. Some of these defects were remedied by the Conveyancing and Feudal Reform (Scotland) Act of 1970. In particular, it gave the vassal, or even his neighbours, the right to apply to the Lands Tribunal for Scotland for the variation or discharge of irksome land conditions, in some cases subject to payment of compensation to the superior.[2]

However, despite the 1970 Act disadvantages remain. The enforcement problem has not been completely solved, and the system still operates arbitrarily. 'Inequity may arise not only from the harsh enforcement of some particular land condition which is now outdated, but also from the failure of a superior to enforce a condition which is still of real practical benefit to others.'[3] There has been an increasing tendency in recent years for feudal superiors to be transferred from individuals to companies or trusts, whose primary interest is more likely to be financial rather than any concern with the use of the land. Also, the system results in a multi-tier structure of land ownership which makes conveyancing procedures more complicated and costly. On the other hand, the system has compensating benefits. The most important among these is that the perpetuity of landholding avoids the disruptions and social problems that can occur when a long lease expires. On balance, however, in 1970 the government felt that the drawbacks of the system conferred net disadvantages and pledged that the land tenure system would be reformed,

50

and that this reform should involve the abolition of feudal tenure. The Land Tenure Reform (Scotland) Bill of April 1974 was a little more modest, prohibiting new feu duties, and providing for the legal redemption of feu duties in return for a capital sum as property and land changes hands.

Characteristics of the Scottish property market

A considerable virtue of this study is that it is based on the actual prices at which properties changed hands rather than on 'assessed' or estimated prices.[4] The Scottish property market has a very unusual mode of operation, but one that makes market analysis more rather than less relevant. The reason is that in many property markets supply price is the key factor. The seller sets his price usually in terms of last year's price (or the price of an equivalent property on the same street) *plus* an increment to reflect generally rising prices.[5] In Scotland supply price is not very significant simply because the supplier does not fix a price. He may offer, on a solicitor's advice,[6] some guidance via a minimum price (offers over £x,000) or by asking for offers 'about £x,000'. This is not necessarily a clear indication of the price at which the property will change hands. The actual price is determined in most cases (i.e. excluding the infrequently used auction or 'public roup') by buyers making written sealed offers.[7] Therefore, the actual price is very much a market demand price, highly responsive to variations in demand conditions, except that buyers offer on the basis of incomplete information (i.e. they lack knowledge of the number of serious competitors and of the strength of their offers). Although it may be argued that the price at which the property is exchanged is less of a 'true' market price than if it had been sold at a public auction, the price is very sensitive to changes in market conditions. In particular, conditions of excess demand may generate sharp upward movements in price. Also, there is a strong element of indeterminacy in price since keen potential buyers have to guess at competitors' offers.

The Register of Sasines[8]

The Register of Sasines is the national land register for the whole of Scotland, dating from the Scots Act of 1617 and regulated by the Land Registers (Scotland) Act, 1868. It is unique to Scotland in Britain. The English parallel, the Register of Title at the Land Registry, is not comprehensive covering only part of the country, records less information, and most important of all is a private register not open to the public.[9] The Register of Sasines, on the other hand, is a public register and its contents can be made available without restriction subject to the huge task of extracting the information. The Register is principally a legal record of property transactions such as changes of title, conditions affecting the nature of feus, etc. All dealings are included, not only houses, but land, shops and other non-residential properties. Its primary value for research is that since 1905 market prices paid at the time of transaction are recorded; thus the Register is a valuable, even a unique, source for details of property values. [10] Every writ or deed affecting land is registered and recorded in the record volume; a précis of each writ is recorded in the minute book. Both these are kept in chronological order, and an index of all persons and all places concerned in each minute is prepared annually.

If data had to be obtained from these records, the process of extracting information for a single property would be quite laborious. Fortunately, in 1871 a scheme was introduced whereby a separate record was kept for each property, thus providing a complete history of the property without the need for searching the minute book. This record is called a *search sheet*. The search sheet gives a complete abstract of all the deeds which affect the property. The most important contents, from the point of view of this research project, are:

1 The address of the property.
2 The type of the property.
3 The age of the property.
4 In some cases, the size of the plot (or failing that, frontage).
5 The feu duty of the property.
6 The number of dwellings in the property.
7 The date and nature of any changes in size or use.
8 The date of each transaction (including for newly-built properties the date of completion).
9 The price of each transaction.[11]
10 The names and type (individual, company, institution, etc.) of the buyer and the seller.
11 In many cases, where the buyer and/or seller are individuals, sex and occupation are given.
12 The source of finance for the purchase.

In virtually all cases the information required for this research was obtained from the search sheet without resort to the record volume.[12]

The sampling procedure

The basis of the sample of Edinburgh residential properties was a stratified unequal cluster sample. This was designed specifically to construct time series of prices for houses at the small zonal level rather than for the cross-sectional analysis also undertaken in this book. All areas of the city were sampled using strata in the form of zones about 71 acres in area.

These zones were triangular in shape, obtained by dividing $1000m^2$ square grids into four diagonally. This yielded 590 zones covering the entire city. The size and shape were determined by the need to aggregate zones into concentric rings and radial sectors for other aspects of the study. In particular, triangles were found to aggregate more easily than mini-grid squares and also enabled major radial routes to be followed less cumbersomely. The sample size consisted of 20 per cent of the Edinburgh search sheets, [13] and *all* the properties on one out of every five streets within each zone were sampled. This cluster sample was selected in order to minimise differences in type between houses for the purpose of constructing a street price index from the prices of those houses that happened to come on to the market, taking account of the infrequency of turnover on any individual house. [14] Since streets can vary widely in length, a procedure was devised to ensure that both long and short streets were represented.

The procedure was as follows:

(a)   For zones containing eight or more streets, the sample frame was divided into one stratum of the five largest streets and another of the remaining streets. One street was randomly drawn from the first stratum, and one street in every five in the second stratum. Where the number of smaller streets was not a multiple of five, one street was drawn from the residual if it consisted of three or four streets.

(b)   For zones containing three to seven streets, the three longest streets were selected and one of these randomly drawn for the sample.

(c)   For zones containing one or two streets, one street was randomly drawn in order to ensure coverage of even the sparsest zones.

(d)   Where streets crossed zonal boundaries, only the section of a selected long street within the zone was included in the sample. Shorter streets were considered available for sampling if at least 80 per cent of their length was located in the zone in question.

Method of data collection and processing

The basic information was extracted from the search sheets by part-time research assistants working during office hours in Register House. The data were entered on record sheets, which were laid out in a form permitting coding to be carried out on the same sheet. This was not difficult since much of the information was quantitative (prices, dates, feuduties, etc.). The research assistants subsequently coded the information at home, and the coded sheets were then despatched in bulk from Edinburgh to the research centre in Canterbury. The coding operations were then rechecked, with special attention given to the occupational codes since the multiplicity of occupations implied that these had to be coded according to predetermined guidelines rather than automatically. All the data were punched on to 80-column punch cards and verified. The information was scrutinized once again on the computer by a data check programme, and was then transferred to magnetic tape. Thus the extraction and processing operations were carried out using procedures with repeated built-in checks so as to minimize the risks of data error.

The only phase where no major checks were possible other than duplication of the whole research was at the initial data extraction stage. However, some sample checks were made. Also, the search sheet is a simple document, and the risks of transcription error are low. Moreover, most of the research assistants were very experienced people who had been Sasines Register employees in the past, but had given up the work usually for domestic reasons.

Description of the data

The rest of this chapter presents the basic factual information about the sample as a whole obtained from the Sasines Register. In particular, this information relates to the number of sales per zone, dwelling type, changes in use and size, frontage and plot area, feu duties, sales by type, occupational and other information about the buyers and sellers, age distribution of properties, prices, annual turnover rates, seasonal variations in sales and sources of finance.

Sales per zone

There was a marked variation in the number of sales between zones during the period under study (1905–71); the actual range stretched from one to 1,126 properties. Out of the total number of zones containing private residential properties (423), in only 55 did the number of sales exceed 200. This relatively low density of sales necessitated a revision of the original intention to develop street and even zonal price indices,[15] because such an operation was hardly justified by the small sample size. As a result, attention was shifted towards larger geographical areas. Particularly from the point of view of testing theoretical hypotheses relating to urban spatial structure, the most convenient size and shape of area for deriving price indices were found to be segments obtained via the superimposition of five concentric rings on eight radial sectors.

Dwelling type

The basic information on dwelling type is summarised in table 3.1. The majority of properties in the sample consisted of flats; this is the typical distribution in a Scottish city. Although some of the search sheets contained more details about property types (e.g. whether or not a house was detached), the frequency of this kind of data was much too patchy for use to be made of it. [16] Price information on multiple properties proved very difficult to handle because of the wide variety of quality between blocks and the difficulty of accounting for heterogeneity of individual components within a multiple property. Fortunately, multiple properties accounted for less than 2 per cent of the total sample.

Table 3.1

Type of dwelling

Type	Number	Percentage of total
Houses	6,357	41·6
Flats	8,650	56·5
Multiple properties	287	1·9
Total	15,294	100·0

Changes in use and size

Changes in use affected a sizeable proportion (2,436) of the properties. Over half of these (1,394) consisted of subdivisions. Although most of these subdivisions meant division into two or three properties, examples could be found of up to more than twenty units. However, the number of subdivisions decreased steadily the greater the degree of subdivisions. Of the other changes in use, 354 involved a major change in use (probably residential to commercial use). These two factors explain why we would expect to find a positive association between properties that undergo at some stage a change in use and price. Other changes in use refer to demolitions (316), land transactions (262) and garage transactions (68).

Frontage and plot area data

The size of site data in the Sasines Register are incomplete. In the sample frontage was obtainable for 3,371 properties (22 per cent) while plot area was available for 2,445 properties (16 per cent). [17] Frontage fell within the 20–50 feet range for 2,550 houses, i.e. about three-quarters of the properties for which such data were available. As for area, the distribution was skewed towards small plots. As many as 2,092 properties occupied sites smaller than one-quarter of an acre, while only 38 houses were situated on one-acre-plus plots. The modal size range was 0·067–0·125 of an acre (975 houses).

Feu duties[18]

Feu duty information was available for 11,504 properties. Of these, for 6,119 the feu duty fell in the range £1–5, with another 3,301 in the range of £5–10. The feu duty was greater than £15 only on 635 properties.

Sales by type

Each property transaction was classified by type of sale, reflecting all combinations of individuals, local authority, companies and organizations, plus sales by builders to each of these. In fact, a very high proportion of the total transactions (32,525 out of 41,199) was made up of sales by 'individual to individual', and this proportion fluctuated over time within the ranges of 61–64 per cent in the period 1905–09 and in the 1930s to 87 per cent in the 1940s and in 1970–71. The other sizeable category 'builder to individual' fluctuated considerably in response to changes in housebuilding rates. It was high before 1914, between 1925 and 1939 and in the late fifties, accounting in these periods for shares within the range 15–30 per cent. In other periods it was well below 10 per cent, and actually fell to 3·3 per cent in 1970–71. All the other categories were very small, apart from 'company to individual' which accounted for 3–5 per cent of total sales. Companies also bought from individuals, though on a smaller scale (about 1½ per cent of total sales). The major factor in this type of sale was conversion to non-residential use.

Buyers and sellers

Individuals accounted for about 97 per cent of all buyers and (apart from before 1910, in the 1930s and the late 1950s) for almost 90 per cent of the sellers. The gap is due to sales by builders and the fact that companies sold residential properties far more frequently than they bought them.

This is due to the decline in the investment return available from private rented housing compared with the returns obtainable by investing the cash proceeds of sales in other outlets.

The most striking change within the separate individuals categories (classified by sex and marital status) is the growth of joint ownership by husband and wife (28·3 per cent of total buyers in 1970–71 compared with 9·1 per cent in 1905–09). Since this was accompanied by a commensurate fall in the percentage of 'one male' buyers (59·4–42·2 per cent) and of married women buyers (10·3–3·5 per cent), it suggests not so much joint purchase as the fact that the real purchaser was, if married, increasingly permitting joint ownership on the title deeds. In other words, it is more a reflection of changing social customs than of the emergence of new methods of payment and finance.

Occupations of buyers and sellers

Occupational data were obtained from the Register for both buyers and sellers in almost 15,000 of the 41,200 transactions. These were originally classified into 808 different occupational groups, but it soon became clear that this number was unmanageable and that no firm criteria could be established for aggregating them into a smaller but still highly dis-aggregated set of groups. The main problems were the generality with which some occupations were defined ('engineer', 'sales worker', etc.) and the changes in the relative status of occupations over time which made it very difficult to devise a large number of groups ranked by class or status for the period as a whole. Consequently, the way in which the occupational data are used later in the book (see chapter 9) is via aggregation into a small number of broad categories.

Age distribution of properties

Reliable data on the age of dwellings were obtainable for almost 95 per cent of the sample. For practical purposes of analysis and because of less precision in the very early years, all properties built in 1871 and earlier were classified together. This accounted for about one-sixth of the total sample. The overall percentage distribution by year is given in table 3.2.

Age distribution information is valuable for at least two reasons. First, it enables tests to be made of the hypothesis that intending purchasers prefer new houses to old, and, more particularly, it permits estimates to be made of the quantitative impact of age on house price. Increasing age may be associated with obsolescence in the sense of a need for higher repairs and maintenance expenditures and because of changing tastes

Table 3.2

Age distribution of sample, 1872–1970 (%)

Year	%	Year	%	Year	%	Year	%
pre-1872	16·66	1896	2·47	1921	0·10	1946	0·56
1872	0·22	1897	2·12	1922	0·14	1947	0·11
1873	0·56	1898	1·60	1923	0·27	1948	0·19
1874	0·72	1899	2·01	1924	0·56	1949	0·02
1875	0·50	1900	0·98	1925	0·76	1950	0·09
1876	1·13	1901	0·77	1926	1·51	1951	0·04
1877	1·30	1902	1·44	1927	1·05	1952	0·33
1878	2·50	1903	0·89	1928	0·87	1953	0·75
1879	0·88	1904	1·21	1929	0·66	1954	0·79
1880	0·96	1905	1·27	1930	0·98	1955	1·55
1881	1·57	1906	0·98	1931	1·38	1956	1·26
1882	1·15	1907	0·68	1932	2·08	1957	0·72
1883	1·39	1908	0·45	1933	2·51	1958	0·32
1884	1·35	1909	0·31	1934	2·33	1959	0·45
1885	0·56	1910	0·27	1935	1·38	1960	0·36
1886	0·77	1911	0·10	1936	1·51	1961	0·69
1887	1·69	1912	0·12	1937	1·95	1962	0·83
1888	1·60	1913	0·06	1938	1·00	1963	0·60
1889	1·29	1914	0·14	1939	0·61	1964	0·92
1890	1·52	1915	0·02	1940	0·21	1965	1·06
1891	0·36	1916	0·00	1941	0·07	1966	0·54
1892	0·31	1917	0·00	1942	0·06	1967	0·60
1893	0·90	1918	0·00	1943	0·00	1968	0·40
1894	0·58	1919	0·00	1944	0·00	1969	0·14
1895	0·89	1920	0·03	1945	0·02	1970	0·23
						Age not known	5·26

about sizes of rooms, layout and exterior design. Second, if the property sample is large enough and is representative of all areas of the city (both these conditions being fulfilled in this study), the age distribution provides a reasonable surrogate for *private* housebuilding activity.

Viewed in this manner, table 3.2 enables peaks and slumps in private residential building to be identified over the last hundred years. Relatively high levels of activity are found in the following periods: 1877–78,

1881–84, 1887–90, 1896–99, 1902–05, 1926–27, 1932–37, 1953–57 and 1961–65. Serious slumps occur in 1872–75, 1891–95, 1908–14, the years of World War I, 1920–24, World War II, 1945–52, 1958–60 and since 1966. Peak years (as represented by the crude indicator of >1·5 per cent of the overall age distribution) consist of the following: 1881, 1887, 1888, 1896, 1897, 1898, 1899, 1926, 1932, 1933, 1934, 1936, 1937, 1955. With one or two exceptions, these data point to three main periods of private housebuilding activity in Edinburgh: the late 1880s, the late 1890s and the 1932–37 recovery period.

The use of the term 'slump' in the post–1945 period is a little misleading, particularly since the levels of activity in the good years are also relatively modest. Private housebuilding *within* the city boundaries in the post-World War II period has been almost uniformly low, primarily because a substantial proportion of the new private houses built for households holding jobs in Edinburgh was located outside the city boundaries because of land shortages and suburbanization forces. The developments that were located within the city boundaries tended to be small (see above, p. 33). A secondary explanation of secularly low level of private building was the competition of public sector housebuilding, particularly the powers of Edinburgh City Corporation that enabled it to purchase most of the land that became available within the city.

An interesting question is whether the cyclical patterns found in Edinburgh are peculiar to that city or replicated in other Scottish cities. The companion national study to the Edinburgh project yielded samples for the other three large Scottish cities – Glasgow, Aberdeen and Dundee. The sample sizes were much smaller, particularly in the latter two cases, so that the age distributions are less reliable. Nevertheless, it was possible to draw some conclusions from an inter-city comparison. [19] First, Dundee's housing stock was much older than Edinburgh's (21·1 per cent built before 1872), while in Glasgow (12·2 per cent) and Aberdeen (11·5 per cent) the reverse was true. Second, the cyclical patterns were broadly similar, but there was by no means perfect synchronization. For example, the housing boom of the 1870s occurred in 1875–77 in Glasgow, 1878–80 in Aberdeen, and 1874–76 in Dundee as opposed to 1876–78 in Edinburgh. Such divergences can be found again and again. The great housing boom of the late 1890s, for instance, petered out in Aberdeen in 1898, in Edinburgh in 1899 and in Dundee in 1900, but in Glasgow not only did it begin a little later (1898) it continued, apart from a minor dip in 1901, through to 1905–06. These differences suggest the importance of local factors as determinants of the turning points in housebuilding activity, even if an approximately uniform cyclical pattern moulded by national (and international) forces can still be identified. The stress on local determinants provides a Scottish parallel to the arguments found in Saul's study of housebuilding in England in the period 1890–1914: [20] that to describe the pre-1914 building cycle as a 'foreign investment-emigration cycle in disguise' is an oversimplification: and that there is an intimate relationship between local economic conditions, the state of the local housing market and the urban housebuilding cycle.

The differences continue into the inter-war and postwar periods. Private housebuilding was almost continuously depressed in Glasgow (an indirect reflection of inter-war conditions in the staple industries on which the economy of Glasgow was based – shipbuilding, iron and steel, coal, cotton and engineering), and even the nationwide private housing boom of the 1930s had virtually no impact in Glasgow. Only in the period 1926–28, when the basic industries were doing relatively well, was Glasgow's private housebuilding industry active. [21] In Aberdeen and Dundee the 1930s housing boom was visible, in 1933–35 and 1934–38 respectively, but was not as vigorous as in Edinburgh, an indication of the much greater buoyancy of a service-based city. In the post-1945 period, private housebuilding in Glasgow and Aberdeen has been even more limited than in Edinburgh. The same explanatory forces observed in the Edinburgh case were operative: land shortages, suburbanization, competition for land from the public sector. In Dundee, however, the situation was different. Land problems were not as severe, much of the existing private housing stock was very old and of poorer quality, and social and economic conditions favoured a limited growth in private housing demand – particularly in the most recent period. Accordingly, private housebuilding in Dundee was strong in 1954–56, 1961 and in 1965–69. Once again, the analysis points to the importance of local determinants in private housebuilding patterns.

Prices

The basic series of Edinburgh residential property prices is given in table 3.3. The series is obtained by taking the mean price of all properties in the sample that were sold in a particular year. However, to prevent distortions due to artificial prices (e.g. the compulsory purchase price preceding demolition) all prices below a certain level were excluded, as were especially high prices. [22] This resulted in the elimination of 164 and 99 sales respectively from the data used to construct the index. A further 1,333 sales had to be excluded because the prices were unknown, leaving

Table 3.3

Edinburgh house prices, turnover rates and sources of finance, 1905–72

	Price (£s)	Price (£s) for Scotland (excluding Edinburgh)*	Edinburgh new house prices (£s)	Exclusive turnover rate (%)	Sources of finance (%)		
					Cash sales	Building societies	Other
1905	–	502		2·25	37	4	59
1906	–	545		1·64	30	6	64
1907	–	686		1·16	37	2	61
1908	–	528		1·35	36	5	59
1909	–	528		1·25	41	3	56
1910	583	518		1·28	43	9	48
1911	667	516		1·15	58	4	38
1912	555	502		1·36	56	5	39
1913	610	536		1·40	60	6	34
1914	491	500		1·03	64	8	27
1915	612	487		0·86	74	1	25
1916	429	510		0·69	68	5	26
1917	566	548		0·92	76	3	22
1918	543	635		1·26	66	2	32
1919	684	717		5·34	63	6	31
1920	778	742		6·86	56	7	37
1921	878	737		3·98	65	4	31
1922	806	753		4·06	58	6	35
1923	840	769		4·61	57	7	35
1924	897	738		5·00	54	7	39
1925	869	727		4·23	51	8	41
1926	886	733		4·49	48	6	46
1927	806	702		4·48	54	7	39
1928	813	725		4·35	49	9	42
1929	758	697		4·14	49	20	31
1930	732	664		4·44	47	23	30
1931	780	586		3·60	44	28	28
1932	698	589		3·24	40	33	27
1933	643	569		4·04	40	36	24
1934	678	635		3·81	42	31	27
1935	713	590		3·44	41	32	27
1936	679	589		3·72	41	35	24
1937	731	643		3·96	39	40	21
1938	741	653		3·70	40	39	21

Table 3.3 continued

1939	760	636		3·11	38	38	24
1940	629	662		1·34	62	16	22
1941	797	728		1·58	59	22	19
1942	801	845		2·54	58	22	21
1943	1,021	999		3·03	52	22	26
1944	1,258	1,139		3·13	50	28	21
1945	1,616	1,430		4·16	44	32	24
1946	1,674	1,580		5·62	44	38	18
1947	2,072	1,786		5·71	39	39	22
1948	2,159	1,835		6·63	40	42	18
1949	2,075	1,799		7·27	40	40	20
1950	2,075	1,701		6·06	40	40	20
1951	2,178	1,709		6·34	39	36	24
1952	2,087	1,612	2,060	6·27	34	40	26
1953	1,677	1,384	2,250	6·66	33	43	24
1954	1,627	1,376	2,350	7·36	33	49	18
1955	1,725	1,408	2,330	7·16	28	50	22
1956	1,742	1,379	2,360	6·42	36	41	23
1957	1,719	1,361	2,790	6·77	39	41	20
1958	1,775	1,360	2,750	6·84	39	43	18
1959	1,841	1,455	2,750	7·69	36	45	18
1960	1,908	1,565	3,020	7·43	37	48	15
1961	2,064	1,671	2,810	7·08	42	42	16
1962	2,327	1,765	3,220	7·61	39	45	16
1963	2,462	1,872	3,820	7·68	37	49	14
1964	2,923	2,101	4,680	7·48	38	49	13
1965	3,370	2,348	4,320	7·85	37	48	15
1966	3,532	2,592	4,940	7·43	35	51	14
1967	3,629	2,773	6,390	7·90	29	59	12
1968	4,028	3,053	6,330	7·40	36	49	15
1969	4,023	3,220	6,070	7·91	32	52	16
1970	4,071	3,820	5,860	8·31	31	54	15
1971	5,212	*	5,770	*	28	60	12
1972	*	*	8,450	*	*	*	*

*Not available. The data for the rest of Scotland were obtained through
a 5 per cent sample of residential properties drawn from the Register
of Sasines covering the whole country apart from Edinburgh.

38,709 prices for the index. [23] The years 1905–09 had to be excluded because of insufficient sales in the sample, and the sample size for the period 1910–18 is also a little precarious (within the range 56–116). Apart from these exceptions and during World War II (when the number of sales ranged from 174–478), the number of prices included in estimation of the annual mean price varied from 327 to 1,256. Coupled with the size of our sample relative to the total private housing stock and the method via which the sample was drawn, this suggests that the price series provides a reasonable measure of changes in residential property values in Edinburgh City as a whole over the past sixty years. On the other hand, the range of price variation within any one year (as measured by the standard deviation) was considerable, but this is inevitable in view of the heterogeneity of residential properties, especially in a city where the private housing stock includes both large detached villas and tiny tenement flats.

The movements in Edinburgh house prices over time are evident from the data shown in table 3.3: year-to-year fluctuations in the period 1910–18, but no trend; a sharp upward movement between 1918 and 1921, a relapse in 1922 and 1923, followed by a return to the level of 1921. After 1926, however, prices start to fall, though irregularly, for several years, and the trough is not reached until 1933. Prices then start to edge slightly upwards until the outbreak of the war. A sharp drop in 1940 is followed by a continuous rise, particularly after 1942, with the result that house prices at the end of the war were double the pre-war level. The increase continues, not unexpectedly in view of postwar building controls, to 1947 and then house prices remain at this more or less constant but high level until 1952. Coincident with the relaxation of controls and the resurgence of private housebuilding prices fell sharply in 1953 and to a much lesser extent in 1954. After 1954, the trend is continuously upwards though the rate of change varies from year to year, with the sharpest increases taking place in 1961–65, 1967–68 and 1970–71.

It is interesting to compare the movement of residential property values in Edinburgh with that observed both in Scotland as a whole and in the other three leading Scottish cities. The Scottish series is also presented in table 3.3. From 1920 onwards, prices in Edinburgh moved ahead of the national level. Although the gap widened in the 1920s, it tended to narrow slightly in the following decade. After World War II, however, the gap widens once more. This is indicative of the housing market boom experienced in Edinburgh, particularly in the 1960s. In comparing the national and the Edinburgh series, it should be noticed that the peaks and troughs do not always coincide: examples are the peak of 1923 and 1924 and the trough of 1931 and 1933.

The inter-city comparison is rather more hazardous because the small sample sizes available for Glasgow, Aberdeen and Dundee yield only very crude measures of house price, at least before the 1950s when the sample sizes are substantially larger. However, the striking feature of such a comparison is that Edinburgh's reputation as the most expensive housing market in the United Kingdom outside London and southeast England is relatively recent. Prices in all three cities were higher than in Edinburgh in the early decades of the century. Edinburgh began to pull ahead of Glasgow in 1931 and the gap progressively widened so that by the late 1960s house prices in Edinburgh were about 80 per cent higher. In Dundee, house prices were at levels similar to Edinburgh, though perhaps a little higher, throughout the inter-war period, but Edinburgh began to move ahead after 1948. By the late 1960s, house prices in Edinburgh had risen to a level 35 per cent higher than in Dundee. In Aberdeen, house prices were a little higher than in Edinburgh both between the wars and after 1945 up to the late 1950s. From 1960, however, Edinburgh moves ahead so that by the late 1960s Edinburgh house prices are about 25 per cent higher. Nevertheless, Aberdeen remained the second most expensive housing market in Scotland.

Table 3.3 also gives estimates of *new* house prices built within the boundaries of Edinburgh City since 1952. These figures were obtained from the residential development information yielded from the survey of private sector land purchases. The series does not show the continuous upward movement in new house prices that has characterized housing market conditions in the United Kingdom from the mid-fifties until 1973, when a (probably temporary) drop occurred. The explanation for this is the wide variety of new houses (ranging from small apartments and terraced houses to luxury villas and apartments) and the small scale of housebuilding within the city, so that the occurrence of a single atypical development in any one year could distort the price estimate for that year to a considerable degree. Accordingly, it would be wrong to use this information as a measure of year-to-year variations in new house prices. However, the trend of new house prices is clearly upwards. The most significant point of interest is the wide divergence between new and old house prices in Edinburgh over the last twenty years. Generally speaking, the price of a new house has been 50 per cent higher than that of an old house. This is, to some extent, an overestimate since this comparison is not standardized for size and quality. Nevertheless, even allowing for this, the gap between new and old house prices remained large. It is probably wider in Edinburgh than in many other British cities, because of the scarcity of new housing within the city itself creating conditions of excess demand for such houses. The other main explanation of the differential is the heavy increase in postwar land prices.

Turnover rates

Table 3.3 also includes a series measuring turnover rate. The standard method of deriving a turnover rate is simply to divide the number of annual sales by the total number of saleable properties available in that year (i.e. the part of the housing stock *potentially* available for sale). However, the Sasines Register also lists as a sale the transfer of a new house from the builder to its first owner. This is more satisfactorily interpreted as an increment to the housing stock rather than as turnover in the existing housing stock. As a result, these transactions were excluded from the numerator to yield what may be called the 'exclusive turnover rate'. This is the series shown in table 3.3.

Although there are year-to-year fluctuations in the turnover rate, the intensity of which may be used to draw inferences about the state of the housing market and which should show some correspondence with changes in national mortgage credit conditions, the most striking characteristic is its upward trend. Apart from the war periods when it slumps and the immediate postwar periods when it jumps above its trend position, [24] the trend in the turnover rate is clearly upwards, rising from below 2 per cent before 1914 and around 4 per cent between the wars to 8 per cent by the end of the period. The obvious explanation of this trend is increasing mobility both within and between cities.

A comparison was possible between the exclusive turnover rate on pre-1918 dwellings and that on post-1918 dwellings. Perhaps surprisingly, with the exception of the period between 1936 and 1943, the turnover rate on older properties was consistently 1−2 per cent higher than on the newer ones. There are three feasible explanations of this fact. First, filtering processes tend to affect older much more than newer housing. Second, a sizeable proportion of the older housing was rented, frequently at controlled rents. The abolition of rent controls and the insatiable demand for owner-occupation (and the rising prices that accompanied this demand) induced landlords, when the opportunity arose, to put their properties on the market for sale usually to owner-occupiers. Third, and probably most important, suburbanization of households into new and relatively new housing outside the city showed itself in higher turnover rates on old central city properties, but the associated turnover on newer properties would be reflected in higher county rather than city turnover rates.

Seasonal variations in sales

There are marked seasonal variations in property sales. The peak months are May (17 per cent of annual sales in the sample) and, surprisingly at first sight, November (9·8 per cent). In fact, there are traditional and legal reasons for the dominance of these two months in the Scottish property market. Feu duties are payable at six-monthly intervals in May and November, and May is the traditional month for the transfer of feus and for major land market transactions.

Apart from May and November, the range varies between January (5·9 per cent of annual sales) and June (8·6 per cent). The peak property selling season converges around May, since more than 42 per cent of annual sales occur between April and July. On the other hand, housing market activity remains considerable even in the trough season of December to March, since more than one-quarter (26·3 per cent) of annual sales take place during those four months.

Sources of finance

Some information on sources of finance was available for each property transaction. The percentage distribution for three categories (cash sales, building societies and 'other sources') is shown in table 3.3. The composition of the 'other sources' category has changed over time. In particular, there has been a shift in the recent past from the banks in favour of insurance companies and local authorities. The main features of the changes over time are clearly evident in table 3.3. First, the most striking development has been the steady increase in the role of the building societies in financing house purchase, from about 5 per cent of total purchases before 1914 to 50–60 per cent in the late 1960s and the first two years of the seventies. Although there are a few minor down-turns in the building societies' share (e.g. in 1956 and in 1968), with the exception of the two war periods the upward trend is firm.

Second, there has been a slight downward trend in cash sales, but this is much more modest than might have been expected. Cash sales accounted for a high share of total sales in the war periods, and perhaps surprisingly for a higher share of sales between the wars than before 1914. The highest peacetime share was in 1921 (65 per cent) and cash sales did not dip below 30 per cent of the total until 1955. Even by the 1960s cash sales accounted for 30–40 per cent of the total.

Third, in view of the relative stability of cash sales, other types of mortgage lending institution have been the main sufferers from building society expansion. Apart from a mild revival in the mid-twenties, an even more modest recovery in 1951–53 and a below-trend share in World War I, the proportion of property sales involving 'other sources' has declined steadily over time from around 60 per cent in the first decade of the century to 12–15 per cent in recent years.

Fourth, it is unwise to generalize from these conclusions by extending them either nationwide or to other cities. Different housing markets may vary substantially in their relative reliance on alternative sources of mortgage finance. In Glasgow, for example, the share of cash sales has dropped only very recently, and the building societies have been less involved. As for the 'other sources' share, this has increased markedly since 1961 (when it jumped from 9 per cent to 23 per cent). These differences can be explained by conditions peculiar to the individual housing market. Cash sales are more common in Glasgow because properties are cheaper. Also, a higher proportion of the housing stock dates from before 1914 and its average quality is poorer. As a result, building societies have been much more cautious about extending their activities, particularly since the early 1950s. The tightness of mortgage funds has made the building societies very selective about lending on older properties, and as a consequence the local authority has stepped in as a significant supplier of mortgage funds (this explains the rising 'other sources' share). The same factor also accounts for the continued high share of cash sales.

Notes

[1] The superior could waive these conditions, sometimes in return for a monetary consideration.

[2] The Act included several other reforms. It introduced a new form of standardized heritable security. It simplified conveyancing procedures. It also gave a vassal whose feuduty is 'unallocated' the right to secure from his superior, failing which from the Lands Tribunal, an allocation limiting his liability to payment of his own share. Unallocated feuduty refers to the situation where a property subject to a single feuduty has been subdivided, but the proprietor of each part can still be required by the superior to pay the whole feuduty.

[3] Scottish Home and Health Department (1972), p. 9.

[4] On the other hand, a corollary is that the urban house price structure is based in any year upon the experience of recent movers rather than of all residents. However, for a durable good that is transferred between owners very infrequently this is inevitable unless one is happy to fall back on the artificial 'assessed' price method.

[5] In periods of falling prices, the seller usually fixes last year's price and hopes that an offer will not fall too far short of this figure.

[6] Solicitors rather than estate agents tend to have control over the property market.

[7] Under Scottish property law, the transaction is made when a written offer (and this is the only offer which counts) is accepted in writing rather than at the time when contracts are exchanged as in England. This sometimes means, particularly in periods of excess demand, that would-be purchasers make offers in advance of obtaining a mortgage, and much reliance is placed on the solicitor's capacity to arrange a mortgage subsequently.

[8] The term 'Sasine' is derived from an old French word coming from the same root as 'seizing' in the sense of taking possession. The term was first applied to the legal ceremony of transferring land, whereby the seller handed to the purchaser a handful of earth and stone, thus symbolically giving him possession. The ceremony was recorded in a written deed called an Instrument of Sasine and these deeds were recorded in the Register of Sasines. The modern equivalent is a deed of transfer or disposition.

[9] Compulsory registration of title applies only to London (since 1898–1902), Eastbourne (1926), Hastings (1928), Middlesex (1937), Croydon (1939), Oxford (1954), Oldham (1956), Kent (1957), Leicester (1957), Canterbury (1958), Manchester and Salford (1961), Huddersfield (1962), Blackburn (1962) and Reading (1962). The Register is so private that it can be inspected only under the authority of the registered owner.

[10] It is true that information on property values can now be obtained from building society data (e.g. the Nationwide Building Society) and with greater difficulty, from Inland Revenue sources, but such information is very aggregative, referring only to broad regions, and is available only for recent years. However, in some parts of the country, e.g. the West Riding of Yorkshire, the prices of some individual property transactions are registered in the area Registry of Deeds. Professor E.M. Sigsworth and R.K. Wilkinson are undertaking research into property values using this source.

[11] Since the names and details of transactions are noted, it is possible to distinguish between market value sales and transactions at artificially low values to, say, other members of a family or to a part owner.

[12] The records are distributed among thirty-three divisions, each corresponding to a Scottish county, and the counties are grouped in six districts (Central, East, Edinburgh, Glasgow, North and South). At H.M. Register House, Edinburgh, where the records are kept, there is a room for each district. For further details of the operations of the Register see *Report of Committee on the Registration of Title to Land in Scotland*, Cmnd. 2032, 1963.

[13] The sample is well under 20 per cent of the housing stock since council houses (not included in the Register of Sasines) account for over one-quarter of the housing stock.

[14] As it turned out, the construction of street price indices was impossible because of low turnover rates, time clustering of sales and the variability of properties and prices within streets.

[15] The number of properties per street varied from zero to 328. However, out of 607 streets only 26 contained more than 100 properties while another 26 streets had between 50 and 99 properties. Combined with the modest turnover in properties (an average of only 2·7 sales per property over the 65-year period), this fact ruled out any attempt to construct meaningful price indices at the street level, even if it had been possible to assume that the degree of property homogeneity was very high.

[16] A qualification to this comment is that flats are usually specified by floor. In the absence of lifts, prices tend to be rather lower on the second floor and above.

[17] These proportions look much healthier when it is remembered that this type of information (certainly plot area) is usually obtainable only for houses, not flats.

[18] The role of feu duties in the Scottish land tenure system has been described above; see pp. 49–51.

[19] The tables have not been published because of space constraints.

[20] S.B. Saul, 'House building in England, 1890–1914' *Economic History Review,* 2nd series, no. 15, 1962, pp. 119–37.

[21] The age distribution of dwellings data for Glasgow clearly point to the secular strength of Glasgow's economy before 1914 and its secular weakness since that time.

[22] The minimum–maximum ranges were £0–5,000 in the period 1870–1939, £100–10,000 in 1940–59 and £100–20,000 in 1960–71.

[23] Multiple properties were also excluded.

[24] There is also a relapse in the 1930s, presumably because housing market activity shifted towards new houses and because this shift was not accompanied by extensive filtering which would have tended to boost the exclusive turnover rate.

4 Determinants of Edinburgh's House Price Structure in 1966

The aim of this part of the study is to make a contribution to the literature on the determinants of relative urban house prices by using cross-sectional data referring to all property transactions in the sample for 1966. After discussion of some data and methodological problems, the next step is to estimate a 'best fit' equation using stepwise regression methods for the full sample and for a smaller subsample for which plot area data were obtainable. Subsequently (see chapter 5), the sample is used for indirect tests of alternative residential location theories (namely accessibility, spatial, environmental or area preference, and housing characteristics, i.e. locationally-insensitive, models). One advantage of the spatial model is that its data requirements are so easily met that it can be tested dynamically (over the period 1910–71). This advantage is capitalized on below (see chapter 6) in order to permit some of the ideas associated with the work of Homer Hoyt to be tested.

Classification of independent variables

Table 4.1 lists all the independent variables that were used in the regressions,[1] and classifies these according to whether they represent space and topography, accessibility, environment, quality of nearby properties or house characteristics. These classifications indicate the most obvious variables for testing specific types of models, e.g. accessibility and 'trade-off' theories. However, it is obvious that there is considerable overlap both between categories (e.g. environment and quality of nearby properties) and in the assignment of variables to each category (e.g. distance must be included in both the spatial and accessibility groups). The dual functions of some of the variables are a little less obvious and require a brief comment. The effect of the 'bus route through zone' variable effect is interpreted according to its empirically derived sign. If positive, it indicates the relevance of accessibility; if negative, it should be interpreted as an environmental

Table 4.1

Classification of independent variables

			Influence of size and/or quality	
Spatial/ topographical:	distance direction height			
Accessibility:	distance car ownership zone on periphery frequency of buses bus route through zone	positive		
Environment:	class no industry in zone open space bus route through zone	negative		
Quality of nearby properties:	amenities		—	Q
	rooms per person		S	Q
	population structure: under 15		S	—
	over 64		S	Q
	tenure groups		—	Q
House size and quality:	type		S	Q
	change in use		S	—
	age		—	Q
	source of finance		—	Q
	area of plot		S	—

disamenity reflecting noise and disturbance and risk of traffic accidents to children. There has probably been some shift over time in the influence of proximity to bus routes as a factor in house prices. In the past, such as in the inter-war period, main road (and bus route) locations were regarded as a desirable feature in a house, largely on accessibility grounds. This advantage has been eroded by the growth in car ownership, which gives a more flexible form of travel to the household, and hence an alternative form of accessibility on the one hand, and has been associated with the increase in traffic, and hence environmental disturbance on the other. Another example of dual function is the directional dummy variables which stand as surrogates for environmental features that are located sectorally. For instance, in Edinburgh in the full best-fit equation the negative coefficient for the composite northeast directional variable probably reflects, *inter alia,* environmental disamenities of this part of the city (dirt and noise, docks, warehouses and industry) that are inadequately captured by included variables.

The car ownership variable, though assigned to the accessibility category, is difficult to interpret unequivocally, partly because it had to be measured at the enumeration district rather than the individual household level. One interpretation is to consider a high car ownership score as measuring a high *average* degree of accessibility from the zone to the city centre, independent of distance. However, an alternative is to treat car ownership as a surrogate for social class, or income.

Third, to the extent that a high car ownership score is correlated with a high proportion of houses with a garage, it may be a partial measure of the effect of a garage on house price (i.e. a housing attribute measure). Our results show that car ownership is an important variable, but its precise impact is hard to specify. Wilkinson (1973, pp. 78–9) has suggested that difficulty of specification has compensating advantages because 'it draws attention to the ambiguities that may arise in using apparently quite straightforward specifications of housing attributes and serves to underline the need both for understanding the structure of housing attributes and services and for developing clear criteria for adopting particular measures'.

An attempt is made with the last two categories in table 4.1 to suggest *a priori* whether they would affect the size and/or quality of dwellings. This is consistent with Kain and Quigley's argument (1970(a) and (b)) that quantitative aspects of housing have been overemphasized to the exclusion of, possibly more important, qualitative considerations. In many cases it is impossible to isolate a size or quality effect. For example, rooms per person obviously reflect size, but because of the association between overcrowding and slum properties its more important effect is probably qualitative. The age structure variable of percentage of population over sixty-four will be indicative of small houses, but also old occupants are less likely to spend on maintenance and repairs. The house type variable distinguishing between houses and flats takes account of the fact that houses are, in general, considered more desirable to purchasers than flats apart from their tendency to be larger.

Areal level of independent variables

Although the dependent variable (house price) is always expressed in terms of the individual dwelling,[2] the independent variables fall into three categories, each relating to a different level of spatial aggregation – the dwelling itself, the sampling zone and the census enumeration district (see table 4.2). To a substantial degree, this is justified by the fact that many of the independent variables are intended to represent environmental considerations which make sense only at the neighbourhood level. However, the choice between zonal measures and those relating to the census of population enumeration district was determined not on theoretical but on pragmatic grounds – namely, the availability of data. It would have been desirable to have all the variables obtainable only at the enumeration district level available for the zonal level if data had permitted. It should also be noted that two variables do not figure in any of the quoted regressions. These are access to schools and access to shops. Because of the spatial spread of services in Edinburgh, there was insufficient variation in accessibility to these important services (unless we had chosen to indulge in subjective qualitative rankings) to justify their inclusion in any of the tests.

Table 4.2

Level of aggregation of independent variables

Dwelling	Zone	Census enumeration district
Type	Distance	Car ownership
Age	Peripheral location	Social class
Change in use	Bus route	Owner occupation
Area (where available)	Open space	Council tenure
Paid outright	No industry	Rooms per person
Building society finance	Bus service frequency	Dwelling amenities
Local authority purchaser	Access to parks	Population under 15 (%)
	Height	Population over 65 (%)

House prices compared with land values and distance

Before 1970, most of the studies in this field (e.g. Brigham, 1965; Yeates, 1965; Wendt and Goldner, 1966; Mills, 1969) were concerned with the relationship between land values and distance and the determinants of land values generally. Very few gave specific attention to house prices, primarily because of data scarcity. Although this imbalance has recently been corrected, the land value–distance theory and findings have continued to exert an influence on the form and content of analysis on relative house prices. For example, it is commonly assumed that the demand for a house is a derived demand for land and hence that the house price and land value gradients are similar. The justification for this is the assumption that construction costs, and implicitly housing quality, are invariant with distance. Only Muth (1969) has given any attention, primarily at the theoretical level, to the possibility that construction costs may vary with distance from the CBD (Central Business District) core.

However, difficulties arise in the equation of the land value with the house price gradient. First, particularly in the inner city, poor housing may be located on potentially very valuable land, but where the value cannot be realised until demolition and clearance makes large-scale land assembly possible. Second, the demand for land for non-residential purposes (offices, shops, public buildings, etc.) will vary with distance from the CBD, and will normally be much stronger close to the CBD; this fact alone would pull the land value gradient out of shape relative to that for house prices. Third, there may be a tendency for housing of a particular quality or type to be built in particular districts located at predictable distances from the core. The most obvious example of this complex point is that flats, which are usually cheaper and smaller than houses, may be built at more central locations. Finally, house prices refer to far more heterogeneous units than land prices, and – in addition to marked quality differences – houses may be built on plots of land of widely divergent size. In particular, especially for high quality housing, there may be a tendency for site size to increase with distance from the core.

The overall effect of all these considerations is probably *either* that the house price gradient is flatter than the land value gradient *or* that the house price–distance function has an altogether different shape. Certainly, the commonly observed negative exponential function of land value studies is by no means ubiquitous in the analysis of urban house prices. In some cases, the 'pure' house price–distance function may be positively sloped, though the negative relationship may reappear after

75

appropriate standardization procedures (e.g. for household income levels) have been carried out. Alternatively, the prevalence of low quality inner city housing combined with the continued value of accessibility may lead to an inverted – U quadratic house price–distance function. Furthermore, an implication of the considerably greater heterogeneity of houses compared with undeveloped land is that it is much harder to explain a high percentage of the variation in house than land prices, unless very detailed quality and housing characteristic variables are available. This suggests that satisfactory house price variation results may be obtained with much lower R^2s than those achieved in previous *land value* studies.

Multiple regression or factor analysis?

In their study of housing quality in Saint Louis, Kain and Quigley (1970b) used factor analysis to consolidate 39 quality variables into five factors accounting for 60 per cent of the variance in housing quality. These five factors – basic residential quality, dwelling unit quality (interior), quality of proximate properties, non-residential use (in neighbourhood), and average structure quality – were then fed into multiple regression equations along with other (non-quality) housing attributes. In a series of papers Wilkinson (1971, 1973 and Wilkinson and Archer, 1973) has gone much further in the use of factor analysis, promoting it to his main statistical technique and arguing that it is more appropriate for the analysis of relative house prices than multiple regression analysis. His argument is based primarily on multi-collinearity between housing attributes:

> These broad categories of the dwelling and the environment, however, are themselves multi-dimensional concepts, the services and groups of services which they provide being conceptually distinct but statistically interrelated. Under these circumstances of extreme multi-collinearity the traditional estimation technique, the multiple regression of house price on all the attributes of the dwelling and its location, has proved unsatisfactory, producing estimates that are both unstable and far removed from their true values (Wilkinson and Archer, 1973, pp. 358–9).

Whatever the general force of these arguments, they are not particularly strong in the context of our study. First, the risk of multi-collinearity is much more serious for internal attributes of dwellings, which were the main variables in Wilkinson's research, since these are more likely to be closely related than neighbourhood or locational characteristics. For instance, four-bedroomed houses almost universally have garages. The correlation matrix for the variables in our analysis, few of which refer directly to dwelling attributes, showed that there was no serious problem due to high inter-correlation between variables. Second, factor analysis is more appropriate when there is little *a priori* justification for selection of particular variables on theoretical grounds, so that the selection of key variables out of a large number of potential candidates can be determined empirically. In our study it is possible, we believe, to justify the inclusion of each variable theoretically, and there is no need for a technique for sorting out the effect of a large number of variables for which *a priori* specification is impossible or difficult.

Third, the charge of coefficient instability can be rejected in this case. Tests of instability of the regression coefficients under different variants and specifications of the models, and particularly of alternative formulations of the 'best fit' model via inclusion and exclusion of particular variables and by feeding in additional plausible but, in the end, non-significant variables, showed that the regression coefficients were very stable. Since, in almost every case,[3] the variation in the coefficients was very small, in the range $\pm 0.1-3$ per cent, the results of these tests were encouraging.

Fourth, and related to the coefficient stability finding, use of multiple regression rather than factor analysis allows us to quantify the monetary value (in the sense of contribution to house price) of locational and house type characteristics. Since estimation of monetary values of particular determinants appears to depend heavily upon model specification (i.e. which variables are included or not) and on the selected equation, the empirical discovery that the regression coefficients changed little in response to slight changes in specification means that we can be fairly confident about the *approximate* monetary impact of house price determinants.

Finally, the choice between multiple regression and factor analysis is, of course, a false one. Both Kain and Quigley and Wilkinson himself made some use of multiple regression analysis, after having identified some of the key variables with the aid of factor analysis.

The distance effect

From the point of view of testing residential location theories, one of the most important variables in any study of the determinants of relative urban house prices is distance from the city centre (or an alternative locational variable such as travel time or an accessibility index). Although one or two studies have omitted distance variables and nevertheless achieved high R^2s (e.g. Cubbin, 1970; Massell and Stewart, 1971), this is usually to be explained by the homogeneity of the samples. From the point of view of our analysis, the distance variable is important in several of the models tested, namely the pure spatial model, accessibility models (and their more specific variants, 'trade-off' hypotheses), the 'best fit' multiple regression result, and in dynamic tests of Hoyt's radial sector theory (see below, pp. 83, 102 and 111–20).

The house price–distance function has also had a notable role in the development of the theory of residential equilibrium (e.g. Beckmann, 1969, and Solow, 1972). In particular, a condition of locational equilibrium is that house prices decline with distance from the CBD, but that the rate of fall in house prices declines with increasing distance. This suggests a non-linear distance function, i.e. negative exponential. The fact that this hypothesis was not supported in our study is not, in our view, a major defect. There is no reason why an equilibrium condition of an abstract model built upon restrictive assumptions should be assigned priority over an empirically derived relationship in a real-world city. In addition, this study has a significant advantage over residential equilibrium theory. The latter is invariably unidimensional in scope, in effect exploring the house price and residential distribution pattern along a linear ray from the CBD. Our study recognises the obvious fact that a city is an areal rather than a linear phenomenon, and hence includes direction as well as distance. It also takes account of topography more satisfactorily by including the height of residential land. Both these refinements are particularly useful not only from the point of view of greater realism, but also permitting direct testing of Hoyt's and other spatial theories.

Before discussing the treatment of distance in our analyses and their results, it is relevant to refer briefly to the distance effect in other house price (and land price) determinant studies. In most cases where distance or an accessibility measure has been used, its impact has been significant. The few exceptions include Kain and Quigley (1970b), some of Anderson and Crocker's (1971) results for St. Louis[4] and Kansas, and Wendt and Goldner's (1966) land value–distance relationship.[5] In all these cases, the function was negative but insignificant. Most of the significant relationships observed in other studies are also negative (or positive where accessibility rather than distance is used), but Wilkinson (1971 and 1973) found a positive distance effect, Frieden (1961) failed to find a rent gradient in Los Angeles, while Ridker and Henning (1968) also discovered that house prices increased with distance beyond a travel time of 38 minutes from St. Louis CBD.[6]

Ball (1973) criticized Wilkinson for failing to explain the contradiction with theory of his finding. However, it is quite possible for the house price–distance function to be positively shaped, since there is no inevitable equivalence between the house price–distance function and the land value gradient. In most cases, however, as our own results show, a positive distance function will become negative if the relationship is standardized for income or its surrogates and for house type. Unfortunately, it is not possible to make direct comparisons between the distance findings obtained in the different studies, partly because the mix of independent variables changed from one study to another, but mainly because the distance effect was measured in so many different ways. Linear distance (Brigham, 1965), the logarithm of distance (Evans, Anderson and Crocker), travel time (Wabe, Ridker and Henning), various accessibility measures (Apps, 1971; Lane, 1970; Brigham, Wendt and Goldner) are some of the most popular choices.

In our study distance was treated simply as road distance of the residential zone from a defined point in the CBD (the intersection of The Mound and Princes Street), though experiments were also undertaken with linear, logarithmic (negative exponential) and quadratic distance functions. In view of the alternatives such as travel time, 'constructive mileage',[7] a job accessibility index,[8] or multiple accessibility measures (see Wendt and Goldner), why was the simpler form of distance measure preferred? The justification rests on several grounds. First, many studies that have experimented with alternative distance measures have shown that the choice makes little difference (for example, see Lowry, 1964). Second, travel time, which might have been an attractive alternative to road distance, could not be used for two reasons: it would have been difficult to implement in Edinburgh in view of the dispersed model split (bus, car, foot, and even train), and since our study includes longitudinal analysis since 1910 it was impossible to make travel time estimates over this period.

Third, there was little reason to prefer the more difficult to measure accessibility index approach. Edinburgh is a very clear-cut example of a single CBD structure so that the case for a multiple accessibility measure was weak. Moreover, the regression equations used included accessibility measures apart from distance such as car ownership, public transport accessibility and location on the city periphery. Once the road distance decision had been made, whether the function should take logarithmic, linear or quadratic form was not determined *a priori* but derived empirically from the equations. Surprisingly, the logarithmic functions never worked well, and the best fits were obtained with either the linear or quadratic relationship depending upon which model was being tested and which sample was being used.

Although there is no reason why the house price—distance function should have the same shape or slope in every city (or in the same city over time),[9] the findings in some studies that distance was insignificant is unconvincing on theoretical grounds. In most cases, the failure to perceive a distance effect is due to mis-specification, particularly the failure to include variables whose exclusion obscures the distance effect. This is not to say that the distance relationship is simple to interpret. In our study its meaning varied according to the model examined, though it should be pointed out that in *all* cases in 1966 where distance was included, whether alone or with other variables in the 'best fit' equation, a pure spatial model or an accessibility model, or again with the large or the small sample, its influence was significant.

In Edinburgh, the 'pure' price—distance effect is strongly positive, not only in 1966 but in all postwar years.[10] Introducing other variables reduces the value of the distance coefficient, but it remains positive until social class is introduced when it becomes significantly negative. Its (negative) value increases when the car ownership variable is added. In other words, once social class and car ownership are included in the regression equation (variables which, to be consistent with residential location theory, should be treated as surrogates for income (see p. 98 below)), the familiar negative price—distance effect becomes clearly marked. House prices rise with distance from the core, even in Edinburgh where there are fine middle-class properties close to the city centre (Gordon, 1966). However, for a given class of housing, the price—distance effect is strongly negative.

These findings have a general significance far wider than this study. Simple correlations between house price and distance (in our study +0·50) are very misleading. Superficial observation of how house prices vary with distance and the well-known generalization (based on both residential location theory and real world fact) that the wealthy tend to live on the outskirts of cities may suggest that the negative distance effect does not exist. However, it is crucially important to standardize for income and social class, for age of dwelling and other house type characteristics. When this is done properly, it is believed that — with only a few rare exceptions — the negative house price—distance function will become apparent. This is not inconsistent with expensive houses being located in the suburbs.

In some of the models (the 'best fit' small sample, the pure spatial and the accessibility model (see pp. 83 and 102)), the quadratic (an inverted $-U$) gave as good as or a slightly better fit than the linear, with a maximum point (house price peak) in the range 2·3–2·8 miles. [11] The fact that the peaks are not located at the city centre is shown even more convincingly in the computer maps of house price trend surfaces (for an example see fig. 4.1 on p. 92). The relevance of the quadratic house price–distance function is related to the peculiar locational distribution of the housing stock in Edinburgh, which may or may not be applicable to other cities. This distribution includes some very high quality older middle-class housing located near the city centre but with the best quality newer housing being found within the 2–3 mile ring, especially in the west-north-west sector, rather than on the periphery of the city where in some sectors the quality of suburban housing is mediocre. Apart from this, the argument in favour of a quadratic relationship can be made more generally on the grounds that inner-city zones are invaded by commercial and other non-residential properties with the remaining inner-city residential areas consisting of poor quality, inexpensive housing with a limited future located on potentially valuable land.

Social class

Our results confirm the generalization, familiar from Burgess and Hoyt onwards, that social class of the neighbourhood has a positive impact on residential property values. However, in the 'best fit' results for both the large and small samples it was either of marginal or of negligible significance, primarily because the more powerful car ownership variable is highly correlated with social class. In the results for the environmental area/preference model (see p.102), from which car ownership is excluded, class becomes very significant once again.

The social class variable has an additional significance that transcends its t value in the regression results. This is the impact already noted that the introduction of social class has on the distance coefficient in stepwise regression procedures. Before social class is introduced, the distance coefficient is positive (and varies in significance according to which other independent variables are included). This finding, that houses are dearer with increasing distance from the CBD, conflicts with most a priori theories such as the housing/transport costs trade-off hypothesis or more general accessibility models. The introduction of social class, and a fortiori car ownership, changes the sign of the distance coefficient and restores the concept of a negative price–distance function. This suggests that the higher-priced properties desired by the higher social classes are predominantly located in the suburbs rather than near the CBD, but once we standardize for social class house prices nevertheless decline with distance from the city centre. This finding highlights the critical importance of correct specification for interpreting the results of multiple regression analysis.

A possible problem in interpretation of the social class variable is that values for this are derived indirectly from census of population enumeration district (ED) data rather than from information on the individual properties, streets or zones. [12] However, in practice this was not a serious difficulty. A test of the validity of the ED values with the sellers and buyers occupational status data from the Sasines Register itself revealed a clear distinction in class status between high class and low class EDs as reflected in the occupations of housebuyers and sellers. In particular, in the above-average EDs from the class status point of view, high socio-economic status buyers and sellers (defined by occupation, i.e. professional and managerial, and store-owning self-employed) were as important as other buyers and sellers put together (intermediate and junior non-manual on the one hand and manual workers on the other). In the below-average EDs, on the other hand, the high class buyers and sellers were no more important than manual workers considered alone. In these areas they accounted for only 37 per cent of the total buyers and sellers as opposed to 55 per cent in the above-average EDs.

'Best fit' results

The 'best fit' results in the sense of high explanatory value and inclusion of significant variables are presented in table 4.3. The quoted equations refer to the large sample (all the residential properties in our sample sold in 1966, excluding multiple properties), to the small sample (a sub-set of the previous sample for which plot area data are available), and to a reduced predictive equation for the large sample. Since the virtue of these equations is their empirical explanation rather than subscription to a particular theoretical viewpoint, [13] it may be useful to discuss the equations in turn in some detail.

The large sample

The first column of table 4.3 presents the 'best fit' equation for the large sample, where best fit is defined as the highest R^2 obtained by the use of

Table 4.3

'Best fit' equations

	Large sample	Small sample		Reduced predictive model
		with area	without area	
Constant	2,818·78	2,506·85	−3,268·58	2,389·06
Type	−1,828·21***			−1,822·58***
Age	−3·88**	−2·93	21·94***	
Change in use	326·12***	−738·40*	1,764·42**	
Paid outright	−386·66***			
Building society financed	−248·34**	−231·51*	−144·44	
Area		2·99***		
Owner occupation	−8·41***	−12·76**	−21·31***	
Distance	−371·86***	2,142·53***	5,547·02***	−193·87***
Distance^2		−396·47***	−876·81***	
Car ownership	2,884·15***	3,960·55***	6,391·69***	3,788·78***
Zone on periphery	−1,288·65***	505·07*	1,177·43**	
Class	7·08*			
No industry	315·87***	315·90*	645·52**	
Rooms per person	1,223·07***	962·17***	2,211·31***	680·00***
Population under 15 (%)	21·18**			
Population 65 and over (%)	−43·31***			
Open space	7·90***			
Amenities	4·63**	−33·31**	−50·84***	
Direction (NE composite)	−697·49***			−676·43***
Direction (WNW)		616·49***	1,227·77***	509·55***
Bus route through zone		−1,525·79***	−1,721·33***	
R^2	0·6429	0·7633	0·4843	0·6051
$\frac{dP}{dD}$ = 0(miles)		2·70	3·16	
Number of observations	1,176	215	215	1,176

*** significant at 0·01 level
** significant at 0·05 level
* significant at 0·1 level

statistically significant variables. The first point to be noticed is that despite including eight more independent variables than the best equation of table 5.1 the R^2 is raised by a mere 4 per cent (see p. 102). Similarly, this 4 per cent gap separates this equation from the reduced predictive model equation given in the last column of table 4.3, which explains the variation in houseprices with *eleven* fewer variables(!). Second, several *a priori* important variables are excluded from the 'best fit' equation because they lacked significance. These include: height (which had the 'wrong' sign and was insignificant), probably subsumed in the low-lying northeast directional variable; the peak WNW sector which becomes significant only if class and amenities are excluded; council housing which, rather surprisingly, is insignificant − probably to be explained by the extreme residential segregation in Edinburgh (see pp. 156−62) which eliminates most council housing from our predominantly private sector zones; bus service frequency which was insignificant, while the 'bus route through the zone' variable lacked inter-zonal sensitivity since 93 per cent of the zones were crossed by bus routes; parks (i.e. access to a public open space) were insignificant, probably outweighed by the more general open space scores; local authority purchases were ignored because too few observations were involved; while plot areal data were available for little more than 20 per cent of the total observations, and hence were examined separately as a sub-sample.

The 'best fit' equation for the large sample is reasonably satisfactory; a R^2 that explains more than 64 per cent of the house price variation is not too bad a result in view of the fact that the data base excludes many of the possibly important dwelling characteristic variables; all the independent variables quoted are statistically significant, though class is barely significant probably because it is overpowered by the car ownership variable; most of the variables have their *a priori* expected sign.

However, one or two of the signs require comment. The positive sign for the change in use variable suggests at least one of two possibilities: dwellings that can be changed in use (e.g. commercial conversion, division into two or more dwellings) are more valuable because of their potential adaptability and/or they also tend to be larger. The fact that the sources of finance variables quoted ('paid outright' and 'building society financed') both have negative signs is indicative of the fact that the main alternative source of finance, the insurance companies, favoured the more expensive properties. The negative sign for the northeast composite directional variable is to be expected since the main industrial zones of Edinburgh (the Burgh of Leith) lie in this quadrant, the area is situated on low-lying land, and is characterized by the presence of environmental disamenities not directly measured in the analysis. The zone on periphery's negative sign may be interpreted as a reflection of the limited accessibility of peripheral locations (or, more precisely, that lower accessibility relative to the city centre outweighs increased access to open space).

The only sign somewhat difficult to explain is the negative sign of the owner-occupation variable. However, there are two factors peculiar to the city of Edinburgh which should be noted. First, Edinburgh is so highly segregated (in the sense of public and private sector housing distribution) that a low owner-occupation score implies a high private-rented zone not the presence of council housing. Second, mixed residential areas (i.e. owner occupied and privately rented) are frequently more desirable in Edinburgh than the high owner-occupation zones which are often found in rather drab, lower middle-class suburbs. Also, the inclusion of other correlated independent variables such as social class and car ownership reduces the owner-occupation effect, and, as the size of the regression coefficient indicates, its quantitative impact is not very large (£84 for a change of 10 per cent in the owner-occupation score).

The quantitative effects of particular variables in the large sample are interesting: the fact that a house was on average about £1,830 dearer than a flat; the linear distance function suggesting a rate of decline in house prices of about £370 per mile; the marked price trough in the northeast quadrant, with properties on average £700 cheaper than elsewhere. The car ownership and rooms per person variables are highly significant (note their continued dominance in the predictive model equation), though their very large regression coefficients are somewhat misleading. For instance, although a reduction in overcrowding via an increase of one in the rooms per person ratio raises house prices by £1,223, such an increase in the rooms per person ratio would be quite massive. The absence of industry in a zone increases the value of a house by £316.

As interesting as these large quantitative impacts is the very small monetary effect of some plausibly important (and indeed statistically significant) variables: these include age, social class, open space and amenities. The tendency for ten years on a property's age to reduce its value by less than £40 or an increase in the higher social class score of 1 per cent to add little more than £7 are particularly worthy of note, though an obvious reason for the former is that older properties in Edinburgh are frequently more desirable and better built than new houses, while it has already been suggested that the social class effect is swamped by car ownership. Finally, the high negative value of the zone on periphery variable should not be treated too seriously, in view of the small number of observations (less than 4 per cent of the total sample).

The small sample

The major defect of the large sample is the sparsity of dwelling characteristics. However, for about 20 per cent of the properties plot area data were available, and since this is an important dwelling attribute (e.g. in Alonso's, 1964, theory) it suggests that the sub-sample should be subject to further analysis. Table 4.4 compares the mean values for the

Table 4.4

Mean value of variables, large and small samples*

	Large sample	Small sample
Type	0·591	—
Area	—	745·07 square yards
Age	55·56	21·83
Change in use	0·170	0·028
Owner occupation	61·95	70·44
Paid outright	0·35	0·27
Building society financed	0·51	0·58
Price	3,508·13	6,003·32
Distance	2·59	4·00
Distance^2	8·45	16·99
Height	192·28 ft.	297·33 ft.
Open space	30·17	45·16
Council housing	12·97	14·55
Bus frequency	332·03	166·67
Car ownership	0·45	0·73
Population under 15 (%)	19·74	24·70
Population over 64 (%)	15·39	12·73
Class	25·94	41·34
No industry	0·20	0·48
Amenities	79·93	95·69
Rooms per person	1·66	1·79
Zone on periphery	0·039	0·074
Bus route through zone	0·93	0·76
Distance (log)	0·35	0·58

*Mean values for the directional dummy variables are not reported in this table.

large sample (1,176 properties) and for the small sample (2·5 properties). It is clear that the small sample is by no means a microcosm of the large, and consequently there is little reason to expect coefficients for the same variable to be of similar magnitude. The main differences between the large and small samples are that the latter are newer (22 years on average rather than 56), further out (4 miles rather than 2·6 miles), much more expensive (over £6,000 as against £3,500), on higher ground and in environmentally preferable residential areas. Also, the smaller sample is much more homogeneous than the large (as shown by much smaller standard deviations around the mean values). Finally, all the small sample consists of dwelling houses whereas three out of five of the large sample are flats.

The additional variable, area, is highly significant. The simple regression of price against area takes the form

$$P = 3,419 \cdot 83 + 3 \cdot 47A \qquad (R^2 = 0 \cdot 6198).$$

The best fit for the smaller sample explains more than 76 per cent of the price variation, compared with 64 per cent for the large sample and 48 per cent for the small sample without area but with the other independent variables retained. The small and large sample best fits do not share the same independent variables, and where they are shared their interpretation is rather different. In the small sample age structure of the population disappears, sources of finance are barely significant, class and open space are no longer relevant, while age ceases to be significant. Also, the signs for peripheral zone and for change in use are reversed, but again the very small number of observations (15 and 6 respectively in the small sample) rules out reading too much into this. Car ownership, distance, rooms per person and direction remain highly significant. However, in regard to distance a quadratic function with a peak at $2 \cdot 7$ miles fits much better than the linear function, and the significant directional variable now becomes the WNW peak. The bus route through zone variable is more meaningful (with a non-zero dummy value in only 76 per cent of the affected zones), and is strongly negative suggesting that environmental considerations overpower the public transport accessibility effect. It should also be noted that the amenities variable has the wrong sign, though the mean value is so high for the small sample that this does not need to be taken too seriously. Despite these differences, and making due allowance for the heterogeneity of the samples, the results for the large and the small samples are broadly complementary. They both confirm that the evidence does not clearly support a mono-causal explanation of relative house prices, and suggest that spatial, accessibility and environmental factors all have some relevance.

A brief comment should be made on the results obtained when the small sample is run without the area variable. The fact that two coefficients change in sign (i.e. age and change in use) while the size of almost all the coefficients increases drastically in value is additional evidence of the importance of plot area as a house price determinant. The sign changes are easily explained: until area is included older properties and properties experiencing change in use at some time or another appear more expensive; however, these apparent facts merely reflect that the dwellings with a larger plot area tend, first, to be older and, second, to have greater change in use potential. Once area is accounted for, the signs of both coefficients become negative and cease to have much significance. The only other point of interest is that exclusion of area extends the quadratic price peak by almost half a mile further from the CBD. Thus, the larger plot areas tend to be further out, a finding fully consistent with Alonso's (1964) theory. All the other differences between the two small sample equations (with area and without) are obvious and fully consistent with each other. The major significance of the results is the extent to which the R^2 can be raised by inclusion of a single dwelling characteristic variable. In a sense, this increases the satisfactory nature of the large sample results, i.e. the fact that almost two-thirds of the house price variaition can be explained without major dwelling characteristics data, apart from type and age.

Reduced predictive model

An alternative to the 'best fit' equation is given in the last column of table 4.3 which explains 1966 house prices in terms of six independent variables: type, distance, direction (2 dummies); car ownership and rooms per person. These variables explain over 60 per cent of the variation in house prices, and all the variables are highly significant (as shown by the t values). In theoretical terms, the equation must be interpreted as a 'hybrid', since distance and direction are spatial variables, distance and car ownership are accessibility terms, while rooms per person (overcrowding) is an environmental influence. The high degree of significance of the sole housing characteristic variable (type) supports the importance of drawing a distinction between houses and flats.

A crucial question is whether economy in the sense of minimizing the number of independent variables consistent with obtaining a high R^2 is worth possible loss in specification due to excluding key variables from the viewpoint of theory. The answer probably depends upon the objective of the exercise. This 'efficient' equation may be particularly useful for predictive purposes, either for general forecasting of house prices at specific locations or else for the more practical professional purpose of providing information for future rate (or property tax) assessments. Apart from the location of the property and whether it is a house or flat the only independent variables that need forecasting are car ownership and rooms per person. Values for both variables are obtainable at the ED (enumeration district) level from the census of population, and present little difficulty for either interpolating between census years or for forecasting future values. Of the two, rooms per person is probably a little harder to predict due to the problems involved in estimating future building, demolitions and changes in population at the small area level. Nevertheless, it remains a relatively easy forecasting model to implement.

The lack of a structural model

A possible objection to the 'best-fit' equation reported here is that it must be a reduced form version of some unspecified structural model, and that unless the latter is specified prior to reduction biased estimates of regression coefficients may be obtained. Two types of structural model might have been used. First, a simultaneous equation model might have been developed to include both housing demand and supply functions. Second, if housing is such a heterogeneous commodity (one of the reasons why the first type of structural model might have been too difficult and over-ambitious), a structural model might be developed that decomposed the aggregate commodity 'a house' into its component parts, each representing a flow of services considered to have utility to households. This is, in effect, the hedonic price index approach (Cubbin, 1970), which crops up in another guise in this study as the locationally insensitive model. However, had detailed housing characteristics data been available it would have been feasible to incorporate the hedonic approach into a spatial price determination analysis as the first phase (see below).

Is the failure to develop a simultaneous equation supply and demand model serious? Despite its theoretical appeal, there is strong justification for not adopting this course here. Traditional supply and demand analysis is not as relevant to housing as for other goods and services, because of the extreme heterogeneity of housing, and in any event would be very difficult to apply. Indeed, it may not be stretching facts too far to argue that each house is unique, because of the combined effects of differences in location, neighbourhood and environmental characteristics, dwelling size and quality. If this were the case, the supply function would have to be specific to each individual house and hence would be inelastic. Similarly, the demand function does not have to take account of population changes, partly because of the cross-sectional nature of the results but mainly because population has remained relatively stable in Edinburgh over the study period as a whole (see p. 31). Even if the 'unique commodity-inelastic supply' hypothesis is too radical, the supply of housing is notoriously inelastic with the *maximum* annual contribution of housebuilding to the housing stock not more than a few percentage points increase. In Edinburgh in the postwar period the supply of housing has been particularly inelastic. Due to the shortage of land and other factors most new housebuilding in the region has taken place well outside the city boundary.

Apart from the supply inelasticity argument, the need for a structural model is reduced since the aim of this part of the study was to explain *spatial variations* in house prices rather than their *level.* The only sensible way of proceeding on simultaneous equation lines in this case would have been to examine spatial variations in demand and supply. The practical problems here are insuperable: in many zones changes in supply would have been zero; the identification problem would have been unsolvable since *effective* demand is constrained by the need to match the number of households and the number of dwellings (excess supply might conceivably have been handled by vacancy rates, but how could excess demand be measured? [14]); demand—supply interactions within each zone are not independent of demand and supply conditions either in adjacent zones or in zones having similar neighbourhood characteristics or similar types and quality of dwellings.

The hedonic price approach attempts to deal with the heterogeneity of housing by dividing housing units into component characteristics, each of which offers the household a particular flow of services (house size, garden size, number and type of rooms, type of heating system, garaging facilities, particular quality characteristics, and so on). Had detailed housing characteristics data been available for this study, there is no doubt that a more conceptually satisfactory structural model could have been used. Instead of regressing locational, neighbourhood, environmental and other relevant characteristics against house price directly, the estimation procedure would have been divided into two sequential phases. First, the composite and, some might argue, rather meaningless house price could have been broken down into component parts via the hedonic approach. Second, the monetary values of each component could have been used as a new set of dependent variables to explore how each is influenced by spatial, neighbourhood and other characteristics. For instance, one of the components in the first phase might have been amount of floor space so that a £ per square foot of housing space could have been derived, and the total value of housing space in each house (size of house multiplied by the £ per square foot coefficient obtained from the first run) used as the dependent variable in a spatial determinant equation. Despite the theoretical appeal of this approach, its advantages are academic in the context of this study simply because the required data were not available.

The problem of the residuals

The unexplained residuals are a little higher in our study than in some of the other house price determinant inquiries, approximately one-third of the total variance in the large sample and one-quarter in the small sample. As the difference between the large and the small samples suggests (due solely to the area of dwelling variable), the unexplained residuals are explained to a considerable extent by the fact that dwelling characteristics are under-represented in this study though feature prominently in others. These include such features as whether the dwelling is detached, the number of bedrooms, bathrooms, the existence of a garage, garden size and other characteristics not reported in the Sasines Register. To the extent that this is the explanation, the loss from the point of view of testing residential location theories is not serious. However, from the locational point of view − even in the fairly comprehensive 'best fit' equation − some environmental externalities have been excluded (e.g. pollution, noise, congestion, dirt), though these are partially reflected in surrogate fashion in the northeast directional variable. As Ball (1973) has pointed out, a critical question is whether part of the unexplained variance is spatially related, though it is recognised that this is exceedingly difficult to test. [15] In this study, this problem was analysed by visual inspection of computer spatial mapping of the residuals for the selected equation. These residuals did not display any noticeable spatial pattern.

The trend price surface

Figure 4.1 shows a contour map of the house price distribution derived, using a quartic trend surface, from a regression equation in which the independent variables were grid reference numbers. It is clear that the price surface, despite our reliance on a linear negative distance function, is not consistent with that of a CBD peak tapering off in all directions. Instead, there is a strong price peak in the WNW sector about three miles out, a secondary peak in the SE quadrant and a large price trough in the NE quadrant. The distance relationship turns out to be satisfactory, primarily because the countervailing effects of this trough on the price peaks tend to cancel out the latter.

Since the high residential characteristics of the WNW and SE sectors are well known, as is the industrial blight of the NE quadrant, the fact that they show up so strongly on the computer map gives some support to an environmentally based residential location model. This is not necessarily

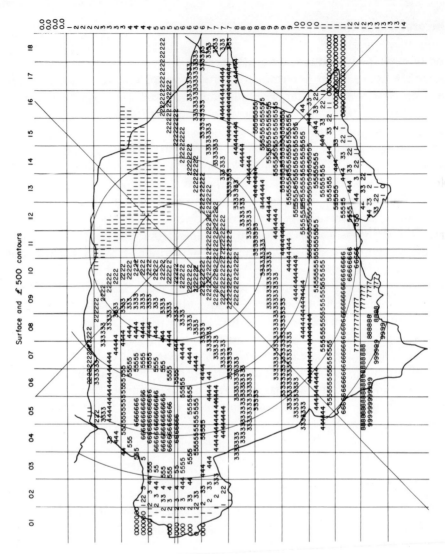

Fig. 4.1   Map of Edinburgh prices in 1966 with quartic surface and £500
contours.

in conflict with an accessibility model if the concept of environmental
accessibility is substituted for employment (CBD) accessibility. The two
price peaks could be treated as nodes of attraction while the trough is a
node of repulsion. Distance-decay functions are probably steeper around
environmental than job accessibility peaks. The obvious reason is that
close proximity to the peak (e.g. the importance of visual factors) is

92

necessary to benefit from its environmental attractions. On the other hand, the depressing effects of a price trough may spread over a much wider area, partly because visual blight can often be seen at greater distances than visual amenities, partly because status considerations may repel middle-class owner-occupiers considerable distances from low-status areas. This hypothesis receives some support in fig. 4.1 in the sense that the trough is greater in spatial extent than either of the peaks.

Notes

[1] Some of the variables listed, such as sources of finance or tenure groups, represent sub-sets of two or three variables, a few of which were used simultaneously in *some* of the runs.

[2] Most of Wilkinson's analyses referred to an average neighbourhood price.

[3] One exception was social class which exhibited some signs of instability.

[4] Kain and Quigley's results also refer to St. Louis.

[5] However, this result is based on distance from San Jose CBD, which is not an important commercial and employment centre. The findings may have been different had the San Francisco CBD been used as the distance origin. Also, not surprisingly given the character of residential development on the west coast of the United States, significant results were obtained when a multiple accessibility measure was used.

[6] In view of the contradictions between Kain and Quigley, Anderson and Crocker and Ridker and Henning, too much significance should not be attached to results from St. Louis. Similarly, in the United Kingdom it is dangerous to generalize from studies of Greater London (e.g. Wabe, 1971; Lane, 1970; Evans, 1973). The very high class close-in residential areas are atypical even of the largest cities.

[7] See Wendt and Goldner. This concept standardizes distance for traffic congestion, road alignment and surface, grades and other factors reflected to some extent by vehicular speed. It is derived from Mohr (1964).

[8] A straightforward version of this might take the form $A_i = \sum_j d_{ij}.E_j$, where A_i = job accessibility in zone i, E_j = employment in zone j and d_{ij} = distance between zones i and j.

[9] Variations between cities may be explained in terms of such factors as the degree of concentration in the CBD, the level and distribution of income, transportation technology, and differences in household locational, travel and work preferences.

93

10 See the dynamic tests of Hoyt's model below, pp.111—20. The 'pure' 1966 result is:

$$Price = 1232 + 878 \text{ Distance (in miles)} \qquad R^2 = 0\cdot2513$$

11 This is for models including house type characteristics. Without house type characteristics the range extends from 2 to 3·5 miles.

12 For a discussion of occupational class indices for up to thirty-four zones within the city of Edinburgh, see pp. 167—77.

13 Indirect tests of particular theories are described on pp. 101—4.

14 The number of households in a zone cannot exceed the number of dwelling units available to accommodate them, and there is no way of measuring the number of unsuccessful competitors for purchasing each house.

15 For a discussion of some of the problems see Fisher (1971).

5 Indirect Testing of Residential Location Theories

Introduction

The data permit indirect testing of several of the main residential location theories. The tests are indirect because, although we have information on the price and certain characteristics of the individual dwelling, the multiple regression relationships attempt to represent the macro-spatial structure of the city. Direct testing would be possible only if data were available on the income levels of individual households and on their budget expenditure patterns. This reflects the fact that most residential location theories are micro in nature, explaining house prices in terms of the relationship between the characteristics of a residential property and the behaviour, preferences and utility function of the individual household. The limited range of housing attributes available from the Sasines Register and the absence of information about individual households (apart from partial data on the occupations of buyers and sellers) inevitably imply that much reliance has to be placed on neighbourhood quality, accessibility and spatial variables.[1] This explains the macro bias in the results of this study.

The absence of income data has another major drawback in interpreting the meaning of regression coefficients. This has been explored by Nourse (1967) in an air pollution context, though the point is much more general affecting many of the variables included in this study. The observed relationship between quality and value subsumes both the income and the price effect of quality changes. For example, if house prices decline in a neighbourhood affected by air pollution, it is not possible to attribute the whole price decline to pollution without taking into account the income of families in the neighbourhood. The regression coefficients for the effects of quality variables on house price assume that income remains constant. If changes in income distribution are introduced, the coefficients would change in value regardless of whether housing or neighbourhood quality changes or not. This is because the income elasticity of demand for services associated with improved housing quality (such as clean air or access to open space) is high.

95

Four alternative theories are examined, relying on housing characteristics (locationally-insensitive), spatial, accessibility, and environmental/area preference concepts respectively.

Housing characteristics (locationally-insensitive) model

A feasible approach to the determinants of relative house prices is to ignore their location and the environmental characteristics of the neighbourhood, and to argue that house prices are determined solely by the characteristics of the dwelling itself, such as floor area, number and size of bedrooms, age, garden size, house type, whether freehold or leasehold, presence of a garage and central heating. Although this approach is implausible, since all past and potential housebuyers know that *where* a house is makes a big difference to how much they might be prepared to pay for it, it is useful for providing a sharp contrast to the other models tested. Unlike them, it may be described as locationally insensitive. Also, it has been given some attention in the literature. Cubbin (1970) is an extreme example, though housing characteristic variables were also given prominence in Massell and Stewart (1971), Kain and Quigley (1970 a and b), and Wilkinson (1971, 1973, and with Archer, 1973). If on theoretical grounds we regard the housing characteristics approach as a non-starter from the residential location point of view, the inclusion of house type, size and quality variables can nevertheless be justified as standardization rather than as explanatory variables within a residential location model.

The 'pure' spatial model

One possible approach to the determinants of urban house prices is to express these in spatial and topographical terms. The variables used in this study (apart from individual house characteristics) are distance from the CBD (including experiments with functions of different shape), direction (division of the location of properties into eight radial zones: NNE, ENE, ESE, etc.) and height.[2] This could be regarded as a theoretically neutral test predicting house prices in terms of spatial variables. Alternatively, it may be treated as a test of Hoyt's radial sector theory.[3] Although Hoyt's theory manifests itself in the form of *spatial* price variations, it in effect subsumes social class considerations since, to take an obvious example, the repulsion of high and low price radial sectors is explained by the repulsion of high and low class residential areas. Another virtue of the spatial model, upon which we capitalize below,[4] is that it can be used for dynamic analysis, since the variables used are independent of time and are not subject to data shortages, provided that we can meet the easily satisfied condition of being able to identify the location of each property sold in the market. Although the spatial model tested here is a very simple one, it is worth pointing out that in its three-dimensional approach (distance, direction and height) it goes further than previous work, particularly in the theoretical literature. The standard theory of residential location, with its unidimensional features to suit the mathematics, is difficult to apply because its assumption of a circular city located on a flat featureless plain is so much at variance with almost all real world cities.[5]

Accessibility models

Accessibility models, or in their micro-behavioural form 'trade-off' models in which households trade-off housing costs against transport (travel-to-work) costs, are undoubtedly the most common type of residential location theory (for examples see Wingo, 1961; Kain, 1962; Alonso, 1964; Schnore, 1965; and Evans, 1974). Although the theories are usually specified in precise, formal terms, their predictions are fairly general. First, house prices decline with distance. The house price gradient will become steeper if the regression equation is standardized for social class and income. This is to correct for the tendency for the wealthy to live in the suburbs of most cities, and presumably in more expensive houses. Second, house prices will be higher in areas having above-average accessibility, such as neighbourhoods with good public transport services (e.g. on bus routes).

The theoretical framework for accessibility theories is most easily derived from individual residential location behaviour. Consider a household utility function in which a household's given income (Y) is assumed on utility maximization principles to be allocated among housing expenditure (h), travel costs (t), all other goods and services (g) and savings (s). Thus,

$$Y - h - t - g - s = 0 \qquad (5.1)$$

If we assume that expenditure on all other goods and services (g) is fixed and that savings are constant for a given income group, then

$$h = (Y - g - s) - t \qquad (5.2)$$

97

and since $(Y - g - s)$ have been assumed constant, they can be made equal to a constant sum C, so that

$$h = C - t \qquad (5.3)$$

This is the familiar 'trade off' relationship between housing expenditures and travel costs. Since it cannot be tested directly in the absence of household expenditures, the model has to be transposed into house price determinant terms for evaluation in our study. This is relatively easy. Since it is reasonable to assume a direct relationship between house price (P_h) and individual household housing expenditure (h), and if we assume that travel cost (t) varies inversely with accessibility (A), then equation (5.3) can be re-interpreted as

$$P_h = f(A) \qquad (5.4)$$

where $\quad f > 0$

According to equation (5.4), variables that improve accessibility ought to have a positive effect on house prices while those that reduce accessibility tend to depress house prices. Clearly, this general function also explains the negative distance effect since increasing distance, as a friction of space, will normally be associated with reduced accessibility.

However, a more direct test of equation (5.3) is possible if surrogates are used to make up for the absence of household income data. In the context of testing equation (5.4) zonal car ownership rates are used as an accessibility variable. An objection to this is that car ownership measures *mobility* rather than accessibility. A response to this objection is that, since the regression equation is standardized for distance, car ownership reflects accessibility since a positive coefficient implies that at a given distance households in zones with higher car ownership rates will have, on average, greater accessibility. However, a conceptually more satisfactory way of interpreting the accessibility regression equation is to use the car ownership rate as a surrogate for zonal income. This is plausible in a United Kingdom context where car ownership is still sufficiently below saturation point for small zone car ownership rates to reflect income, and the empirical findings elsewhere in the study showed that car ownership overpowered social class as an income surrogate.

If this approach is permissible, it allows a more direct test of equation (5.3). We know that C is a function of income (because for a given income group $C = h + t$, and rich households will spend more than poor on housing and transportation expenditures) so that equation (5.3) may be rewritten as

98

$$h_i = Y_i - t \qquad (5.5)$$

where Y_i = income level of group i.

Repeating the previous conversion of h into P_h, using distance from the city centre (D) as a surrogate for t and the car ownership rate (A) as a surrogate for zonal income, and allowing income group i to be located in space so that the subscript $_i$ refers to the average income level in zone i, equation (5.5) becomes

$$P_{h_i} = b_1 A_i - b_2 D_i \qquad (5.6)$$

This is the core of the equation tested in table 5.1, and is probably more conceptually satisfying than interpreting the regression as a test of equation (5.4).

Although the relevance of accessibility models will be determined empirically by their predictive power, it may be useful here to indicate some of the theoretical and practical objections. Undoubtedly, the trade-off model has weaknesses:[6] it ignores the nature of the search process (i.e. the severe restrictions on household residential locational choice in space and time); it disregards the existence of commercial and other non-residential competition for land and housing;[7] and, most important of all, it fails to supply an adequate explanation of price differences between houses that are similar in the sense of having equal accessibility to the CBD but which vary in their physical attributes and in their broad environment surroundings (see also Wilkinson and Archer, 1973, p. 358).

Stegman (1969) has developed two further criticisms of the 'trade-off' theory. First, with the development of the multicentric city, decentralization of both industry and population, increased car ownership and changes in the structure and organization of available transport systems, a suburban location frequently offers greater accessibility than a location close to the CBD (not a direct contradiction of accessibility models, but rather of the negative distance function). Second, households in any event attach more importance to quality, amenity and environmental variables in their location decision than to accessibility *per se*. Finally, in a different context though very relevant to the residential location question, Devletoglou (1971) has challenged the relevance of strict utility maximization based on instantaneous response to infinitesimally small price differences by arguing that real world *consumer* behaviour is subject to thresholds. In the residential location context, these thresholds mean that small differences in house price (or, conversely, small variations in distance and CBD accessibility) will not induce households to vary their locational decision. The mere existence of these thresholds (regardless of their magnitude) blurs the house price—distance effect because each household has a zone of indifference within which neither house price nor distance matter.

Environmental or area preference residential location models

A defect of the familiar accessibility models of residential location is that by virtue of their emphasis on CBD accessibility they rule out the obvious explanation of house price differentials in areas equally accessible but with widely divergent neighbourhood attractiveness. The other end of the spectrum is a branch of residential location theories based on the hypothesis that what counts in the residential site choice is not location *per se* or even accessibility, but rather the environmental attributes of the area in which the house is situated (see Ellis, 1967; Stegman, 1969; and Richardson, 1971). *Ceteris paribus*, favourable environmental attributes attract competition for particular houses and this boosts price; conversely, unfavourable attributes reduce the number of potential buyers and tend to depress price. Favourable attributes include such factors as the absence of industry, access to open space and parks, the presence of local good schools, and the attraction of high socio-economic status areas. Unfavourable attributes include noise, pollution, overcrowding, poor quality and old dilapidated neighbourhoods, and proximity to heavy industry and to council housing. For houses of a given size, type and structural quality, the relative balance between these favourable and unfavourable environmental attributes of the neighbourhood in which the houses are located stratifies them by price.

It should be noted that environmental preference and accessibility models are not necessarily contradictory, though selection of one rather than the other implies a particular view about priorities and value scales in the locational preferences of households. Nevertheless, if we hold distance from the CBD and other accessibility measures constant, the price differential between houses of the same type will tend to be accounted for in terms of neighbourhood environmental differences. Conversely, for houses of a given type in different neighbourhoods with similar environmental characteristics, it is reasonable to expect price differentials to reflect variations in accessibility. Furthermore, another way of reconciling environmental and area preference theories with accessibility models is to substitute accessibility to favourable (and repulsion from unfavourable) environmental sites for CBD accessibility. However, the

100

distance-decay functions from environmental peaks and troughs may have a different shape from those around the CBD. In particular, on *a priori* grounds we would expect the distance functions around environmental attributes to be much steeper than those around employment centres since these attributes are only influential if households are close to them (in some cases, close enough to be *seen*).

Results of the tests of alternative theories

Results of tests of the different models are shown in table 5.1. Before comparing these results, it is necessary to offer a new brief explanatory comments on each. The housing characteristics equation cannot be regarded as a proper examination of a locationally insensitive model since the Sasines Register contains little information about the characteristics of individual dwellings appropriate to such a test (e.g. direct information about house size). Nevertheless, the four significant variables quoted explain as much as 44 per cent of the total variation in house prices.

The spatial model, results for which are reported in the second column, attempts to explain relative house prices in terms of distance, direction and height. All the housing characteristics variables are included as standardization measures. Their inclusion has other advantages: all the variables are highly significant; they raise the R^2 by about 0·02; and, rather more important, the quadratic price peak that is obtained when standardization is carried out (i.e. 2·785 miles from the CBD) is more consistent with the results obtained from other tests. As for spatial variables, distance, height and five of the sectoral dummy variables are all significant. The quadratic distance function (with its predicted price peak about 2¾ miles out) performed rather better than the alternative linear function, and much better than the familiar logarithmic function. Height had the right sign, and was of plausible magnitude, i.e. a height of 100 feet making a price differential of rather less than £240. As for the sectoral variables, these revealed a price peak in the WNW sector, a secondary price peak in the SSE, and a very marked price trough in the industrial northeast quadrant.

The accessibility model tested in the third and fourth columns excludes all the housing characteristic variables except type (which distinguishes houses from flats) on the practical criterion that this improved results. Apart from the variables quoted (distance, car ownership, and location of properties in zones peripheral to the city), experiments were undertaken with public transportation variables, namely whether a bus service passed

Table 5.1

Tests of residential location theories

	Housing characteristics	Accessibility			Environmental or area preference
		spatial	linear	quadratic	
Constant	5,840·44	4,896·56	2,681·67	1,850·44	1,515·79
House type	−2,488·53***	−2,354·34***	−1,733·64***	−1,717·13***	−1,743·35***
Age	−15·05***	−10·40***			−3·46**
Changes in use	307·23***	406·79***			300·86***
Paid outright	−221·40***	−239·99***			−239·70***
Distance		479·56***	−118·27**	589·68***	
Distance^2		−86·09***		−127·58***	
Height		2·36***			
Direction:					
NNE		−939·50***			
ENE		−930·94***			
ESE		−1,016·23***			
SSE		129·00			
SSW		−214·40			
WSW		−527·04**			
WNW		493·82**			
Car ownership			4,830·27***	4,949·90***	
Zone on periphery			−856·35***	−611·64***	
Class					26·75***
No industry					343·30***
Rooms per person					1,744·07***
Population under 15 (%)					28·05***
Population 65 and over (%)					−62·34***
R^2	0·4401	0·5180	0·5708	0·5794	0·6028
$\dfrac{dP}{dD}$ = 0 (miles)		2·785		2·311	

*** significant at 0·01 level
** significant at 0·05 level

through the zone and, if so, the frequency of services. Although they were significant and raised the R^2 by about 0·01, they were left out of the selected equation. The bus route through zone variable had the wrong sign (from the public transport accessibility point of view, though it could be explained in terms of environmental disamenities), and the coefficient was highly unstable in different formulations of the accessibility model. The frequency of bus service variable turned out to be too insensitive, lacking sufficient inter-zonal variation. As for distance, two versions are quoted — one using the linear form, the other the quadratic. The quadratic gives rather the better fit, though it is much more difficult to reconcile with accessibility theory, at least in a centralized city. The linear (or the logarithmic) function is much more consistent with the theory, unless either subcentres have replaced the CBD as the dominant accessibility nodes or traffic congestion severely reduces accessibility close to the city centre. The former condition is certainly not true in Edinburgh, while it is implausible that traffic congestion could begin to have a marked impact from 2⅓ miles out (the quadratic peak in this model). Also, a specific assumption of the variant of the accessibility model adopted in this study was that for a given income group expenditures on all other goods and services apart from housing and travel remained constant, and this ruled out substitution between goods and housing. The lack of substitution makes a linear distance function more plausible than if substitution had been permitted. In general terms, the better fit for a quadratic distance function suggests that environmental features (e.g. the existence of attractive, desirable neighbourhoods) may be more important than pure accessibility effects.

The final column of table 5.1 gives the results of an environmental or area preference model. Apart from the housing characteristic variables, the only variables in the selected equation refer to the absence of industry, social class, rooms per person and two age structure variables. Several other environmental variables were available, namely open space, access to public open space, tenure type (the proportions of both owner-occupied and council housing), housing amenities, and the existence of a bus route through the zone. These were excluded as being insignificant, probably as a result of most of them being highly correlated with included variables. As for the housing characteristic variables, one of them, age, is potentially a very important environmental factor. In practice, although it had the right sign, it was less significant than all the other selected variables, and its quantitative impact was rather small (a price differential of about £35 per decade).

In comparing the results of the tests of all four models, the first point of interest is that none achieved a R^2 as high as reported in many other studies of the determinants of relative house prices. This is not, in our view, a serious defect in view of the use of individual rather than grouped price data and the large sample size. Many of the other studies have used small samples specially pre-selected to hold certain variables constant. After allowing for the lower R^2s, the most striking aspect of table 5.1 is that there are insufficient grounds for selecting one model as giving a

103

markedly better fit. Apart from the housing characteristics equation, which is, as pointed out above, rather crippled by the deficiency of the housing attributes information available, the other three models explain between 50 and 60 per cent of the variation in house prices and *all* the variables in each model are significant and have the expected sign. The importance of distance, direction and height in the spatial model, distance and car ownership in the accessibility equation, and the absence of industry and overcrowding, high social class and a young age structure in the environmental model are all confirmed, while the impact of the main housing characteristic variables, a house being more expensive than a flat and older properties being cheaper, is consistently supported. True, the environmental and area preference model achieves a rather higher R^2, but more independent variables are included. These results suggest the dangers arising out of a strong predilection for a particular theory. An analyst testing the accessibility model alone might be reasonably happy with his findings, and draw the conclusion that his hypotheses were supported by the evidence. Only when the findings of alternative models are set side by side is the weakness of such a position revealed.

Three general conclusions stand out. First, indirect tests are bound to be unsatisfactory. The tests here all relate to the macro-spatial structure of house prices, and for one model to be judged superior to another it would need to be supported by a different type of evidence referring directly to the micro-level, i.e. the actual behaviour of *individual* residential locators. Second, the approximate equally satisfactory results derived from the alternative theories reinforce the dangers of a mono-causal approach. Although there is a certain elegance in starting from a deductive theory, deriving particular hypotheses and supporting these hypotheses via empirical tests, there is much common sense in an alternative approach. This draws upon a wide set of plausible independent variables, derives empirically the 'best fit' via some kind of stepwise regression procedure and then attempts to explain the results by reference to the predictions of different theories and empirical (but frequently non-quantitative) observations outside the data sets as necessary. (This was the method adopted above; see pp. 82–3.) Third, the mixed results of these tests combined with the hybrid nature (from the point of view of theory) of the 'best fit' (see table 4.3) suggest the need for a more complex residential location theory taking account of accessibility, environmental considerations, neighbourhood characteristics and dwelling attributes as potentially important determinants of household location decisions and spatial house prices. The residential site choice and the price-quality trade-off are much more sophisticated decisions than the conventional theories suggest.

Notes

[1] Many studies (e.g. Ingram et al., 1972, pp. 18–19) have stressed the importance of allowing for the heterogeneity of housing (including structure type, number of rooms and dwelling unit quality) in residential location theory. The limited use of such data in this study reflects non-availability not disbelief in their importance.

[2] Another potentially important topographical variable which has the opposite effect from height is location along a seafront (or lakeshore). Although Edinburgh has an extensive coastline most of it, apart from the northwest (e.g. the village of Cramond) and the eastern resorts (parts of Portobello and Joppa), is used for port and industrial facilities. Very few properties in the sample were located on the sea/river front itself.

[3] For a dynamic test of Hoyt's theory see pp. 110–20.

[4] See pp. 110–20.

[5] For a debate on how simple urban models can afford to be, see Richardson (1973) and replies by Solow and Mirrlees.

[6] See Richardson (1971).

[7] Incidentally, it invariably discusses accessibility in terms of accessibility to employment centres, with travel time and costs conceived solely as journey-to-work costs. Senior and Wilson (1972) have recently reminded us of the fact that some households (particularly retirement households) making residential site choices do not contain workers: 'The inclusion of non-worker households in the model is important for policy reasons, but even more fundamentally to achieve a comprehensive picture of residential choice – namely that worker households compete with non-worker households for residential opportunities' (Senior and Wilson, 1972, p. 6.).

6   The Dynamics of Hoyt's Spatial Model

Introduction

The best known model of residential spatial structure derives from the inductive generalizations of Hoyt (1939), based on observations of land value and property rental patterns in 142 United States cities. Although his initial hypotheses were based on cross-sectional studies, he also constructed a dynamic version of his model based on three observations (1900, 1915 and 1936) in six cities (Boston, Seattle, Minneapolis, San Francisco, Charleston, West Virginia and Richmond). The absence of long-run time series of city-wide large samples of house prices or rentals has prevented adequate testing of Hoyt's model. This chapter fills this gap by a spatial analysis of house price variations in Edinburgh over the continuous period 1910–71.

Hoyt's theory

As a preface, it is helpful to recapitulate Hoyt's views. In the 1920s, Burgess (1925) and Haig (1926) had developed the concentric zone model of urban spatial structure which is the basis of the familiar rent gradient concept. Hoyt's work amplified this model by stressing that radial sectors may stratify urban function (particularly residential neighbourhoods) as well as concentric zones. The key feature of the model is a

> sector theory of the location of rent areas in American cities (in which) rent areas ... tend to conform to a pattern of sectors rather than of concentric circles. The highest rent areas of a city tend to be located in one or more sectors of the city. There is a gradient of rentals downwards from these high rental areas in all directions. Intermediate rental areas ... adjoin the high rent areas on one or more sides, and tend to be located in the same sectors as the high rental areas. Low rent areas occupy other entire sectors of the city from the centre to the periphery. On the outer edge of some high

rent areas are intermediate rental areas. In small cities, or cities of slow growth, the highest rental areas may occupy parts of sectors directly adjacent to the business centre. As in the large cities, the low rent sectors extend from the centre to the periphery on one side of the city. (Hoyt, 1939, p. 76)

These last points bring the dynamics of his model into consideration. The high status residential sector initially develops alongside the retail and office centre, but its subsequent growth is influenced by some or all of the following factors: the HPS (high price sector) tends to develop along established lines of communication towards another existing nucleus and among these to move along the fastest transportation lines; the HPS moves towards high ground or along *non-industrial* waterfronts (e.g. Chicago);[1] it tends to develop in the direction where there is open country beyond the urban fringe; the HPS gravitates towards the location of homes of community leaders and elite groups; relocation trends in offices, banks and department stores pull the HPS in the same general direction; and, particularly important, the growth of the HPS is very stable in the sense that it continues in the same direction over long periods of time. Hoyt discusses two main exceptions to this last generalization: the subsequent location of luxury apartment areas near to the business centre; the activities of property developers may bend and influence the direction of the HPS.

The essential spatial structure of Hoyt's approach, therefore, takes the form of one or two high price areas shaped like pie-slice wedges extending along radial lines from the city centre to the periphery. Intermediate price areas will be located either adjacent to the high price sectors or in other parts of the city. Low price areas extend from the city centre to the edge of settlement on one side of the city, usually repelled from the high price sector (or rather *vice versa*). Whereas the high price peak of the high price sector may be located near the periphery and may shift outwards over time (even indicating a positive price–distance gradient), the gradient in the low price area assumes the traditional negative slope. Although the HPS is a key element in the model, it rarely occupies more than one-quarter of the peripheral circumference of the city. Except in the rare cases of close-in luxury apartment zones or the 'gentrification' of older areas, once a residential neighbourhood's status declines it almost never recovers. Accordingly, the growth of a high status sector must be outwards. This suggests a correlation between residential neighbourhood quality and age of settlement, as well as a filtering process in which high class households are replaced by intermediate class households as the HPS shifts over time.

It is obvious from this description that, in spite of Hoyt's reliance on spatial maps and his explanation of residential structure in spatial terms, behind the spatial shifts there lies a process of socio-economic status change. This process could be examined with many kinds of data such as socio-economic status data, analysis of turnover rates and measures of the changing occupational status of owner-occupiers in addition to price data. However, the key aspects of the process are: the socio-economic status of areas increases with distance from the city centre towards the periphery (the original dynamic version of the Burgess model); more precisely (the Hoyt variant), socio-economic status groups concentrate within certain sectors, though within each sector there is a zonal pattern with increasing status as we move from the city centre; finally, all areas decline – though often very slowly – in socio-economic status over time, due to the residential mobility of high status groups into better and newer housing further away from the city centre,[2] and the fact that the properties they vacate are filled by lower status households.

From the point of view of a dynamic analysis of spatial house price variations, it is possible to simplify this process by translating it into the purely spatial terms used by Hoyt to summarize complex status-influenced residential location decisions. According to Hoyt, the expensive houses should tend to cluster along one or two pie-slices, particularly on high ground, and at a considerable distance from cheap housing. More specifically, house prices may *increase* rather than decline with distance from city centre, and if there is a negative gradient, its slope should be very shallow and its steepness should decline over time. Radial sector price differentials ought to be large, and the high and low price sectors should repel each other. Moreover, the high price sectors should remain stable over long periods of time, though they may jump at one point in time from one part of the city to another. Since high-lying land is valued for residential purposes, height should be positively associated with house prices regardless of zonal and/or sectoral shifts. These propositions can be tested with the aid of distance, direction and height variables in a multiple regression model of Edinburgh house prices.

Hoyt's views have been challenged over the years in many quarters: for their spatial determinism (Firey, 1947); the lack of precision in sector definition; the preoccupation with high income groups, and neglect of the general structure of the housing stock; the simplified view of the social structure based on community leaders; the neglect of planning and government controls (Rodwin, 1961); the complications that follow once we move from a mono-centric to a multi-centric city. Some of these are relevant to the Edinburgh case. Particular attention needs to be given to a high proportion (in Edinburgh over one-quarter) of the housing stock of a Scottish city consisting of public housing, the development of which can radically transform previously high price sectors. Also, the community leaders hypothesis is of some relevance in Edinburgh, since Gordon (1971) has shown that community leaders there tended to live in central older properties rather than in peripheral residential suburbs. The stability of this phenomenon (comparing 1962 with 1914) was strong enough to induce in this century some upgrading of 1914 middle-class areas. Thirdly, any study of urban development in Edinburgh cannot neglect the role of the landowner and the private builder in influencing the pattern and form of residential development.[3] A further point of difference relates to major dissimilarities between the United States and the United Kingdom housing market. In particular, Hoyt's generalizations were derived from *rental* values, while the analysis in this study is based on the selling price of houses. However, this should accentuate the class status effects, since owner-occupiers and property owners generally are concerned about long-term capital values, and these are positively related to neighbourhood status.

The sample

The full Edinburgh sample, both for houses and apartments,[4] is used in this analysis. The sample size is 15,300, and the total number of sales over the period 1910–71 is 38,700. The sample thus covers more than 10 per cent of Edinburgh's total housing stock, i.e. including public housing, and is stratified spatially to obtain overall geographical coverage as described in chapter 3.

The spatial model

The spatial model used here is that

Price = f (House characteristics; distance; direction; height).

Since distance, direction and height are (given the simple physical measures employed here) invariant with time, and since the aim of the exercise is to explore the relationship between price and space on an annual basis, the results will throw light on the impact of time (if any) on the spatial variables. However, before looking at the results, a few words of caution about the data are necessary. First, it should be remembered

110

that the *main* purpose of the sample was not overall city coverage on an annual basis as required here, but rather to provide sufficient information to explore the dynamics of price changes at the very small area level.

Second, the spatial pattern used has been arbitrarily imposed in the form of the city divided into quadrants intersecting at the CBD, with each quadrant bisected to yield eight wedges (NNE, ENE, ESE, SSE, SSW, WSW, WNW and NNW). Since Hoyt himself used a mono-centric approach and his maps show large wedges (though not always using the 45° arcs), this is a permissible procedure to the extent that this analysis is a test of Hoyt. However, it is subject to the same charge of spatial determinism. It would have been possible, for instance, to derive continuous price profiles from 0° through to 360°, but it was felt that the quality of the sample did not warrant this. Also, it is easy enough given the availability of computer map trend price surfaces to replace distance from the CBD with distance from peak price reference points. Such surfaces have been generated in this study (see fig. 4.1), but are not used in this chapter.

Neither the mean distance nor mean height of properties sold alters very much over the period, and this is reassuring from the points of view of comparability of year-to-year results and, more generally, of the representativeness of the samples. There is a slight tendency for the mean distance to increase within the range 1·9–2·6 miles, but this is only to be expected in the light of the outward growth of the city over this sixty-year period. As expected, the mean age value increases over the period within the range 18–61 years.[5] But the rate of increase is not regular and there are substantial year-to-year fluctuations. The most important reason for this is that in certain years of low new housebuilding activity sales of older properties tend to dominate the market (e.g. the early 1920s, the late 1940s and early 1950s); conversely, in periods of heavy new building (e.g. the 1930s), the trend increase in mean age of properties sold falls away. These differences between years in the age composition of properties sold reduce the ability to derive consistent results since it is well known that, despite the high degree of substitutability of old and new houses in terms of price, their locational and other characteristics vary widely.

The effect of distance

With these qualifications in mind, it is now possible to examine the spatial results. The first step is to look at the influence of time on distance. Experiments with different types of distance function revealed that over the period as a whole a linear distance function turned out consistently better than either an exponential or quadratic. In table 6.1 two sets of coefficients are reported, coefficient A measuring the distance effect corrected only for house type (i.e. whether the property is a house or apartment), the other (coefficient B) showing the distance coefficient in the full spatial model (i.e. in the regression equation containing all house characteristic variables,[6] height and the sector directional variables). The latter set of coefficients is rather more difficult to interpret, partly because the t value is insignificant in a high proportion of the years, and

Table 6.1

Coefficients of linear distance and height

Year	Coefficient A (type only included)	't' value	Coefficient B (full spatial equation)	't' value	Height coefficient (full spatial equation)	't' value
1910	−142	2·25	−121	1·78	−0·69	0·73
1911	−111	1·84	31	0·42	1·76	1·61
1912	−7	0·11	38	0·46	2·32	2·12
1913	75	1·27	107	1·49	1·74	1·96
1914	189	2·65	331	3·97	−1·48	1·26
1915	22	0·31	6	0·06	0·88	0·73
1916	225	0·39	565	0·76	−10·95	0·92
1917	17	0·29	−85	1·14	0·60	0·49
1918	65	1·81	−5	0·11	−0·75	1·29
1919	−42	1·55	−42	1·24	0·21	0·49
1920	−39	1·01	−42	0·85	0·40	0·53
1921	−9	0·23	5	0·10	1·04	1·39
1922	6	0·16	−10	0·23	0·30	0·47
1923	1	0·02	73	1·87	1·23	2·05
1924	−39	1·30	−71	2·36	1·60	3·56
1925	−42	1·45	−57	1·76	1·12	2·01
1926	−40	1·46	−70	2·14	0·71	1·58
1927	0	0·02	−73	2·44	1·05	2·97
1928	104	3·78	70	2·19	1·10	2·62
1929	3	0·09	−27	0·80	0·43	0·94
1930	32	1·44	29	0·98	0·03	0·09
1931	−120	4·39	−102	3·23	−1·24	2·90
1932	−10	0·50	−26	1·07	−0·50	1·69

Table 6.1 continued

1933	−3	0·23	−23	1·30	0·46	2·13
1934	−43	2·22	−73	3·09	0·37	1·31
1935	−14	0·71	−57	2·68	0·70	2·81
1936	33	1·46	−5	0·18	0·43	1·29
1937	−24	1·14	−79	3·16	0·55	1·89
1938	1	0·06	−31	1·32	0·54	2·02
1939	−1	0·04	23	0·74	−0·45	1·23
1940	−8	0·29	−51	1·27	0·11	0·24
1941	59	1·95	103	2·72	0·54	1·35
1942	12	0·46	22	0·67	0·92	2·57
1943	73	2·38	44	1·13	0·29	0·55
1944	152	3·55	77	1·37	−0·40	0·57
1945	199	3·48	223	3·08	2·07	2·15
1946	68	1·84	−21	0·47	2·07	3·64
1947	187	3·96	108	1·87	0·29	0·38
1948	164	2·82	45	0·64	−0·38	0·41
1949	309	6·78	96	1·77	1·32	1·92
1950	224	4·68	85	1·53	−0·01	0·01
1951	114	2·12	−50	0·75	2·86	3·27
1952	144	3·26	107	1·96	3·80	5·44
1953	71	2·17	45	1·10	3·04	5·96
1954	178	5·85	66	1·75	2·74	5·98
1955	91	3·84	−15	0·47	2·00	5·29
1956	108	4·01	−90	2·34	2·11	4·82
1957	211	8·42	59	1·77	0·98	2·70
1958	230	8·16	32	0·90	0·83	2·04
1959	213	6·73	79	1·84	1·63	3·06
1960	221	7·52	59	1·59	1·29	2·99
1961	202	6·05	106	2·44	1·81	3·40
1962	214	6·03	118	2·61	2·74	4·92
1963	409	9·13	320	5·02	2·33	3·03
1964	398	10·29	192	3·76	1·20	1·88
1965	248	4·71	177	2·45	2·45	2·71
1966	360	7·61	−31	0·49	1·57	2·20
1967	309	6·76	−99	1·49	0·77	1·20
1968	293	4·92	−25	0·31	3·69	3·83
1969	339	5·56	32	0·38	2·32	2·39
1970	315	5·13	−34	0·42	3·06	3·06
1971	268	2·46	−98	0·68	3·33	2·13

partly because of less consistency in the signs.[7] Accordingly, the interpretation that follows is based on coefficient A. These coefficients reflect the impact of social and economic influences that are subsumed in the distance effect rather than the influence of distance purged of all other intervening variables. However, their use can be justified on several grounds. First, the difficulties of obtaining data for every year, apart from house characteristic and spatial variables, mean that a thorough purge was impossible. Second, coefficient A is more consistent with Hoyt's own approach, since the spatial variables in his theory encompass all kinds of other considerations, but particularly status influences and responses. Third, given the impossibility of measuring the precise effect of distance relative to all other variables, this distance coefficient at least gives us a measure of the *maximum* effect of distance.

The most striking characteristic of the distance coefficient is that it changes over the course of the period from being negative (up to 1941, apart from the 'perverse' years of the First World War) to positive (each year during the last thirty years of the study). This is clear support for Hoyt's hypothesis that the high price sector will shift outwards over time. In the Edinburgh context, it is evidence of the fact that suburbanization has eventually eroded away the prestige of the high class inner-city areas (Gordon, 1971). It should also be observed that the switch towards a positive house price gradient is by no means incompatible with the theoretical hypothesis that for a household *in a given income class* house prices decline with distance.[8] The positive gradient is a fact of the macro-structure reflecting the tendency for the rich to live further out than the poor, not a micro-behavioural parameter affecting the decisions of the individual household.

Table 6.1 also shows that for many years before World War II the distance effect was very small. For instance, in almost half the years of the twenties and thirties it was within the range ± £10 per mile. However, since the *t* values for many of these years were insignificant, it would be wrong to rely too much on this finding. Since 1943, on the other hand, the *t* values have been highly significant, and the evidence in favour of the positive house price gradient is clear-cut. But it would seem reasonable to conclude that up to 1940 distance effects were not very strong in Edinburgh. Even in the 1920s, when the B coefficients are more significant statistically, the distance effect only tends to be about ± £70 per mile.

Another question of considerable interest is whether, regardless of sign, the distance gradient becomes shallower over time. The distance coefficients can be interpreted in terms of £s per mile, but they do not lend themselves to inter-temporal comparisons over a period when house prices changed drastically. Accordingly, it is necessary to deflate the distance coefficient by mean price[9] to obtain a meaningful comparison. Table 6.2 shows the results for selected years, namely years which pass significance tests for both distance coefficients. There is some tendency for the house price gradient to become less steep over time, but it is much more noticeable in the B coefficients. However, the change in the relative value of the A coefficients is completely swamped by the change in sign, certainly from the point of view of testing Hoyt's predictions.

Table 6.2

Distance coefficients deflated by mean price (selected years)

| | Coefficient | |
	A	B
1910	−22·8	−19·4
1928	+12·6	+8·5
1931	−15·2	−12·9
1934	−6·4	−10·8
1949	+14·7	+4·6
1956	+6·2	−5·2
1964	+13·7	+6·6
1966	+10·3	−0·9
1970	+7·6	−0·8

Height

The hypothesis that residential land on high ground is more valuable is also tested in table 6.1 where height coefficients are shown for each year between 1910 and 1971. The hypothesis receives some support from this evidence. First, the coefficient has the expected positive sign in all but ten years, and only in two of these ten 'perverse' years is the t value significant. Second, in the majority of years the height coefficient is statistically significant. The main exceptions are the war and immediate postwar years (both wars). From 1951, however, the coefficients are always significant. Third, although the impact of height is in general significant and positive, its quantitative impact on house price is rather small. Apart from 1916,[10] its peak effect is little more than £3 per foot (and then only in 1970 and 1971 when the mean price is over £4,000 and over £5,000 respectively). Although there may be extreme variations in a

115

few individual properties, the range of annual *mean* height values after World War I was 175 feet to 213 feet. This fact places the size of the height coefficient in perspective. In other words, that high-lying residential land is more valuable is. confirmed, but given the topography of residential neighbourhoods in Edinburgh this fact is not sufficiently strong to make height a significant determinant of spatial variations in house prices.

Radial sectors

The more critical tests of Hoyt's hypotheses refer to radial sector prices, to variations between sectors and to the stability of high and low price sectors over time. Table 6.3 shows the mean prices and ranks of each of the eight sectors over the period 1910–71. The ranks indicate in general a high degree of stability over the period. The high price sector throughout has been in the WNW, with top rank in thirty-five of the years; since 1953, in particular, it has been ranked first in every year but three. The adjacent sector NNW has also been ranked consistently high. The other adjacent sector (WSW) was ranked high in the inter-war period, but has dropped in status to some degree since the late 1940s. The most probable explanation of this change is interventionist factors (Hoyt admitted that his model was a pure *laisser faire* theory), particularly the location of public sector housing. There is also a secondary peak in the SSE sector which becomes noticeable from the late 1920s. Finally, a large segment of the city (namely the NNE, ENE and ESE sectors) is consistently of very low rank, reflecting the persistence of low price and low quality housing in the industrial areas of Edinburgh and Leith.

All these results are quite consistent with Hoyt's predictions. They show that the high price sector retains its status over long periods of time; that intermediate price sectors may be found both next to the high price sector (i.e. NNW) or in other parts of the city (SSE); that exogenous forces may bring about fairly dramatic changes in status (e.g. as in the WSW); and that the low price sectors tend to be located at the opposite end of the city to the high price sector (in the east rather than in the west). The overall stability of these results is quite marked, and is in large part explicable by the fact that Edinburgh has grown relatively slowly in this century by contemporary metropolitan standards. The results are all the more remarkable in the light of Edinburgh exhibiting the typical characteristics of a Scottish city, namely that a high proportion of the housing stock is publicly owned and that the location of the council housing stock is determined, at least in theory, more or less independently of neighbourhood status considerations.

Apart from ranks, the price deviations between sectors are also of some importance. The annual mean prices for each sector and for the city as a whole are also shown in table 6.3. These data show that the stability in ranks is not associated with stability in either absolute or relative price variations between sectors. Instead, the range of relative price variation between sectors has narrowed over time, particularly in a comparison of the post-World War II and pre-1939 periods. Also, the narrowing of the sector price differential, certainly since the mid-1920s, has largely taken the form of a pulling down of the high price sector towards the mean city price. In other words, sector price convergence manifested itself as a relative loss in status of the high price sector rather than an upward change in status of the low price sector. Once again, this is consistent with Hoyt's findings since he showed that neighbourhood status tends to decline over time.

On the other hand, it should be noted that the rate of increase in the average price of the lowest ranked and the highest ranked sectors has been approximately the same since 1951. This may be explained partly in terms of the effects of chronic housing shortage and continued house price inflation since 1954 on demand both in high and low status areas, and partly in terms of the very broad sectoral aggregations used in this analysis. Since council housing has been built in every sector of the city, this has made for some levelling out in status in these broad sectors. There has been a tendency, again noted by Hoyt himself in his observations of American cities, for much greater residential differentiation at the small area level, with the highest class residential areas increasingly taking the form of much smaller spatial clusters, more homogeneous in quality and clearly separated from lower (though still high) class neighbourhoods around them. This emergence of smaller but more select high price neighbourhoods than the broad sectors used in this analysis requires a much greater level of spatial disaggregation.[11]

Conclusion

Despite its age and attacks of spatial determinism, the simple model of residential spatial structure associated with Hoyt (and its concentric zone predecessor by Burgess) has had a major influence on contemporary thinking about the city. Surprisingly, at least until one appreciates the massive data requirements, the *dynamic* version of the model has never

Table 6.3

Mean price (£s) and rank of each sector by year,* 1910–71

Year	NNE	ENE	ESE	SSE	SSW	WSW	WNW	NNW	City mean price
1910	185(8)	539(5)	483(7)	701(3)	1,018(2)	534(6)	2,600(1)	630(4)	623
1911	568(5)	722(3)	519(7)	556(6)	570(4)	445(8)	1,994(1)	1,014(2)	667
1912	608(5)	722(3)	531(6)	291(8)	457(7)	657(4)	1,835(1)	782(2)	598
1913	695(4)	890(1)	629(5)	566(7)	448(8)	627(6)	765(3)	772(2)	610
1914	404(6)	394(7)	315(8)	640(3)	591(4)	773(2)	1,173(1)	558(5)	557
1915	–	–	–	–	–	–	–	–	612
1916	–	–	–	–	–	–	–	–	983
1917	–	–	–	–	–	–	–	–	566
1918	398(5)	380(6)	303(8)	605(2)	819(1)	603(3)	326(7)	562(4)	543
1919	527(8)	578(6)	541(7)	681(5)	765(3)	800(2)	1,477(1)	705(4)	695
1920	579(8)	985(1)	681(6)	827(5)	843(4)	904(3)	592(7)	953(2)	828
1921	771(8)	831(5)	809(6)	800(7)	877(4)	1,093(3)	1,142(2)	1,192(1)	895
1922	588(8)	616(7)	683(6)	784(5)	852(4)	869(3)	1,255(1)	978(2)	806
1923	813(6)	821(5)	607(8)	890(3)	718(7)	865(4)	1,862(1)	1,020(2)	859
1924	752(7)	833(5)	813(6)	880(4)	745(8)	1,114(2)	1,669(1)	1,026(3)	897
1925	692(8)	718(6)	705(7)	927(4)	762(5)	942(3)	1,919(1)	1,005(2)	869
1926	615(8)	714(7)	890(5)	861(6)	953(4)	1,058(2)	1,426(1)	957(3)	886
1927	660(8)	717(6)	898(2)	830(4)	685(7)	1,135(1)	887(3)	784(5)	806
1928	740(7)	924(3)	781(6)	819(5)	843(4)	931(2)	684(8)	1,012(1)	823
1929	587(8)	650(5)	646(6)	983(2)	809(3)	991(1)	607(7)	763(4)	778
1930	567(8)	600(7)	691(6)	752(5)	727(5)	1,078(1)	864(2)	732(4)	743
1931	333(8)	504(7)	528(6)	984(2)	1,010(1)	768(5)	915(3)	802(4)	791
1932	508(7)	492(8)	553(6)	888(2)	896(1)	724(4)	732(3)	649(5)	698
1933	520(8)	583(7)	633(6)	686(3)	618(5)	682(4)	731(2)	767(1)	643
1934	493(8)	588(6)	572(7)	697(4)	698(3)	837(1)	795(2)	617(5)	678
1935	545(8)	644(6)	603(7)	680(5)	736(3)	925(1)	707(4)	804(2)	713
1936	534(8)	562(7)	674(6)	733(3)	690(5)	805(2)	834(1)	699(4)	691
1937	538(7)	515(8)	657(6)	727(5)	733(3)	1,048(1)	857(2)	730(4)	731
1938	534(8)	582(7)	712(5)	784(3)	768(4)	803(2)	1,031(1)	711(6)	750
1939	403(8)	550(7)	557(6)	814(3)	891(2)	811(4)	1,077(1)	640(5)	770
1940	500(8)	539(7)	559(6)	601(3)	670(2)	594(4)	1,039(1)	584(5)	629

Year									
1941	660(6)	754(5)	613(8)	759(4)	808(7)	627(7)	1,186(1)	1,048(2)	790
1942	798(4)	728(5)	697(8)	849(3)	719(6)	714(7)	1,267(1)	952(2)	801
1943	755(8)	831(7)	854(6)	1,041(4)	1,026(5)	1,172(2)	1,512(1)	1,083(3)	1,015
1944	900(8)	942(7)	942(6)	1,320(4)	1,403(2)	1,259(5)	1,764(1)	1,353(3)	1,244
1945	1,472(6)	1,732(4)	1,256(8)	1,714(4)	1,655(5)	1,655(5)	1,920(2)	2,151(1)	1,666
1946	1,492(6)	1,500(5)	1,342(8)	—	1,451(7)	1,803(3)	1,919(2)	2,184(1)	1,682
1947	1,537(8)	1,731(6)	1,651(7)	2,339(3)	2,089(5)	2,260(4)	2,419(2)	2,484(1)	2,068
1948	1,745(6)	1,583(8)	1,736(7)	2,413(4)	2,478(3)	2,696(1)	2,662(2)	2,237(5)	2,211
1949	1,716(6)	1,688(8)	1,707(7)	2,368(2)	2,328(3)	2,144(5)	2,223(4)	2,580(1)	2,095
1950	1,518(8)	1,768(6)	1,533(7)	2,600(1)	2,334(3)	2,116(4)	2,555(2)	2,087(5)	2,081
1951	2,040(5)	1,986(6)	1,733(8)	2,267(4)	1,964(7)	2,433(3)	2,952(1)	2,800(2)	2,226
1952	1,942(5)	2,033(4)	1,911(6)	2,345(3)	1,793(7)	1,770(8)	2,434(2)	2,935(1)	2,070
1953	1,501(7)	1,674(4)	1,553(6)	1,828(3)	1,652(5)	1,315(8)	2,141(1)	2,136(2)	1,652
1954	1,452(7)	1,509(6)	1,717(4)	1,786(3)	1,535(5)	1,271(8)	2,130(1)	2,052(2)	1,611
1955	1,271(8)	1,613(6)	1,675(5)	1,857(3)	1,496(7)	1,706(4)	2,381(1)	1,870(2)	1,713
1956	1,434(8)	1,525(7)	1,709(5)	1,977(2)	1,556(6)	1,836(4)	2,385(1)	1,845(3)	1,739
1957	1,387(8)	1,552(5)	1,452(7)	1,845(3)	1,808(4)	1,522(6)	2,208(1)	1,872(2)	1,704
1958	1,319(7)	1,482(6)	1,309(8)	2,033(2)	1,881(3)	1,685(5)	2,258(1)	1,729(4)	1,760
1959	1,654(7)	1,679(6)	1,566(8)	2,050(3)	1,799(5)	1,849(4)	2,345(1)	2,080(2)	1,857
1960	1,606(7)	1,610(6)	1,521(8)	2,286(2)	2,015(4)	1,637(5)	2,632(1)	2,067(3)	1,899
1961	1,680(8)	1,936(5)	1,890(6)	2,330(3)	1,875(7)	1,958(4)	2,869(1)	2,443(2)	2,052
1962	1,914(8)	2,137(6)	2,141(5)	2,534(3)	2,035(7)	2,231(4)	3,139(1)	2,756(2)	2,315
1963	2,028(7)	2,319(4)	1,930(8)	2,756(3)	2,250(5)	2,187(6)	3,738(1)	2,942(2)	2,474
1964	2,129(8)	2,429(6)	2,250(7)	3,739(2)	3,099(4)	2,488(5)	3,294(3)	4,057(1)	2,908
1965	2,704(7)	2,898(6)	2,697(8)	3,805(3)	3,117(4)	3,061(5)	4,481(1)	4,415(2)	3,382
1966	2,775(8)	2,805(7)	2,851(6)	4,134(2)	3,807(4)	3,386(5)	4,323(1)	3,817(3)	3,508
1967	2,586(8)	2,951(7)	3,163(6)	4,266(2)	4,061(3)	3,623(5)	4,034(4)	4,311(1)	3,656
1968	2,951(7)	3,607(6)	3,250(7)	4,328(3)	3,856(4)	3,764(5)	5,404(2)	5,577(1)	4,047
1969	3,113(8)	3,256(6)	3,132(8)	4,863(3)	3,942(4)	3,920(5)	5,200(1)	5,116(2)	4,055
1970	3,197(8)	3,486(7)	3,803(6)	4,511(3)	3,916(5)	4,157(4)	5,601(1)	4,937(2)	4,143
1971	4,408(7)	4,087(8)	4,618(6)	5,115(4)	4,750(5)	5,572(3)	6,869(1)	6,548(2)	5,311

*The mean sector prices are derived from regression equations containing other spatial independent variables. The city mean price, on the other hand, is the simple arithmetic mean of all property prices.

— Insufficient observations (<75) for sectoral prices.

been satisfactorily tested. Any relevant generalizations have been crude and mainly based on United States experience. The mine of data collected for Edinburgh in this project generated the capacity to subject the key hypotheses to empirical verification, and in a different institutional context — that of the United Kingdom. Although some qualifications were needed, the hypotheses stood up to testing remarkably well.

Notes

1 Most of the coastline near Edinburgh is industrial.

2 The same point has been made by Muth (1969, pp. 98–9).

3 In Scotland the land tenure system is called feuing, under which ground rent (feu duty) is paid in perpetuity for use of the services of land. Landowners frequently placed restrictions on the use of land, including density restrictions on residential development. See p. 24.

4 Apartments accounted for about four-sevenths of the sample, with houses making up the remaining three-sevenths. Multiple properties were excluded from the analysis, but these accounted for less than 2 per cent of the sample.

5 It should be pointed out that the maximum age in the study is 100 years, since it was impossible to determine precisely the age of properties built before 1870. Thus all such properties were coded as if built in 1870.

6 Apart from house type and age, these are 'sources of finance' and 'change in use'.

7 For example, over the last thirty years of the study the distance coefficient A was positive in every year without exception, but there were negative B coefficients in nine of these years.

8 This is the standard prediction of the familiar accessibility models of residential location in which housing costs are traded off against transport costs (for a recent analysis see Evans, 1974).

9 These mean prices are shown in the final column of table 6.3.

10 1916 is an extreme year which can be ignored (insignificant and the wrong sign as well as too high a value) since the high negative coefficient for this year is due to the very small number of properties changing hands in the middle of World War I.

11 See pp. 131–5 and 167–77. In view of Hoyt's stress on residential differentiation at the neighbourhood level, this subsequent analysis may also be regarded as an extension of Hoyt's work. In particular, it permits a look beyond the spatial price variations to the social class differences, that, according to Hoyt, underpin them.

7 Spatial Disaggregation

The level of disaggregation

There are several grounds for the belief that small area housing analysis is necessary for understanding residential spatial structure. First, one of Hoyt's major amendments to the Burgess concentric zone model was the argument that socio-economic status groups tended to concentrate within certain sectors (see p. 107). Second, an implication of many modern residential location theories is that neighbourhood characteristics and environmental amenities are important determinants of house price. Since these characteristics are highly localized, it follows that urban house price studies need to be focused at the small area level. Third, general observation of the residential neighbourhoods of British cities shows that housing is very heterogeneous spatially, especially in older parts of these cities. Scottish cities, in particular, probably contain a wider variety of house types than urban areas elsewhere in the United Kingdom.

Originally, it had been hoped that this study would yield price indices for individual streets (or at least for the sample zones). Since the number of sales in many streets was small, fulfilling this hope required two pre-conditions: first, houses on an individual street had to be very homogeneous so that a price observation for a particular house could be taken as representative of the street price at the time of the sale; and second, turnover rates had to be high to yield sufficient observations to build up a price index over time. Unfortunately, examination of the street price data revealed that neither of these conditions generally held. Although price movements between separate properties on a street moved closely in parallel in most cases, the price *level* varied widely, indicating considerable heterogeneity within a street in house type and quality. As for turnover rates, not only were these very low (less than 3 sales per property over the 65-year period) but the turnover of properties on a street tended to cluster in time. As a result, on many streets there were long time intervals with zero or only one or two price observations. Accordingly, any attempt to build up price indices at the street level would have required far too much interpolation. Furthermore, streets containing more expensive houses tended to exhibit wide variations in the movement of property values, and these variations have become much more extreme in recent years. These considerations ruled out the possibility of constructing meaningful street price indices. The same arguments made the development of zonal price indices almost as infeasible because the average number of streets per zone was too low.

As a compromise between adequate spatial disaggregation and sufficiently large samples to generate satisfactory price indices, zones were obtained by dividing Edinburgh into five one-mile rings and splitting each ring into eight segments by drawing radial lines through the city centre at 45° angles. This procedure yielded a maximum of 40 radial sector zones, reduced to 34 because the outer north and eastern rings were located in the sea. One of the main virtues of these subdivisions is that they permit testing of Burgess's concentric zone and Hoyt's radial sector models (see chapter 6). However, this approach to spatial disaggregation has certain implications. First, the zones are of different size, increasing in area substantially with outward movement from one ring to another. On the other hand, the variation in sample size from the point of view of properties per zone is much less because residential densities tend to decline with increasing distance from the city centre. Second, the time series for the zonal price indices are truncated in the case of some of the outer zones because many of the outer suburbs of Edinburgh were not developed until the third and fourth decades of this century. Third, selecting zones with the aid of geometry has a certain cost in that these do not match residential neighbourhoods, although there are offsetting benefits in the form of permitting tests of spatial models of urban structure.

Before analysis of zonal prices, there is some value in examining what happened to prices in the five rings and eight radial sectors from which the zones were drawn.

Rings

The basic data on property prices in each ring at ten-year intervals are shown in table 7.1, while ring price indices spanning cyclical phases are presented in table 7.2. The *a priori* expectation about ring price levels is that these should increase with outward movement because of the tendency for higher status housing to be peripherally located.[1] This expectation is broadly confirmed by table 7.1. However, only in 1950 and 1960 is the pattern of higher prices with distance precisely confirmed. In 1910 the upward price slope dips in the third ring, whereas a decade later prices peaked in that ring. In the years 1920, 1930 and 1939 prices were

Table 7.1

Ring prices

| | Rings | | | | |
	1	2	3	4	5
1910	451	596	559	671	1,050
1920	752	689	1,038	783	904
1930	643	607	971	893	1,072
1939	740	640	821	896	809
1950	1,565	1,802	2,699	2,782	3,415
1960	1,186	1,441	2,529	2,567	3,312
1970	3,031	3,301	4,958	4,888	6,229

Table 7.2

Ring price indices

| | Rings | | | | |
	1	2	3	4	5
1929/1910−14	102	137	148	123	46
1947/1929	313	259	271	289	331
1953/1947	67	82	80	74	110
1970/1953	249	233	239	242	199
1970/1910−14	532	679	770	637	331

rather higher in the inner-most ring, ring 1, than in ring 2. In the inter-war period price levels in the outer three rings stood at approximately similar levels with no clear tendency for the price level to increase with distance. In the more recent periods, on the other hand, prices have been consistently higher in the outer rings, though the biggest shift is found between ring 2 and ring 3. Also, since 1950 prices have been considerably higher in the most peripheral ring (ring 5).

The theoretical expectations of how the rate of change in house prices varies between concentric zones are much less clear, primarily because so little evidence has been made available about the dynamics of property prices. However, the most reasonable prediction is that house prices will increase more rapidly in high price rings (typically the outer rings), particularly during periods of secular income growth. The justification for this is that households will tend in periods of rising incomes to compete strongly with each other for the higher-priced housing, and this intensified competition will be reflected in rising house prices. Table 7.2 divides the secular period between before 1914 and the recent past into four sub-periods. These data give no support to the *a priori* expectation. Between the years prior to 1914 and 1929, the overall price increase was modest, but was sharper in rings 2 and 3. The falling price level in ring 5 is probably misleading, since the main explanation is the unrepresentative small sample of higher priced properties in this ring before 1914. In the period from the late 1920s to the immediate post-World War II peak, prices increased sharply in all rings, though rings 5 and 1 performed best. In the following slump (1947—53), prices fell in every ring apart from the peripheral ring, and dropped most sharply of all in the central ring. In ring 5, however, prices continued to rise.

The differential experience between concentric zones in the house price boom of the last two decades is very surprising. Prices increased most rapidly in the inner ring 1 and most slowly in ring 5. This is not easy to explain. One factor may have been the conditions of chronic housing shortage that persisted everywhere but especially in Edinburgh. As a consequence, there was a state of excess demand in all housing sub-markets within the city, so that the forces making for house price inflation were more or less equally strong anywhere in the city. The more important consideration may have been a revival in inner city residential living. Because of traffic congestion and similar problems, it is possible that there was some tendency to substitute housing costs for transport costs, boosting the demand for and hence the price of inner-city houses (particularly the better quality properties). This argument receives some support from other evidence, since the positive house price—distance gradient becomes progressively shallower over the postwar period (see pp. 114—15). Also, because of the existence of the New Town the inner city housing stock in Edinburgh does not share the blight characteristics so typical in other cities. There is some poor dilapidated housing in and near the city centre but the *average* quality is much higher than elsewhere.

Abstracting from the sub-periods, the final row in table 7.2 shows the rate of price increase by ring over the whole period 1910—14/1970. Ring 5 appears to perform very badly, but again this is due to the misleading pre-1914 data. Between 1929 and 1953 ring 5 did best of all, even if the rate of price increase fell off relatively after 1953.[2] For all-round consistency ring 3 turns out best; the rate of increase in house prices was greatest over the period as a whole and above average in each phase. This performance is, upon reflection, not surprising since the third mile ring

124

should benefit from outward expansion forces yet is not close enough in to suffer from the adverse effects associated with strong suburbanization and decentralization trends. Although prices in the central ring (ring 1) increased more slowly than in any other ring (apart from the spurious findings for ring 5), their rate of increase is not much slower than elsewhere, confirming the suggestion made above that inner-city housing in Edinburgh is far from blighted. On the contrary, the relative performance of house prices in ring 1 has been much better since the early 1950s than in any period between 1910 and 1953.

Sectors

Tables 7.3 and 7.4 present data for prices and price indices for the eight directional sectors for dates paralleling those selected for the ring analysis of tables 7.1 and 7.2. The price levels in these tables are the actual levels obtained by calculating the mean price of all properties sold within each

Table 7.3

Sector prices

	NNE	ENE	ESE	SSE	SSW	WSW	WNW	NNW
1910	492	269	462	475	944	701	900	674
1920	489	372	686	810	825	1,120	1,036	996
1930	428	420	722	739	746	1,082	1,046	718
1939	437	464	667	710	848	843	1,139	655
1950	1,136	1,386	2,339	2,448	2,330	2,200	3,133	1,972
1960	959	1,033	1,938	2,234	2,337	1,878	3,077	1,584
1970	2,055	2,514	4,771	4,751	4,546	4,156	5,923	3,964

Table 7.4

Sector price indices

	NNE	ENE	ESE	SSE	SSW	WSW	WNW	NNW
1929/1910–14	108	129	149	158	100	137	62	117
1947/1929	292	315	307	245	282	240	353	315
1953/1947	67	88	91	86	97	61	86	80
1970/1953	247	227	246	232	221	274	246	220
1970/1910–14	522	816	1,030	772	598	549	466	649

125

sector in a particular year rather than the estimated sectoral price levels obtained by multiple regression analysis used earlier (see pp. 83 and 102). In view of the earlier analysis of the sector price differentials, only very general comments will be offered here on the data summarized in table 7.3. First, throughout the period 1910–70 the lower prices are consistently found in northeast while the higher prices occur in the west. The persistence of this pattern reflects the importance of historical factors: the location of the Edinburgh area's early industrial development; the lower-class social structure of Leith; and the more desirable higher ground to the west and northwest. Second, the WNW has been the peak price sector since 1939, and by a wide margin. In the earlier period, on the other hand, the WSW and SSW sectors competed for the role of peak sector. Third, the secondary peak in the southeast quadrant did not emerge until the post-World War II period. Fourth, the NNW sector fell progressively behind, dropping to sixth place by 1970 even though it stood very well in 1920. Fifth, the sector price differentials are surprisingly wide. There is a large gap between the house price levels prevailing in the Leith industrial and port areas to the northeast and the middle-class suburbs to the west. Moreover, the ratio of peak to trough sector prices remained relatively stable over time, though there was some narrowing in the inter-war period and after 1960. Similarly, there have been no recent dramatic changes in relative positions.

Table 7.4 shows the sectoral price changes over time. Over the whole period 1910–14 to 1970 the peak WNW sector performs rather badly, but this is only because the price index for this sector declined between 1910–14 and 1929 primarily because of the unrepresentative sample of high-priced properties in the WNW before 1914. In all periods after 1929 the WNW sector prices increased most rapidly of all. The rate of increase in prices between 1910–14 and 1970 was most rapid in the ESE sector (which rose from seventh to second rank over the period as a whole), though the rate of increase in the low price ENE sector was also impressive (this sector was the trough up to 1930 and the second lowest since then). The other trough sector, NNE, performed badly, though its rate of change was never the slowest, either over the period as a whole or in any of the sub-periods. However, a comparison of tables 7.3 and 7.4 shows that there is no clear-cut association between sector price levels and their rates of price change. Looking at the sub-periods, prices increased between 1953 and 1970 at approximately the same rate in all sectors, and this similarity is a consequence of the overall chronic housing shortage. In the postwar slump (1947–53) prices fell to a similar degree in all sectors apart from the NNE and WSW where the decline was much steeper.

126

Between 1929 and 1947 the WNW sector price increased the most rapidly, but the inter-sectoral rate differentials were not very wide. The improving ESE sector began to show itself, but the ENE trough also performed very well. In the early period (1910–14 to 1929), the southeast quadrant prices increased the most rapidly while prices in the WNW declined sharply for reasons already explained.

Zonal prices

The analysis of ring prices showed that although property prices tended to be higher with outward movement from the CBD the tendency was far from clear-cut. Certainly, there was no marked trend for the *rate of change* in property prices to be positively associated with distance. As for sector prices, the most noticeable feature was the persistence of wide differentials between the east and the west of the city. Although prices in the west were much higher than in the east, the rates of change in prices were no higher in the western sectors and in some cases rather lower. An interesting question is what happens to these generalizations upon further spatial disaggregation.

Table 7.5 presents the mean prices in each radial sector zone at ten-year intervals.[3] The 1910 data show (by the infrequency of observations in the fourth and fifth rings) that suburban development had hardly commenced with the exception of the SSW sector. In that sector, prices increased with distance (from Merchiston to Morningside, Craiglockhart and Colinton). Both the peak and trough zones were close in: the peaks were 1WSW and 2ESE (St. Leonards) while the troughs were 1ENE and 2ENE (Abbeyhill) and 1SSW (Tollcross). Surprisingly, the peak and trough zones were adjacent to each other. This is not consistent with the hypothesis (advanced by Hoyt among others) of mutual repulsion between high and low price zones, though it supports the alternative hypothesis that city housing and sub-markets can exist at the small neighbourhood level. The other feature of the 1910 price structure is that the WNW sector that later emerged as the peak sector was already beginning to show with high price zones in the first and second rings.

The assumed relationship between high prices and suburban location is unclear from the 1920 data. On the contrary, some of the lowest prices were found on the periphery (5SSE and 4ENE). Of course, there had been very little building since 1910 so that the urban price structure for 1920 reflects the after-effects of World War I and other atypical conditions. Once again, the spatial juxtaposition of peaks and troughs is quite marked

Table 7.5

Zonal prices

	1910	1920	1930	1939	1950	1960	1970
1 NNE	260	522	390	324	1,222	912	1,890
1 ENE	242	494	468	375	1,769	1,423	3,021
1 ESE	385	266	152	50	227	256	500
1 SSE	464	607	511	337	1,339	1,127	3,018
1 SSW	253	560	414	384	1,312	910	2,998
1 WSW	1,475	1,753	1,468	1,618	2,756	2,345	6,075
1 WNW	900	1,153	1,601	1,900	2,438	1,583	3,687
1 NNW	599	823	699	407	2,211	1,290	3,968
2 NNE	510	484	458	481	1,084	983	2,156
2 ENE	214	304	376	336	1,164	964	2,219
2 ESE	1,450	1,875	916	612	2,275	2,800	5,626
2 SSE	469	640	640	677	2,435	2,148	5,124
2 SSW	573	567	620	692	2,108	1,522	3,035
2 WSW	881	1,154	808	1,003	1,739	1,107	2,541
2 WNW	975	1,125	786	705	2,909	3,163	5,323
2 NNW	749	1,126	739	780	2,309	2,323	5,428
3 NNE	—	—	—	—	—	—	—
3 ENE	463	614	900	671	2,191	1,756	4,671
3 ESE	428	513	778	768	2,813	2,691	5,422
3 SSE	525	910	1,012	871	3,042	2,990	5,329
3 SSW	970	1,373	1,087	976	3,135	3,401	6,068
3 WSW	560	888	955	504	2,433	1,663	4,156
3 WNW		395	976	951	2,860	3,459	5,972
3 NNW		392	160	343	666	981	1,953
4 NNE	—	—	—	—	—	—	—
4 ENE	—	400	—	—	753	323	907
4 ESE	546	715	729	711	2,363	2,077	4,303
4 SSE	—	624	1,100	810	2,715	2,738	5,084
4 SSW	1,042	780	812	1,135	4,095	3,609	6,282
4 WSW	656	1,026	1,048	783	2,573	2,288	4,696
4 WNW	—	—	1,550	996	3,463	3,472	6,206
4 NNW	—	—	—	—	—	—	—
5 NNE	—	—	—	—	—	—	—
5 ENE	—	—	—	—	—	—	—
5 ESE	—	—	1,364	623	2,777	2,180	5,370
5 SSE	—	265	890	600	2,281	1,478	3,425
5 SSW	1,050	1,360	2,225	892	4,325	2,800	8,983
5 WSW	—	858	950	677	2,894	2,890	5,167
5 WNW	—	—	837	1,855	4,708	4,530	8,559
5 NNW	—	—	—	—	—	—	—

(e.g. 1ESE and 2ESE), and there are extreme price variations in other sectors, especially the NW quadrant. This finding reinforces the results derived from analysis of the 1910 data. Residential neighbourhoods, and the price levels obtaining there, break up into spatial clusters which although quite large are too small to be analysed satisfactorily in terms of either concentric rings or sectors. The prevailing spatial pattern is much more complex.

The 1930 price data show that the 2ESE peak had disappeared, reflecting a downward change in status for the St. Leonard's area. One of the most striking features of the 1930 price structure is that suburbanization tendencies were beginning to assert themselves. Price peaks occurred in ring 5 (ESE and SSW sectors) and in ring 4 (SSE and WNW). On the other hand, although most of the central city was made up of trough areas (1NNE, 1ENE, 1ESE, 1SSE and 1SSW), there were inner high price zones in the west (1WSW and 1WNW). This was, in part, a reflection of the fact that the repulsion between peak west and trough east prices had started to develop. Another consequence of the same tendency was that the spatial contiguity of the low price zones was becoming marked.[4]

The evidence suggests, therefore, that the inter-war period witnessed increasing residential segregation in Edinburgh. There are several explanations of this trend. First, the social forces stimulating the demand for new suburban housing were probably the same forces making for increased stratification within the lower and middle classes and for a growing emphasis on status considerations in residential location decisions. Suburbanization also accentuated the polarization of inner-city housing into a cluster of low price zones, with the conspicuous exception of the traditionally high status areas of 1WSW and 1WNW. Second, extensive public housebuilding took place between the wars. The location of council housing estates acted as a barrier between high and low-class private housing, increased the price differentials between them and made far greater price homogeneity within zones. Third, housebuilding rates between the wars were high, though the public—private sector mix changed drastically from year to year. The high incremental growth rate in the housing stock probably accelerated the *social* obsolescence of lower quality old housing and depressed its relative price levels.[5]

In 1939, the peak zones are found in the inner city (i.e. the western sectors 1WNW and 1WSW), with the exception of 5WNW. Although there are other high price zones, particularly in the third and fourth rings of the WNW and SSW sectors, the price levels ruling in these zones were much below the peaks. In these two sectors, suburbanization tendencies were strong, though the peripheral ring did not, apart from in the WNW, contain the most expensive properties. It is possible that ring 5 was not, to use Blumenfeld's (1954) term, the *crest* of the wave of metropolitan expansion, and in some sectors was still exurban rather than suburban. Moreover, in the search for cheap building land, builders of lower quality new housing may have been driven to the periphery of the city. All the trough zones, with the exception of 3NNW, i.e. the port and industrial area of Granton, were centrally located. The inner-city low price zonal pattern was becoming dominant, though the persistence of the peak price wedge to the west warns against the dangers of over-generalization.

By 1950, however, this western inner-city wedge had disappeared as an absolute peak, though price levels remained much higher than elsewhere in ring 1. This may indirectly reflect the increasing prominence of the suburbanization – higher price relationship, particularly in the WNW, WSW and SSW sectors. On the other hand, in the southeast quadrant the peak occurs in ring 3 (Liberton, Braid Hills and Duddingston). Trough zones were beginning to emerge in other parts of the city besides the inner rings.[6] In the west, for instance, a low price zone had developed in 2WSW (the Dalry–Saughtonhall–Gorgie area) due to the location of industrial development and of council housing there. Similarly, a low price zone had already begun to show itself, and was even more marked in 1960 and 1970, in 5SSE, i.e. in the Ferniehill–Gilmerton area. The main explanation appears to have been the proximity of council housing, though many of the estates were developed after 1950. The other feature of the 1950 data is that all the thirty-four zones were occupied. Although there was still much public housing development to take place, large-scale private suburbanization *within the city* was more or less complete, with most subsequent new private housebuilding being on a small scale and primarily on 'in-fill' sites.[7]

Examination of the 1960 price structure suggests the continuation of the same features observable in 1950, such as inner-city depressions, higher price suburbanization, the Granton and Portobello industrial area troughs, and the recently developed atypical troughs (2WSW and 5SSE). The overall city price level in 1960 was almost 9 per cent lower than in 1950, but the price fall was much heavier in the inner city than on the periphery (in fact, prices in some peripheral zones remained at about the same level). The price declines were particularly marked in the former inner-city peaks, especially in 1WNW. Of the inner-city zones only the 1WSW remained with price levels above the city average. Moreover, the price gap between the peripheral peak (5WSW) and the inner-city troughs was now massive. The 2WSW trough had become very prominent; indeed, its price level had changed very little since

1939 or even since 1920.[8] The existence of this trough appeared to hold down prices not merely in the 2WSW zone itself, but also in the more peripheral zones of that sector. Although there were industrial developments, council housing and disamenities further out beyond the second ring, the main explanation of the price dampening was probably the fact that crossing a low status area while travelling out to suburbs constrains the status level of those suburbs.[9] The 1960 data also show the dominance of the WNW as the peak sector and that within that sector the average price level increased with distance. The southeast high price zone (2ESE, 3ESE, 3SSE and 4SSE) was large and firmly established, but was undoubtedly only a secondary price peak compared with the west.

The 1970 data present a similar spatial pattern to that of 1960, though the overall much higher price levels reflect the housing demand boom of the 1960s. The most interesting question is how the vigorous house price dynamics influence relative zonal price changes. The general housing shortage coupled with non-residential demand and slightly reinforced by changing tastes in favour of central city living boosted price levels in the inner city (e.g. 1NNW and 1SSW) probably rather more than on the periphery. [10] On the other hand, the Granton and Portobello troughs and to a lesser extent the suburban 5SSE low price area remained noticeable. As for peaks, the price levels in the peripheral high price zones (5WNW and 5SSW) soared ahead of nearby zones. The association between suburbanization and high status was now very strong indeed in the west. The massive price increase in the 5SSW zone reflected the fact that this was the last suburban fringe *within* the city to be developed, so that the price levels obtaining there are due to the location of recently built, and hence very expensive, housing. The differential experience of adjacent zones is, once again, very strong, e.g. 1WSW and 2WSW, 2NNW and 3NNW, 1ESE and 2ESE. In these cases, the zonal ranks are very wide, and provide additional support for the hypothesis that residential neighbourhoods are smaller than implied in Hoyt's mutual repulsion thesis in regard to high and low status radial sectors. Finally, the rising price with distance relationship is clearly in evidence from the second to the fifth rings in the WNW, WSW and SSW sectors, that is, in those sectors of the city where outward expansion was not held back by topographical constraints.

Zonal price indices

Whereas table 7.5 presents what are, in effect, 'snapshots' of the spatial price structure in various years, table 7.6 gives a much more direct indicator of the dynamics of residential neighbourhood change.

131

Table 7.6

Zonal price indices

Zone	1929 (1910–14=100)	1947 (1929=100)	1953 (1947=100)	1970 (1953=100)	1970 (1910–14=100)
1 NNE	93	494	56	239	609
1 ENE	101	320	105	164	556
1 ESE	27	477	69	166	149
1 SSE	110	314	75	305	793
1 SSW	166	207	71	416	1,012
1 WSW	98	247	67	272	438
1 WNW	78	238	59	243	266
1 NNW	105	334	44	434	668
2 NNE	119	232	73	253	511
2 ENE	143	297	87	240	884
2 ESE	44	395	88	253	388
2 SSE	175	213	91	258	873
2 SSW	83	366	91	190	529
2 WSW	157	194	49	255	376
2 WNW	76	407	101	211	660
2 NNW	121	335	93	221	833
3 NNE	–	–	–	–	–
3 ENE	171	310	90	255	1,210
3 ESE	187	287	99	246	1,306
3 SSE	129	258	94	188	589
3 SSW	145	259	90	217	734
3 WSW	107	316	60	368	742
3 WNW	71	351	82	289	586
3 NNW	48	507	98	224	538
4 NNE	–	–	–	–	–
4 ENE	–	–	38	150	–
4 ESE	140	242	102	238	818
4 SSE	275	208	110	203	1,271
4 SSW	129	212	104	197	559
4 WSW	141	309	59	279	713
4 WNW	–	230	72	243	–
4 NNW	–	–	–	–	–
5 NNE	–	–	–	–	–
5 ENE	–	–	–	–	–
5 ESE	–	230	121	190	–
5 SSE	223	281	70	195	856
5 SSW	92	195	126	189	429
5 WSW	–	244	108	217	–
5 WNW	–	590	107	220	–
5 NNW	–	–	–	–	–

The first column of table 7.6 shows the zonal price changes over the period 1910–14 to 1929. In several peripheral zones there is no price index because of the absence of development before the First World War. In general, there is a great variety in price experience. One reason might have been the distorting effects of the war, another may be the unrepresent-ativeness of some of the pre-1914 samples because of their small size. Apart from these distortions, there are early signs of features of the spatial price structure that were to become more marked later in the century. For example, there were no price increases and some price declines in the inner ring (with the exception of 1SSW). Also, prices fell sharply in the 3NNW zone, a zone which was permanently depressed throughout the study period. Most of the changes over this period, however, were out of line with subsequent experience. Prices increased rapidly in 5SSE, a zone which was later to emerge as a peripheral trough; however, public housing development had not yet begun to affect this area. Also, prices actually fell throughout the WNW sector over this period, despite the fact that this sector later became the dominant price peak. On the other hand, prices rose at above average rates in the Abbeyhill–Craigentinny areas, i.e. zones 2ENE and 3ENE, later to be a marked price trough. The probable explanation is that access to industrial areas was still an important influence on residential location decisions, and hence a determinant of house price levels.

The price trends over the 1929–47 period do not fall into a clear pattern. Whereas prices increased rapidly in the later redevelopment zone (1ESE), they were already growing slowly in the WSW trough (2WSW). On the other hand, prices increased rapidly in the 3NNW trough. There were already signs of the WNW periphery beginning to boom, although prices in the 1970 peak (5SSW) grew more slowly in this period than in almost any other zone. On balance, the rate of increase in property prices tended to be rather slower in the south of the city than in the north. A likely explanation of this difference is that land was more plentiful in the south than in the north where land constraints tended to boost house prices.

The period 1947–53 provides a rare example of a fairly sudden price decline due to the particular problems connected with postwar readjust-ment. There is no reason why behaviour should be symmetrical in periods of price expansion and contraction. In fact, prices continued to rise moderately in several, mainly suburban, zones, e.g. throughout the peripheral ring 5 apart from the 5SSE trough and in ring 4 (sectors SSW, SSE and ESE). Prices declined sharply in the first four rings of the WSW sector, though in several sectors experiencing price falls, e.g. ESE, SSW, NNW and NNE, prices held up rather better with increasing distance from the city centre.

Price behaviour in the postwar house price boom between 1953 and 1970 is summarized in the penultimate column of table 7.6. There are some striking rates of price increase in several inner-city zones (1NNW, 1SSW and 1SSE), and prices rose rapidly in the Saughtonhall–Stenhouse area (3WSW). The peripheral ring prices rose relatively slowly, particularly in the south, but the secondary price peak (2ESE, 2SSE and 3ESE) did quite well. On the other hand, there was the expected poor performance in the eastern inner ring (1ENE and 1ESE) and in the Portobello area (4ENE). There is certainly no association between price acceleration and suburbanization. On the contrary, the zonal indices give the impression of relative inter-zonal stability, with one or two conspicuous exceptions. There is no tendency for the high price zones or the most peripheral zones (frequently they coincide) to experience faster price increases than other zones, and there is no correlation between the 1970 price level and the rate of price change, 1953–70. One factor was undoubtedly the conditions of excess demand for Edinburgh city housing and the chronic shortage of newer private housing within the municipal boundaries. Thus, the overall conclusion is that the dynamics of zonal price changes depend far more on overall housing conditions and on the characteristic of each zone, what is happening there and in the vicinity rather than upon their location *per se*. The implication is that general hypotheses capable of being applied to all cities need drastic modification in the light of the specifics of each case. The dynamics of intra-urban house prices involve much more complicated phenomena than the literature, mainly based upon static studies, suggests.

Drawing conclusions on the longer-run trend (1910–14 to 1970) is handicapped by the lack of base year observations in the peripheral zones. The patterns are rather obscure, but notable features include the obsolescence of 1ESE, the rising status of 3ESE and the relative decline of 2WSW. The very wide variations in performance between adjacent zones (e.g. 1ESE and 1SSE, or 1WNW and 1NNW) are also striking, reinforcing the arguments already made on this point.

The trend price surface and zones compared

The zonal analysis undertaken in this chapter has one major drawback. The concentric rings and 45° angle sectors used to derive the zones may be criticized on the ground that they subordinate the realities of the urban spatial structure to the arbitrariness of geometry. Although such a criticism is too strong, the fact remains that a concentric zone pattern is

134

most appropriate in the case of a mono-centric city where transportation is both feasible and of equal efficiency in all directions. The zones used in this study are of value in testing classical hypotheses about residential spatial structure, but the failure of these tests to provide unequivocal support for these hypotheses is itself a reflection of the imperfections in the zonal procedure adopted. An alternative way of representing the spatial structure is to take all the price observations of sales in a particular year, give each of the properties involved a precise locational reference on a grid map of the city and to use these co-ordinates to generate a spatial price contour map of the city as a whole with the computer.

Figure 4.1 shows a computer trend price surface for one year that was analysed in depth in chapters 4 and 5, namely 1966, though there is no problem — other than the space needed to illustrate them — in constructing similar trend price surfaces for any year within the study period. This map was obtained by using a quartic trend surface and representing the contours in £500 intervals. Since both the boundaries of the city and the zones used in this chapter are also shown, the map provides a clear indication of the way in which price peaks and troughs in particular and the trend surface in general cut across these zones. The price peak in the Barnton area in the WNW, the secondary price peak in the southeast in the fourth ring (Liberton and Craigmillar), and the spatially narrower peak in 5SSW (Colinton and Oxgangs) are clearly visible, as is the massive price trough in the northeast quadrant. These locations of troughs and peaks were identified correctly in the zonal analysis, so that even though the contours and zonal boundaries do not coincide, the zonal pattern adopted was sensitive enough to pick up the main features of the urban price structure. Also, it must be remembered that the trend price surface itself is the result of a smoothing operation, in some ways as crude as the mean prices derived for the zones.

Notes

[1] This is not inconsistent with the finding that the price of a house of a given size and quality may decline with distance from the city centre.

[2] Over the period 1929–70 house prices increased appreciably faster in ring 5 (726 per cent) than in any of the other rings (494–520 per cent).

[3] The zones are identified by ring number (increasing with outward movement) and by sector. For example, 4SSE means the south-south-eastern segment of the fourth ring.

[4] On the other hand, the high price zones were not yet spatially clustered. Apart from 1WSW and 1WNW, the other peaks were located in the peripheral rings but were spatially separated, i.e. in the WNW, SSW and ESE sectors.

[5] For further discussion of the factors behind increasing spatial segregation see pp. 164–7.

[6] The prevailing price levels in the 1ESE trough were far lower than in the other troughs, reflecting the influence of widespread purchase for demolition and slum clearance rather than continued residential use.

[7] Of course, there has been extensive private housebuilding in the Edinburgh area in the past two decades, but much of it has occurred outside the city limits.

[8] On the other hand, there had been up-and-down fluctuations in the intervening years.

[9] The occupational status data of table 9.4 give some support to this hypothesis, particularly in the third ring.

[10] The redevelopment zone, 1ESE, and the northeast trough, 1NNE, are the exceptions to this generalization.

8 The Determinants of Land Prices

This chapter inquires into the determinants of land prices as illustrated by the purchases of both the local authority and private builders and other private buyers in the years since 1945.

Edinburgh City Corporation purchases

The data base is given in table 8.1. This presents the information available on the fifty-one land purchases made by Edinburgh Corporation since the war. These all took place between 1952 and 1967. For all but five of the purchases it was possible to extract information from the Sasines Register on date of purchase, seller, price and size of parcel. Although the Register specified the approximate location of the land areas involved, it is difficult to locate them precisely in space. However, for all but four of the sites it was possible to identify the purchases by distance zone and by sector. The distance zones were constructed by means of annular rings from the city centre (taken to be the junction of Princes Street and the Mound) at ¼ mile intervals,[1] while sectors were made up of eight pie-slices of equal base angle radiating from the centre.

Prior to the unit price determinant analysis, it may be helpful to present some general comments on the distribution of the data.

Spatial distribution

The spatial distribution of the land purchases can be described in terms of table 8.2 and fig. 8.1. There has been no corporation land purchase since the war within 1¾ miles or beyond 4½ miles from the city centre, and about one-half of the total purchases occurred in the 3–4 mile band. Although more recent purchases have tended to be located at distances further out from the centre, the correlation coefficient between distance and date of purchase ($r = 0.5151$) is perhaps rather lower than we might expect *a priori*. The explanation of this probably lies in differential rates of pre-war radial sector development. Thus, in certain sectors (e.g. WNW,

Table 8.1
Local authority land purchases, 1952–67

Distance from centre (miles)	Direction from centre to periphery	No. of purchases in zone/ sector segment	Dates of purchases	Area (sq. yds)	Price (£s)	Price per acre (£s)	Seller type
1¾–2	NNE	1	1956	8,275	1,500	877	D
2–2¼	ENE	1	1954	2,337	1,050	2,175	E
2½–2¾	ENE	1	1952	66,840	775	56	C
2–2¼	ESE	2	1957	330,103	16,656	244	E
			1961	169,884	n.a.	–	E
2¼–2½	ESE	1	1966	60,984	72,000	5,714	B
2¾–3	ESE	1	1957	26,712	4,810	871	E
3–3¼	ESE	1	1957	31,518	3,760	577	E
3¼–3½	ESE	1	1956	358,160	31,500	425	C
3½–3¾	ESE	1	1958	73,568	9,400	618	B
4–4¼	ESE	1	1952	14,060	374	129	C
1¾–2	SSE	1	1952	145,960	5,200	172	B
2¾–3	SSE	1	1953	99,268	5,800	283	E
3–3¼	SSE	1	1955	155,074	3,365	105	E
3½–3¾	SSE	3	1967	31,247	32,280	5,000	C
			1967	40,995	37,250	4,398	C
			1967	12,100	1,769	708	F
3¾–4	SSE	2	1954	467,379	12,990	134	F
			1960	117,787	25	1	A
3–3¼	SSW	1	1955	458,314	8,700	92	C
3¼–3½	SSW	1	1967	82,135	37,000	2,180	A
2¾–3	WSW	1	1952	22,990	475	100	B
3–3¼	WSW	2	1952	50,133	1,050	101	B
			1953	119,596	2,800	113	B
3¼–3½	WSW	1	1954	56,691	77,000	6,574	B
3½–3¾	WSW	2	1957	36,300	3,175	423	E
			1966	85,668	35,375	1,999	B
3¾–4	WSW	1	1962	24,926	4,800	932	B
4–4¼	WSW	3	1967	119,306	30,500	1,237	F
			1967	307,727	166,455	2,618	F
			1967	117,612	52,550	2,162	F
4¼–4½	WSW	3	1966	130,680	122,500	4,537	F
			1967	51,265	10,000	944	C
			1966	n.a.	149,340	–	F
n.a.	WSW	3	1952	179,080	2,250	61	B
			1953	n.a.	12,400	–	F
			1966	15,904	8,111	2,468	C
1¾–2	WNW	1	1955	13,165	2,300	846	D
2–2¼	WNW	1	1952	230,868	6,580	138	C
2¼–2½	WNW	1	1955	290,884	10,050	167	E
2½–2¾	WNW	2	1956	173,853	17,235	480	E
			1959	115,013	5,850	246	A
3–3¼	WNW	2	1958	96,994	n.a.	–	B
			1965	44,731	8,000	866	E
3¼–3½	WNW	2	1965	24,805	22,500	4,390	B
			1965	n.a.	660	–	C
3½–3¾	WNW	2	1954	361,968	17,500	234	C
			1965	9,632	1,108	557	E
3¾–4	WNW	2	1952	135,186	3,360	120	B
			1965	108,363	1,903	85	E
n.a.	WNW	1	1952	61,633	1,083	86	C

Seller type code: A = government department; B = builder; C = individual; D = non-profit making organisation; E = company; F = farmer.

138

Table 8.2

Distance distribution of purchases

	Distance from city centre			
	< 3 miles	3−4 miles	> 4 miles	n.a.
No. of ¼ mile bands	5	4	2	−
No. of purchases	15	25	7	

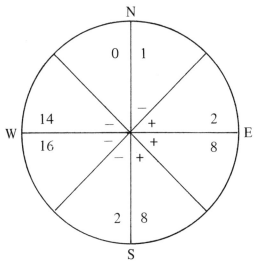

Fig. 8.1   Sectoral distribution of purchases and dummy variable signs

ESE) land was still available for housebuilding after the war at distances less than 3 miles from the city centre well into the period after building activity had resumed.

The sectoral distribution of purchases emerges clearly from fig. 8.1. Almost 60 per cent of the land purchases have occurred in the WNW−WSW quadrant with a high proportion of the remainder in the southeast quadrant. The reasons for this uneven distribution would appear to be the availability of land, as reflected in physical and topographical constraints on the one hand and prior urban development on the other, and the relative price of land. For instance, land purchases in the NNW sector and the northeast quadrant are few because these areas are bounded by the Firth of Forth and are smaller than the others, while the earlier development of Granton, Newhaven and especially Leith limited the amount of undeveloped land available. In the southeast and SSW sectors,

139

physical constraints such as the high ground around Arthur's Seat and Braid Hills and land above mines liable to subsidence have hampered development, though there have nevertheless been many corporation purchases in this zone. In the WSW sector there had been substantial urban development of the city prior to the war around long-established industrial areas in the valley of the Water of Leith, but beyond this the presence of land suitable for building accounts for substantial corporation purchases in several areas, but notably around Wester Hailes. There was relatively little pre-war expansion of Edinburgh into the residential WNW sector. Hence there have been many local authority land purchases in this direction, some of which have been relatively near to the city centre. Another feature of the spatial pattern of purchases is its clustering[2] as adjacent sites were bought to permit the development of Edinburgh's large postwar council housing estates, particularly in the Gilmerton, Wester Hailes, Craigmillar, Clermiston, Silverknowes, Muirhouse, and Wester and Easter Drylaw districts.

The other factor in the sectoral distribution pattern is that the majority of the purchases has been in the cheaper land areas of the west and southwest rather than the dearer east and southeast. This is shown by the signs of the dummy variable regression coefficients in fig. 8.1 (obtained from the multiple regression analysis discussed below). Although few of the direction variables achieve statistical significance, it is interesting that adjacent sectors tend to have the same sign with the dearer land located in those areas where there were topographical and other restrictions on the amount of land available for development.

Time distribution

The time distribution of purchases is shown in table 8.3. All the postwar purchases in the City of Edinburgh have taken place in this sixteen-year period. The time-phasing of purchases (the heavy land-buying at the beginning of the period, the hiatus in the middle, and the resurgence of land purchases at the end) reflects the changes in housing subsidies and in central government's attitude to public housebuilding and simultaneously influences the subsequent rate of council housebuilding in the city.

Table 8.3

Time distribution of purchases

1952	1953–57	1958–62	1963–64	1965–66	1967
9	18	6	0	10	8

Size distribution

The size distribution of purchases is summarized in table 8.4. The total acreage purchased by the corporation in Edinburgh since the war amounts to 1,185·6 acres with an average site size (over the forty-eight purchases where area could be measured) of almost 25 acres. The blocks of land purchased are underestimated in table 8.4 because these data refer to individual purchases, whereas, as we have already pointed out, there were several clusters of adjacent sites. Since all the sites were within 4½ miles of the city centre, these facts are indicative of the substantial blocks of close-in land still available for development in the postwar period.

Table 8.4

Size distribution of purchases

Acres						Average size
> 50	20–50	10–20	5–10	< 5	n.a.	
7	16	9	8	8	3	24·7

Distribution of sellers

It was possible to extract information from the Sasines Register about the sellers of land, and from this the six-fold classification of table 8.5 has been derived. Whereas *a priori* we might expect the urban land market in modern times to be dominated by estate and property companies, table 8.5 shows that individual landowners and even farmers remained important as suppliers of urban land for development. Also surprising is the extent to which the local authority purchased land from builders. Other evidence from the private land purchase survey undertaken in our project shows that certain Edinburgh builders were very active in the land market, holding land parcels for considerable periods of time and engaging in speculative buying and selling.

Table 8.5 also anticipates the results of our multiple regression analysis by giving the regression coefficient signs for seller type. The negative signs for government departments and non-profit organizations are easy to understand given that the purchaser was the local authority. Conversely, we would expect builders to profit from their greater knowledge of the land market by extracting higher selling prices. The other signs are less obvious, particularly the negative sign for companies. The positive signs for builders, individuals and farmers could reflect either land quality

141

differentials (not picked up in the locational variables) or 'hardness' in market negotiations. Why companies should either lack expertise or hold poorer land is unclear.

Analysis of land prices

(i) The model

What determines the variation in the unit price paid in local authority land purchases over this period? Our hypothesis is that land prices reflect the combined influence of time, location and land market variables. More specifically:

$$P = f[T, M, D, A, S]$$

where P = unit price of land (£s per acre), T = time, M = distance in miles, D = direction of sector in which land purchase occurs, A = area of site purchased, and S = seller type.

Time may influence price in several ways. The most important is that the degree of urbanization increases over time, certainly during the period of this study when the main changes differentiating the present-day residential structure in Edinburgh from the pre-war pattern took place. Time may also stand as a surrogate for increased competition in the land market, a factor not unrelated to the forces of urbanization. Although time may represent the impact of inflation, this cannot have been an important influence over a period when the average price of land increased

Table 8.5

Distribution of sellers

Type of seller	Number of sales	Dummy variable sign
Government department	3	—
Builder	13	+ *
Individual	12	+ *
Non-profit making organization	2	—
Company	13	— **
Farmer	8	+

* significant at 0·1 level
** significant at 0·05 level

142

2,400 per cent but the retail price index rose by a mere 72 per cent. Obviously, the *a priori* expected sign for the regression coefficient of T is positive.

In this model, location of land is measured in two ways: by distance, measured by the mid-point of annular bands 0·25 miles thick, and by direction, using the eight sector division of fig. 8.1. The latter is measured by the use of dummy variables and the sign will obviously vary from one dummy to another; the signs are shown in fig. 8.1. Virtually all urban land value theories suggest that the price of land will decline with distance from the CBD due to accessibility considerations, competition and changes in the supply of land.[3] We naturally expect the distance sign to be negative.

Land market influences, apart from increased competition caught up in the time variable, are measured by two variables — size of parcel and seller type. We may hypothesise that there are economies of scale in land purchase, that buying a large site may enable the purchaser to negotiate a lower unit price, so that the sign of A would be negative. The dummy variables for S (see table 8.5) will assume different signs according to the 'leverage' of the seller, his market behaviour and his information. The sign may also reflect quality of land differences, though there is no *a priori* reason to expect these to vary systematically from one type of seller to another.

(ii) Regression analysis

The above model was tested using multiple regression techniques. For this purpose, the fifty-one land purchases had to be pruned to forty-one. Eight of the purchases had to be excluded because of a missing data item (total price, area or distance), and two eccentric purchases were eliminated because it was clear that their prices did not reflect competitive market forces.[4] In each regression run the time, distance and size variables were included, but the dummies were introduced in sequence, first singly then as combinations of D and S, so as not to reduce the degrees of freedom too much. Experiments were made with non-linear time and distance variables, but these transformations brought about no improvement.[5] There was no evidence of multi-collinearity in the correlation matrix, and the Durbin-Watson statistic was satisfactory. Also, there were no signs of systematic bias in the residuals.

The results are illustrated with an equation in which the dummy variables represent aggregated sectors and seller types. Since both the cheap and the dear land sectors are contiguous it is reasonable to divide the city into two zones, one of cheaper ($D=1$) and the other of dearer land ($D=0$). Similarly, the three seller types associated with higher selling prices are aggregated together ($S=1$ for builders, individuals and farmers; $S=0$ for other sellers). The justifications are the small sample size of some seller types when each is considered independently and the belief, in the absence of evidence to the contrary, that the factors (market behaviour characteristics and/or land quality differentials) making for higher selling prices are common to all the 'hard' seller types. The full equation[6] is:

$$P = 1{,}692{\cdot}52 + 208{\cdot}24T^{***} - 735{\cdot}89M^{***} - 517{\cdot}38D^{*} - 6{\cdot}29A + 1{,}059{\cdot}47S^{***}$$
$$(6{\cdot}05) \qquad (2{\cdot}44) \qquad (1{\cdot}50) \qquad (0{\cdot}939) \ (2{\cdot}77)$$

$R^2 = 0{\cdot}5949$ d.f. = 35   D.W. = 2·326

*** = significant at 0·01 level.
*   = significant at 0·1 level.

(iii) Interpretation

This equation explains three-fifths of the variation in unit land prices paid by Edinburgh City Corporation since the war. In view of the fact that there are no variables in the model that refer to the detailed characteristics of each site (topographical and physical features, environmental aspects, or amenity value), this result is highly satisfactory. The signs of all the regression coefficients accord with our *a priori* hypotheses, and these signs remain the same throughout all the regression runs. As the *t* values show, time, distance and seller type were all highly significant (at the 0·01 level) while direction was significant at the 0·1 level. Inclusion of the D and S variables raised the R^2 by 0·13 without any distorting side-effects on the other variables. The size of site variable had rather a low *t* value, but the regression coefficient had the expected negative sign.

    The price of suburban land in Edinburgh, as reflected in local authority purchases, increased at an average rate of £208·2 per year over the period 1952−67. This is quite an impressive rate of expansion when we take into account the very low land prices ruling at the beginning of the period, though the increase is much more modest if compared with the phenomenal rise of more recent years, especially in southeast England. It is also possible that there may be a systematic difference in the level of price paid by the local authority and that paid by private buyers, and this hypothesis will be examined in subsequent studies. The distance effect on land prices can be quantified as a decline of £735·9 per mile with increasing distance from the city centre. If this appears at first sight rather small, it must be remembered that we have no observations within the inner ring up to a radial distance of 1¾ miles, and that is where we would expect the most substantial declines to occur. These results also enable us to quantify the relative impact of time and distance. The time effect overshadows the distance effect; the city would have to expand radially at the rate of 484 yards per year for the local authority or developer to be able to offset rising land prices by outwardly expanding on to cheaper land. Or, to put the same point more realistically and taking account of the fact that housing development is sequential over time but may 'leap-frog' over space, the local authority would have to purchase land 1·44 miles further out merely to absorb the increase in land prices over the previous five years.[7]

Apart from its statistical insignificance, the economies of scale effect is rather weak: each additional acre in a land parcel tends to reduce the price per acre by only £6·29. Finally, the explanatory power of the dummy variables suggests that the direction of land development and the characteristics of suppliers of land are relevant determinants of the variation in urban land prices.

Private land purchases

As shown in table 8.6, there are major differences in the land parcels purchased by the corporation and by private buyers (typically builders). Although the mean distances are similar, the characteristics of the parcels vary in all other respects. The typical private purchase was a much smaller plot, bought more recently at a much higher unit price. The higher price per acre paid by private builders reflects a mix of factors: the date of purchase, the smaller sites, and that some of the corporation's land purchases were negotiable at a price rather lower than the parcels might have realised on the open market.

Table 8.6

Comparison of public and private land purchases

	Mean values	
	public	private
Distance from CBD (miles)	3·22	3·00
Area (acres)	25·40	2·15
Price per plot (£s)	19,810·9	23,228·2
Price per acre (£s)	1,172·1	5,028·5
Time (years)	8·1	16·2
Number of purchases	41	182

The private land purchase equation most directly comparable with the 'best fit' public land purchase regression (see p. 144 above) is given in the first column of table 8.7. The minor differences between the two are found in the directional and seller type dummy variables. The cheap land purchased by the public sector was in the west, while the cheaper private land purchases were in the east. Also, the 'hard' sellers (i.e. where seller type was positively associated with price per acre) were different (builders, individuals and farmers selling to the corporation; individuals, property companies and the unspecified category selling to private buyers). The results are remarkably consistent with those observed for Edinburgh City Corporation's purchases, once account is taken of the fact that the average unit price of private purchases was more than four times that of public sector purchases.

Time and distance were again the dominant explanatory variables, with time even more important relative to distance than in the public sector. The trade-off between space and time in this case is over 1,024 yards per year, more than double what was discovered in the public land purchase analysis. The quantitative impact of parcel size was rather larger than in the public sector case and was also statistically significant. But while direction was rather more significant, the reverse was the case with seller type. However, the explanatory power of the equation as a whole was much lower (the R^2 falls from 0·5949 to 0·3036).

The differences that do exist are not difficult to explain. Distance is less important for private housing because the journey to work constraint is not as restrictive as with working-class housing, and the small lots that were available close to the city centre would not attract the competition of the corporation because it is uneconomical to provide public housing on small gap sites. Similarly, the stronger impact of time probably reflects that it may act as a surrogate for the growing land shortage (and hence increasing competition) so that the scarcity of sites within the city pushed up the price for whatever land became available. The negative association between plot size and price (about £41 per acre) is a possible indication of the premium paid for favourably located but small 'gap' sites.

As for the directional variables, why was land for council housebuilding cheaper in the west while that for private housing was cheaper in the east? Part of the explanation is that many of the corporation purchases occurred early in the postwar period when land to the west of the city was relatively plentiful and cheap, while large sites in the east (with the exception of the southeast) rarely came on to the market. This scarcity of land in the northeast where Edinburgh and Leith pressed closely against each other coupled with constraints in the southeast (Holyrood Park,

Table 8.7

Determinants of private land values

	1	2	3
Constant	−2,488·90	−3,163·82	−3,351·48
Distance:			
linear	−1,148·89*** (2·43)	−1,623·13*** (3·46)	
log			−10,877·24*** (3·80)
Direction			
East composite	−1,982·23** (2·10)	−1,226·65* (1·32)	
WSW		2,406·27** (1·83)	3,001·32*** (2·38)
Time	698·94*** (8·09)	686·40*** (8·07)	669·66*** (7·99)
Area	−40·92** (1·67)	−39·78** (1·73)	−41·03** (1·79)
Non-development		2,098·25*** (2·34)	2,128·78*** (2·39)
Transactions type:			
seller dummy	951·60 (1·06)		
buyer dummy		4,035·40** (1·71)	3,964·72** (1·68)
individuals to smaller builders		5,770·57*** (4·02)	5,733·63*** (4·06)
organizations to property cos.		−2,731·89* (1·35)	−2,970·47* (1·49)
property co. to small builder		7,556·14*** (2·83)	7,560·91*** (2·83)
builder to small builder		2,840·85* (1·36)	2,717·71* (1·31)
d.f.	176	170	171
R^2	0·3036	0·4105	0·4129

*** = significant at 1 per cent.   ** = significant at 5 per cent.
 * = significant at 10 per cent.

environmental amenity constraints around Duddingston, etc.) meant little land was available for private purchase in the east. In general, of the sites that became available those in the west tended to have a higher amenity value and environmental considerations are obviously more important for the private sector, while proximity to workplaces was a dominant factor in the selection of sites for council housing (and hence a willingness of the corporation to countenance higher prices in the east).[8] In other words, once the ultimate users of the land and their needs are taken into account it is quite consistent that the corporation would pay more for land in the east while private buyers (e.g. builders) were willing to pay more in the west. Private and public purchasers were rarely directly competitive,[9] though there have been more examples of conflict of interest between private and public residential land use in the postwar compared with the inter-war period. The importance of environmental quality and neighbourhood characteristics is probably the main reason for the much lower R^2 in the private land case. Many of the detailed and very localized site considerations that would make one piece of land more attractive to a builder of middle-class housing than another are omitted from the very restricted list of independent variables used in table 8.7.

The seller type results are not particularly striking. In the case of private land purchases the variable is not even significant. As for seller types, the builder is a 'hard' seller when disposing of land to the corporation but a 'soft' seller in the private market, primarily because many of the latter sales were to property-holding companies frequently linked via joint directorships with the builder himself.

To sum up, a direct comparison of public and private land purchases suggests that the same key forces, time and distance, were operative in both markets. The greater dominance of time in the private land market indicates that this market was more competitive, particularly since the time distribution of private purchases is skewed much more heavily towards the recent past when land shortages, especially within the city, have become more acute. However, the results for plot size, direction and seller type provide strong evidence of very imperfect substitutability between land for public and that for private purchase. The small plots that are useful for private builders are uneconomic for council housing estates.[10] The environmental quality and neighbourhood amenities that put a premium value on certain sites in the private land market are found in different areas of a city from the proximity to workplaces and level sites that are so important in the land market for public housing. The significance of seller type in the public but not in the private land market is also suggestive of differences in the structure of the two markets. The stronger competition prevailing in the private market is not so conducive to the price level reflecting the varying degrees of market knowledge of specific seller types. Purchases in the public sector, however, were often the result of protracted but non-market negotiations, where some sellers (e.g. builders) would be able to exercise power based on their detailed market knowledge, but where other sellers (such as government departments, non-profit organizations and even some private estate companies) did not extract the hardest market price because the land was being bought for public use.

The equation comparable to that for public land purchases does not, in fact, give the best fit for private sector purchases. Even with the limited data available from the Sasines Register, better results can be obtained (raising the R^2 by 0·11) with a slightly different composition of variables. Table 8.7 (columns 2 and 3) shows equations using a linear and logarithmic distance function respectively. The major differences between these equations and column 1 are more disaggregated transactions type variables, a better fit for the WSW direction than for the east composite variable, and the fact that land purchased but not developed was significantly more expensive than other land. Of these differences, the last is the more important. It indicates the importance of speculation in the city land market and that purchasers who could afford to hold land were prepared to pay a high price for it in anticipation of even higher prices in the future. The positive association over three transactions type variables between unit price and sales to small builders perhaps suggests that the latter had little monopsony power but had to pay high prices in order to obtain sites in a very tight market, and also the fact that small builders were more likely to purchase choice sites on which they could build individual custom-made houses.

The better-fit equations have little effect on the quantitative impact of the main variables time, distance and plot size. The negative size coefficient remains around £40 per acre, that of time falls within the range £660–700 per year, though distance decay increases by about 40 per cent per mile (see column 2). The t values for distance are also rather higher, with the logarithmic function yielding a slightly improved fit. However, even in these equations more than half of the variation in price per acre remains unexplained. Environmental amenity characteristics and specific and highly localized site characteristics probably rank high among excluded variables. Indirect support for this view is provided by the statistical significance of these influences in the *house* price analysis of chapters 4 and 5.

Land prices in the private and public sectors compared

Table 8.8 presents the crude prices per acre paid by private purchasers and by Edinburgh City Corporation over the postwar period. These prices are obtained via unweighted averages, i.e. treating each transaction as having equal value regardless of the acreage involved. Given the small number of transactions involved it is unreasonable to expect smooth price trends. The unit cost of building sites varies so much because of differences in location, plot size, prevailing conditions in the land market, and other factors. The results are seen in the wide range of price variations in the

Table 8.8

Private and public land purchases in Edinburgh, 1952–72

	Private			Public	
	no. of sites	price per acre (£s)	range of prices per acre (£s)	no. of sites	price per acre (£s)
1952	–	–	–	9	107
1953	2	68	63–72	2	198
1954	6	566	329–925	3	848
1955	9	662	99–1,159	4	303
1956	10	1,106	292–3,297	3	594
1957	8	836	81–2,727	4	529
1958	9	1,280	325–4,673	1	618
1959	5	1,031	555–1,717	1	246
1960	6	1,726	625–4,196	–	–
1961	9	3,758	794–10,899	–	–
1962	6	2,894	961–4,808	1	932
1963	7	5,147	380–22,850	–	–
1964	14	5,014	1,479–9,601	–	–
1965	14	6,691	1,067–17,636	4	1,475
1966	14	3,809	799–10,889	4	3,672
1967	17	6,748	861–26,073	8	2,397
1968	3	11,793	7,330–17,647	–	–
1969	6	8,148	965–17,812	–	–
1970	11	15,173	3,570–65,047	–	–
1971	9	9,352	735–23,045	–	–
1972	5	14,005	1,879–22,734	–	–

land purchases of the private sector, which shows that unit prices paid in any year can differ by a factor of ten or even twenty. These facts suggest that the data of table 8.8 should be treated cautiously.

Nevertheless, certain features of table 8.8 are clear. First, the land market varied over time in intensity, being particularly active in both the public and private sectors in 1954–58 and in 1964–67. Second, private purchasers almost always paid much more for land than the corporation, the only exception being the years up to and including 1954. Third, despite the year-to-year fluctuations the data show convincingly the rising cost of building land over the twenty-year period, with only 1956–59 standing out as a phase of relative price stability. [11] Finally, the extremely wide differentials in unit land price even within the same year are powerful evidence of the heterogeneity of the land market. This reaffirms the need for spatial analysis at the intra-urban level.

Conclusions

The theory of urban land values is fairly well developed. Its evolution has been based on *a priori* reasoning and casual observation, and there has been an acute shortage – probably due to the lack of data – of quantitative empirical studies to test its predictions. This chapter is a modest attempt to provide some of the needed support. Our findings suggest the importance of the degree of urbanization and increased competition in the land market (as reflected in our time variable), of distance and other locational characteristics, and of the nature of the urban land market itself – particularly the expertise and behaviour of the different participants in the market. These results should reassure those who have faith in the accepted theory.

Notes

[1] It was impossible to obtain greater accuracy in the distance measures, partly because of the imprecision in the locational descriptions given in the Register, and partly because some of the sites were quite large and would have overlapped two or more rings if the bands had been narrower.

[2] Several clusters could be identified: seven sites in Silverknowes, Easter and Wester Drylaw and Muirhouse districts; seven in Clermiston, three in Wester Hailes and five in the Gilmerton, Stenhouse and Ferniehill districts.

³ With outward movement the supply of land tends to increase for two reasons: there is a large area within each successive annular ring; and a higher proportion of the total land will normally be unoccupied.

⁴ The first exclusion was the sale of 25 acres in 1960 at £1 per acre by the Secretary of State for Scotland. The second was the sale of less than 12 acres in 1954 by a private builder at a price of £6,574 per acre, a price which was more than £6,000 per acre too high for that area at that time. The explanation is that this was not purely a land transaction, since there were buildings on the site compensation for which was included in the selling price.

⁵ This does not imply that the land value gradient is linear. Most of the curvature in the gradient is likely to be found close to the CBD, and no observation in this study was closer than 1·875 miles.

⁶ The mean values are a plot of 25·4 acres located 3·22 miles from the city centre and sold in 1959 at a price of £1,172·12 per acre.

⁷ Strictly speaking, this figure needs to be adjusted for the 'pure' inflation effect since the alternative spending power of £x thousand in year $t + 5$ is less than £x thousand in year t. Given the rate of inflation over the period of this study, and comparing two land purchase decisions in constant prices five years apart, the compensating outward movement would be about 1·2 miles.

⁸ The fact that public sector purchases were on average a little further out reflects the scarcity of close-in large sites rather than a preference of the corporation for distant sites. Its land purchase policy throughout the inter-war period had been significantly influenced by its desire for accessible sites (Smith, 1964, ch. 9).

⁹ For instance, steep and undulating sites are favoured by private builders because they are conducive to attractive estates and fine views but are avoided by the corporation because of the need to keep down public housing construction costs.

¹⁰ It should be noted that whereas the *average* parcel size for private land purchases was only 2·15 acres, only 8 out of the 48 corporation purchases for which size data were available were less than 5 acres.

¹¹ These results are confirmed by the analysis since 1959 by Goodwin, Macdonald and Seale (1974). This research team used the same data source but estimated the average annual prices from mid-year to mid-year. They also present some interesting comparisons with the rest of Scotland.

9   The Spatial Segregation of Social Classes

Introduction

Within cities the various types of housing, offices, public buildings, industry, the major shops, and environmental amenities are not distributed randomly in space. Particular kinds of land used tend to be concentrated in particular areas and concepts such as 'natural area', 'bid rent curves' and 'neighbourhood' have become familiar in urban analysis. In addition, urban sociologists have focused on the more qualitative correlates of the division of the city into relatively homogeneous areas. Park (1926), in a statement which is often cited, observed that 'social relations are ... frequently and ... inevitably correlated with spatial relations'. In the 1920s and 1930s the 'Chicago school', of which Park was a leading figure, contributed an extensive literature on the spatial structure of Chicago which has continued to exert a major influence on more recent work by urban sociologists and geographers.[1]

Although the Chicago school was distinguished primarily by its detailed empirical analysis, its research relied upon the relatively abstract ideas of ecological theory. Fundamental to this theory was the analogy drawn from biology in which the city is seen as a community where, via atomistic (i.e. subsocial) competition between individuals, people are spatially distributed according to an impersonal quasi-market mechanism. The location of the residence of each family, therefore, is dependent upon its ability to compete for space. The influence of Darwin's evolutionary theory may be detected in the notion of 'the survival of the fittest' implicit in the Chicago models and underlined further in the use made in urban analysis of such concepts as 'dominance', 'invasion', and 'succession'.

To this sub-social level the ecologists added an analytically distinct social dimension which took more account of the distinctively human capacity for modifying the natural environment.[2] This more social approach to spatial structure involves an emphasis upon what the sociologists call a 'consensual cultural superstructure' which derives from common residence in a city and which modifies and limits atomistic competition. Hence, competition in the city is understood in terms of ecology and economics with success in the struggle being largely a function of income and wealth, while consensus, both in the city as a whole and in its natural areas, is the product of the evolution of common social values and therefore a matter for sociology.

There is an obvious affinity between classical human ecology and the functionalist theory of social stratification and institutions which came to dominate mainstream sociology in the United States.[3] Both are founded upon a biological analogy, and in both the city and society respectively tend to be raised to the status of the prime object of study and become the distinctive subject matter of a separate academic discipline. In addition, though their emphases may be regarded as different, they share the same conception of a system characterized by impersonal and atomistic competition but regulated and modified by shared social values. This congruence between the main school of urban theory and the dominant sociological model has exerted a powerful influence on studies of social segregation, particularly in the United States. This is seen most clearly in the attention which American urban sociologists have focused upon 'neighbourhoods', characterized by shared values and behavioural patterns and distinguished from other groups by their own specific status ranking. This concentration upon status rather than class[4] has been fostered by explanations of spatial segregation and social class stratification that stress differences between people in terms of impersonal conflict within a quasi-market system. Hence, the interesting sociological question for these researchers is how social customs and values in urban neighbourhoods reinforce the framework of natural inequality. The emphasis upon status rather than class differences has promoted a concern with patterns of interaction between different groups in an urban area (see Laumann, 1966) and has yielded some interesting research into housing as a symbol of identity and as a universal indicator of social rank.[5]

If classical ecology has much in common with functionalist theory, more recent analysis of the spatial segregation of social classes in the city, particularly in Europe where functionalism has never gained the same influence, has shown closer links with conflict theories deriving from the sociology of Marx and Weber. Accordingly, the emphasis has shifted from the analysis of the city as a system *per se* to an examination of the power and interests of the different groups within the city. An early step in this direction was Rex and Moore's study of Sparkbrook. This advanced the thesis that 'there is a class struggle over the use of houses and that this class struggle is the central process of the city as a social unit' (Rex and Moore, 1967, p.273). According to this view, spatial segregation is not the product of pure natural selection but a function of the differential access of various 'housing classes' to alternative segments of the housing market.

Although this study introduced a new dimension to urban sociology, and its theoretical emphasis upon the differential access of various groups to housing made it possible to allow for state bureaucracies in socio-spatial analysis, it has been criticized severely (Haddon, 1970; Davies and Taylor, 1970; Pahl, 1972). It is unnecessary to provide a detailed account of the debate here, particularly since many of the more specific criticisms follow from a major theoretical inadequacy of the Sparkbrook study. This is Rex and Moore's misinterpretation of Weber's writings on the origins of class. Instead of following Weber's contention that class is a function of an individual's ability to *dispose* of goods, capital or skills to secure income and other benefits in a market, they focus on the differential ability to *use* such resources in securing a favourable position in a relatively autonomous 'housing market' and argue that there is a specifically *urban* sociology as represented by 'the class conflicts of the city as distinct from those of the workplace' (Rex and Moore, 1967, p.274).

Against this it is argued, notably by Haddon (1970, pp.129–32), that to concentrate upon the use of power in the consumption of housing, rather than on power acquired through the disposal of resources and skills in the market in which these resources and skills are the subject of bargaining, is to confuse a sympton of urban conditions for a cause. As a result, more recent urban sociological theory has assigned much greater significance to the role of the labour market. Instead of being regarded as the object of study of a separate branch of sociology, the city is viewed as 'an arena, an understanding of which helps in the understanding of the overall society which creates it' (Pahl, 1972). Housing and housing areas are not only the indicators of individual success in the competition for space and of status ranking and identity, but become indicators of class power deriving from the labour market.

Despite this major theoretical reappraisal, the notion of space and of spatial segregation has remained central. Indeed, space becomes the basis for the distinctive contribution of urban analysis to an understanding of wider social processes. For Harvey, 'Urbanism is a social form, a way of life predicated on, among other things, a certain division of labour and a certain hierarchical ordering of activity which is broadly consistent with the dominant mode of production'. In addition, 'the city may also be the locus of the accumulated contradictions and therefore the likely birth-place of a new mode of production' (Harvey, 1973, p. 203). Harvey draws upon Marxian dialectical method in an attempt to reformulate traditional 'urban' concepts in a 'relational' way so that, like the city itself, spatial

155

structure is no longer a subject of study *per se,* but is regarded as simultaneously determined with the socio-economic system.

This brief discussion shows that throughout the theoretical debates spatial structure, and especially the spatial segregation of social groups, has remained a crucial area, particularly from the point of view of empirical testing. Whether they have emphasised spatial segregation as the product of natural selection, or of competition between 'housing classes', or developing from changing modes of production, or whether they have focused upon housing as a source and symbol of status and shared values or of class and political conflict, all researchers have treated spatial structure as a fruitful field in which to explore their ideas.

The occupational data obtained from the Register of Sasines are of considerable interest since, despite their limitations (see pp. 162–3), they offer an opportunity for examining the spatial distribution of social classes in an entire city over a long period of time. Census data collected at the enumeration district level have become available only comparatively recently in Britain and boundary changes often make longitudinal analysis difficult. The Sasines data not only permit cross-sectional descriptive analyses of the Edinburgh spatial class structure, but also the existence of house transaction records from 1905–71 makes possible a dynamic analysis of changes in spatial structure. By relating these empirical findings to the geographical, economic, social and political history and social structure of Edinburgh some evaluation may be made of the various theories discussed above.[6]

Social class segregation in modern Edinburgh

Census enumeration district statistics have been published in Britain only since 1961. Their comprehensiveness makes them a most valuable aid to the analysis of urban spatial structure. They also provide an opportunity for comparative inter-urban analysis. Before examining the Sasines occupational data, therefore, it is appropriate to look at the 1966 enumeration district statistics, the most recent year available within the study period.[7] From the census tables it is possible to measure, first, the degree of social class segregation and, second, the geographical implications of this segregation in Edinburgh.

Duncan and Duncan (1955a) have devised a means of measuring the dissimilarity between the spatial distribution of the residences of social classes and the relative segregation of different social groups. Although alternative indices have been advanced (Duncan and Duncan, 1955b), it is useful to follow the Duncans' method since it has been employed in a number of studies, the results of which may be compared directly with those for Edinburgh. The 'index of dissimilarity' as defined by the Duncans equals the percentage of one social class which would have to change homes in order to be distributed among the enumeration districts of a city in exactly the same proportions as another class. The index is calculated by subtracting the percentage of the city total of one social class resident in an enumeration district from the percentage of the total of another class. This procedure is repeated for each district and the differences summed. The index of dissimilarity is equal to one half of this sum of the differences in distributions. The results for Edinburgh in 1966 are presented in table 9.1

Table 9.1

Indices of dissimilarity in residential distribution, 1966

Social class		1	2	3	4	5	6
1	Professional workers						
2	Employers and managers	27					
3	Non-manual workers	40	28				
4	Foremen, skilled manual and own account workers (other than professional)	59	46	28			
5	Personal service workers, semi-skilled manual workers and agricultural workers	61	50	33	18		
6	Unskilled manual workers	71	62	48	30	28	

Source: Registrar General for Scotland: *Sample Census of Scotland (1966)*, Enumeration District Table 9; Edinburgh, HMSO, 1968.

The six-fold social class classification adopted in table 9.1 is based upon a grouping of the seventeen socio-economic groups employed by the Registrar General for Scotland in the 1966 census.[8] In addition to the six classes included in the table, a seventh (armed forces and persons with inadequately described occupations) was included in calculating the percentage of the total of each class in each district. However, the numerical insignificance of this group would make any attempt to measure its spatial relationship to the main classes meaningless.

The rank order of the indices in table 9.1 shows that the index of dissimilarity between two groups is directly related to the distance between them in the social class structure. For example, for professional workers and unskilled manual workers to be distributed among the Edinburgh enumeration districts in equal proportions 71 per cent of one group would have to change their residential location. For professional workers and the employers and managers group to have an equal distribution, only 27 per cent of one group would have to move. As for the middle groups, despite the widespread belief in the 'embourgeoisement' of the working class in the 1960s, the distribution of non-manual workers is more similar to that of higher white-collar groups than is the distribution of the top grade manual class. In addition, there is a remarkable consistency in the degree of residential dissimilarity between adjacent groups. The only exception is the low index of dissimilarity between the two manual classes, 4 and 5 which could be due to relatively equal access to the superior council housing areas of the city.

The most significant observation to be made about table 9.1, however, relates to the magnitude of the numbers. Other studies to use this index include those of Chicago by the Duncans themselves (1955a and b), Oxford by Collison and Mogey (1959), Oslo by Ramsøy (1966), and the Kent sector of the Outer Metropolitan Area by Taylor and Taylor (1971).[9] A comparison of the Edinburgh indices with these other results shows that residential dissimilarity between social classes in Edinburgh was relatively very high. Certain factors may have inflated the indices. For example, the population was divided into six social classes while the Oxford and Oslo studies employed only five. In addition, the size of city studied may be an influence, a fact which may help to explain the lower degree of residential dissimilarity in the smaller townships of the Outer Metropolitan Area in Kent. Finally, the date at which a study is conducted may have an effect, especially if the social class structure is a function of time.

The studies referred to above relate to years between 1955 and 1971, and the relatively low indices presented by the Duncans for Chicago were based on eight social groups, so that it is a reasonably confident conclusion that Edinburgh in 1966 was very highly segregated. Some indication of the difference between Edinburgh and the other cities is given by the indices of dissimilarity between the highest and lowest class. In Edinburgh the figure is 71 compared with 54 in Chicago, 46 in Oxford, 44 in Oslo, and 53 in the Outer Metropolitan Area of Kent. The intermediate indices for Edinburgh are also significantly higher than in the other cities.

158

The Duncans also developed an 'index of segregation' which measures the degree to which each social class is confined within specific, relatively homogeneous districts of the city. This index is computed by calculating the index of dissimilarity between one class and all the other classes combined. Indices of segregation for Edinburgh in 1966 are shown in table 9.2.

Table 9.2

Indices of residential segregation, 1966

Social class	Index of segregation
1 Professional workers	50
2 Employers and managers	38
3 Non-manual workers	21
4 Foremen, skilled manual and own account workers (other than professional)	22
5 Personal service workers, semi-skilled manual workers and agricultural workers	23
6 Unskilled workers	38

Source: Registrar General for Scotland: *Sample Census of Scotland, 1966;* Enumeration District Table 9; Edinburgh, HMSO, 1968.

These indices show that the classes at the extremes of the social hierarchy are the most highly segregated. This conforms with the findings of other studies. However, the most striking feature of the Edinburgh indices is the high overall degree of segregation. The indices of 50 and 38 for the professional and unskilled manual classes respectively are much higher than the indices for each end of the hierarchy in other cities. The corresponding figures were 30 and 35 for Chicago, 35 and 18 for Oxford, and 37 and 16 in the Outer Metropolitan Area of Kent. The intermediate classes in Edinburgh also exhibit a relatively high degree of residential segregation. Finally, the distribution of indices in Edinburgh is U-shaped rather than V-shaped as elsewhere, i.e. the three intermediate classes (3, 4 and 5) have very similar indices of segregation. This may reflect the greater proportion of the housing stock consisting of council houses in Edinburgh.

Further evidence of the high spatial segregation of social classes in

Edinburgh is given in fig. 9.1. [10] This map shows how the socio-economic class distribution, in particular the high-class share, varies among enumeration districts in Edinburgh. The method used is similar in principle, although different in detail, to one of the methods of measuring class differences between cities developed by Moser and Scott (1961, pp.33, 52–55). While Moser and Scott categorized towns according to the percentage in the top two social classes, defined by the census as professional and intermediate non-manual workers, fig. 9.1 is based upon the proportion of the population of an enumeration district in the top two socio-economic groups as defined in the sample census of 1966. This excludes intermediate non-manual workers. The class scale grades used in the map were determined heuristically. The five-point scale is sensitive enough to show the contrast in residential areas without attempting a spurious precision. But the choice of a different measure, or of other scale boundaries, or of a level of aggregation other than that of the enumeration district could alter the results. Nevertheless, Willmott and Young, in comparing their own social class map of London with those derived by different methodologies, were able to discern a common spatial class distribution (Willmott and Young, 1973, pp.197–8).

Figure 9.1 confirms the high degree of spatial class segregation shown in the indices of dissimilarity and segregation. The low-class areas, as suggested in chapter 2, are confined largely to the low ground of the river valley and the lacustrine flats in the west-southwest, to the sea-port of Leith, and to the area northeast and east of Holyrood Park. Hence, the most clear-cut feature of fig. 9.1 is the black low-class belt stretching from the southwest, through the Old Town, and mushrooming out to cover most of the eastern and northeastern sectors of the city. As explained earlier, low ground and water power fostered the development of railways and industrial areas, and the low residential amenity of adjacent land ensured that it would be used by the poor. Even after 1945, this pattern was reinforced by the development of the Sighthill industrial estate adjacent to the radial routes in the extreme west-southwest and by the nearby council estates on the relatively level land of Wester Hailes and Broomhouse. Large sites in the eastern sectors, close to industrial concentration in Leith and with a topography favouring low construction costs, were reserved by the corporation for cheap council housing, especially between the wars.

The higher class districts in fig. 9.1 are concentrated in areas of superior environmental amenity, particularly in the west-northwest. The postwar council estate at Clermiston is the only low-class concentration, and this was developed only after local political conflict. The amenity of Corstorphine Hill is an important element in the environmental attractiveness of this

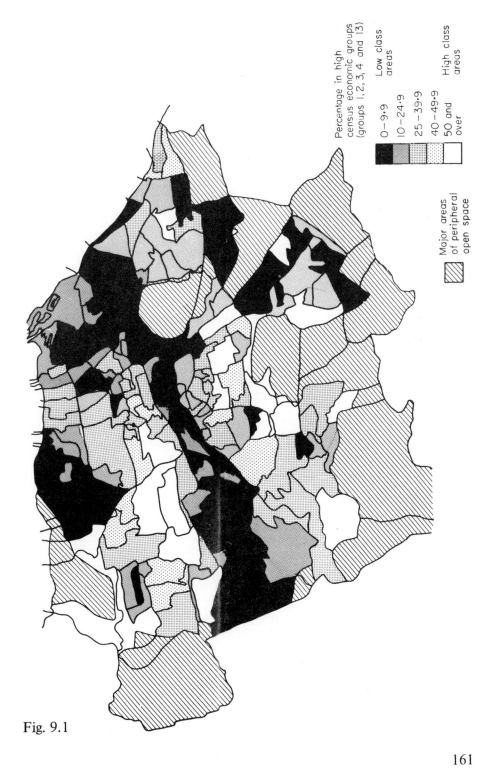

Percentage in high
census economic groups
(groups 1, 2, 3, 4 and 13)

Low class
areas

0 – 9·9
10 – 24·9
25 – 39·9
40 – 49·9
50 and
over

High class
areas

Major areas
of peripheral
open space

Fig. 9.1

161

sector, while Barnton and Cramond are far away from the noise and fumes of the industrial belt for those able to afford transportation to the amenities of the central city. Other high-class concentrations are to be found in the narrow belt surrounding Braid Hills in the south and at Colinton in the southwest, where the topography is also varied and attractive.

Willmott and Young (1973, p.211) suggested that the social class distribution map for London did not reflect the concentric zone scheme developed by Park and Burgess in Chicago. The same is true of Edinburgh.[11] The sectoral distribution pattern is much stronger than any zonal pattern. Also, many areas, which according to the concentric zone model should have declined in class as more affluent families took advantage of improved transport to move to larger sites on the periphery, have retained their high sectoral status. These include the older inner suburbs of Merchiston, Morningside and Grange in the south.[12] In spite of widespread subdivision of properties, the western side of the New Town too has remained, in comparison with central areas in other cities, relatively high in class ranking. Concentrations of low-class housing outside the main southwest/northeast belt have developed on both sides of the city in the form of the council estates at Pilton, Muirhouse and Silverknowes on the fairly level raised beaches of the northwest, and at Craigmillar, Ferniehill, Gilmerton and Liberton in the gently sloping southeastern sector. Figure 9.1 also shows some tendency for social class in modern Edinburgh to increase gradually with geographical distance from the city centre, and the lowest and highest class enumeration districts are generally bordered by districts of intermediate rank.[13]

The evidence suggests that the extreme spatial segregation of social classes in Edinburgh is closely related to the physical geography of the city. This has been crucial in determining the location of the city centre, industry and communication routes and these elements of the spatial structure have repelled wealthy households to more environmentally attractive residential areas. The concentric ring model assumes a feature-less plain, and this assumption is not consistent with the spectacular topography of Edinburgh. The local political structure, heavily influenced by the very high proportion of white-collar and professional employment, and the feuing system have ensured that the impact of geography on spatial social segregation has been mitigated very little.

The Sasines occupational data

Although the Register of Sasines information is very reliable since it is based on legal documents and is an invaluable source for longitudinal analysis of house prices and spatial structure, the occupational data obtained from the Register have certain weaknesses.

First, the responsibility of recording an individual's occupation rests with the solicitor representing one or other of the parties in the transaction. The description of the occupation is often too vague, with labels such as 'civil servant, 'engineer', 'manager' or 'accountant'. In addition, the lack of information on employed or self-employed status is a disadvantage. However, a detailed examination of the Register (covering 50,000 properties [14]) showed that many high status occupations were described with some precision. For example, 'chartered engineers' or 'chartered surveyors' appeared with sufficient frequency to suggest that plain 'engineers' and 'surveyors' could safely be assigned a lower occupational classification.

Second, it was necessary to devise an occupational classification scheme which balanced the need to generate meaningful research results with the quality of the available data. After unsuccessful attempts to draw up a highly disaggregated scheme, a much more modest tenfold division was adopted, on lines suggested by Hoinville and Jowell (1969), based upon aggregation of the Registrar General's (1966) seventeen socio-economic groups. The potentially serious problem remains that occupations change rank over time, due to mechanization, company mergers, changing social activities, etc. A classification to take historical changes into account was considered but eventually discarded on the ground that the marginal increase in accuracy was outweighed by the additional complexities. In view of these limitations, consistent coding was regarded as vital in order to ensure that comparison of different periods, even if not based on ideally classified data, would still be meaningful. [15]

Finally, a large proportion of occupations of both buyers and sellers of property had to be classified as 'not available'. This proportion has increased over time as fewer solicitors have troubled to record occupation. [16] It is important to know whether there is any bias in the 'not available' category. Ideally, they should be a random cross-section of the total population of buyers and sellers in each period. The degree of detail of the occupational information forwarded to the Sasines office is at the discretion of the individual solicitor. Although certain solicitors may represent clients of relatively high social class and may be more inclined to include occupational information, staff at the Sasines office state that there is no evidence that bias from this source is great or that it varies significantly over time. [17]

The dynamics of spatial segregation

The city as a whole

It is possible to measure changes in spatial relationships between social classes over time using the Duncans' index of dissimilarity. The initial focus is on differences in residential location between classes in the city as a whole. The first step is to choose an appropriate level of spatial aggregation.

Indices of residential differentiation vary according to the size of the units into which the city is divided. The smaller the unit the larger the indices, particularly if unit boundaries correspond to those of distinct housing areas. Theoretically, it is preferable to use homogeneous housing zones so that changes in their social class composition may be related to changes in the physical structure of the city. However, examination of the occupational data available for each of the sampling zones and experimental grouping of these zones showed that a relatively high level of aggregation was necessary. [18] The final choice was the zonal pattern derived from rings and sectors used in the house price analysis (see pp. 121–2). With eight sectors of equal base angle and five concentric rings, the inner four of which had a radious of one mile, this meant forty potential zones, reduced in practice to a maximum of thirty-four because of the sea to the north and east. Apart from its geometric simplicity, this scheme was theoretically sensible since concentric rings and sectors are the relevant urban spatial patterns associated with the contributions of the Chicago school and Homer Hoyt respectively. Each of the original sample zones was assigned to one of these thirty-four ring-sector segments, i.e. the one in which the larger part of their area fell.

Indices of dissimilarity were calculated for six sub-periods over the years 1905–71 based upon recorded buyers of property, and these are shown in table 9.3. Zones with less than thirty occupations in any period were omitted. This meant the exclusion of some peripheral suburbs in the early period, certain sparsely populated areas close to the city centre such as those around Holyrood Park and, in later years, depopulated central redevelopment areas. Even so, a minimum sample size of thirty, when divided between five social classes, leaves an average cell size of only six with a relatively high standard error. Nevertheless, most zones in most periods contained far more than thirty observations, [19] and in the calculation of indices of dissimilarity a proportionately higher weighting is given to those areas with large numbers of observations. Also, the professional and managerial classes and the semi-skilled and unskilled

Table 9.3

Edinburgh indices of dissimilarity, 1905–71, by zones

Social class		1	2	3	4	5
1	Professional and managerial					
2	Non-manual	23 22 25 19 24 28				
3	Self-employed	17 19, 23 24 22 32	16 18 19 15 19 20			
4	Skilled manual and foremen	28 34 32 38 41 42	30 29 25 29 28 27	20 19 22 21 24 30		
5	Semi- and unskilled manual	30 46 44 53 59 56	28 43 36 46 48 44	21 31 31 36 41 41	23 23 22 21 22 28	

Note: For each cell the figures are arranged as follows:

1905–19 (15)	1920–29 (21)	1930–39 (25)
1945–54 (28)	1955–64 (26)	1965–71 (26)

The figures in parentheses are the number of zones for which there were thirty or more observations for the corresponding period.

manual classes were combined to form single categories so as to reduce the standard error of cell values in small sample zones. [20] This collapsing of class categories is excusable because the theoretically interesting class divisions are preserved.

The lower right-hand figure in each cell of table 9.3 is the index of dissimilarity for the period 1965–71. These index numbers are much lower than those calculated from the 1966 census presented in table 9.1 There are several reasons for this discrepancy. First, the census data refer to the occupation of *residents* in a district whereas the Sasines refers to *owners*. By using the occupation of buyers rather than sellers in the analysis, the influence of landlords was reduced [21] so as to obtain an improved measure of changing *residential* differentiation. However, this 'filtering' technique is not completely successful, particularly in the earlier periods. Even in recent years the privately rented housing sector in Edinburgh has remained relatively large during a period of prolonged national decline in this tenure group. The ownership of property in lower class residential areas by high status landlords will reduce indices of dissimilarity calculated on the basis of the Sasines occupational data.

Second, the indices calculated from census data are based upon a much larger number of areas than the zones used in analyzing the Sasines data. To the extent that they are smaller and frequently delineated in terms of major roads, railways or other major physical barriers, enumeration districts correspond more clearly to distinct housing areas, and the measures of residential differentiation will be greater.

Third, the Sasines data exclude council housing. Although council housing in Scotland, even in Edinburgh, could not be described as 'one-class' housing, fig. 9.1 shows relatively low-class concentrations in areas of the city with predominantly council housing. These concentrations are obscured in the Register of Sasines data.

Finally, in table 9.3 a five-fold classification of occupations is adopted rather than the six classes of table 9.1. Also, a distinction is drawn between the self-employed (non-professional) class and the skilled manual employee and foremen class, though these groups are similar in terms of income and status. Both these factors tend to reduce the indices.

Despite the differences between the census statistics and the Sasines data in the late 1960s, the rank order of the indices is similar in both to that observed in other studies employing the same methodology. As shown in column 1, the greater the difference in social class the higher the index value. This provides further support for the validity of the data in spite of the large 'not available' category and for the belief that the decision to focus on buyers of property helps to eliminate the influence of ownership of rented properties.

The most interesting feature of table 9.3, however, is the evidence it gives on longitudinal changes in residential segregation. Column 1 shows that over the whole period the degree of residential spatial dissimilarity between the highest (professional and managerial) class and the rest increased considerably. There are at least three main reasons for this trend. First, the decline in the privately rented sector has made for a fall in the average status of *owners* (though there may have been an increase in the status of residents) in low quality housing areas. Second, the movement of higher class families out of central areas and the outward extension of the city has led to a decline in the social status of inner-city residential areas. Finally, associated with this decline in the residential class status of central Edinburgh has been the development of relatively homogeneous suburbs in which classes have become increasingly segregated.[22]

One exception to this general tendency for spatial dissimilarity to increase over time is the lower index recorded for the highest relative to the lowest class in 1965—71 than in 1955—64 (56 against 59). This reflects *inter alia* a return to the central city by some members of the professional and managerial classes [23] as traffic congestion has made the journey to work from the suburbs more irksome and as central redevelopment has led to the relocation of lower class families to more peripheral areas.

There is also a direct relationship between the increase in the degree of residential dissimilarity over the period as a whole between two classes and the distance between them in the class structure. The increase in dissimilarity between the professional and managerial class and the other classes is 5 in the case of non-manual workers, 15 for the self-employed, 14 for skilled manual workers and foremen, and 26 for semi- and unskilled manual workers. This is further evidence of the progressive consolidation during the twentieth century of relatively socially homogeneous suburban areas and for the hypothesis that spatial distance between social classes in an increasingly reliable indicator of the social distance between them. Had a lower level of zonal aggregation been possible, this tendency would have been even more pronounced.

As for the intermediate groups, there is a change in the degree of relative residential dissimilarity of the non-manual and the self-employed groups *vis-à-vis* the professional and managerial class. Prior to the Second World War, the index is lower for the self-employed, whereas since 1945 the non-manual index has been lower. Suburbanization is the main explanation of this change. Both the professional and managerial and the non-manual classes have suburbanized to a similar extent, but many of the self-employed have continued to live in or near the city centre for business reasons. Finally, residential dissimilarity between the skilled manual and foremen and the non-manual groups has declined slightly over time while it remained constant between the two manual categories until the most recent period when the index rose sharply. The probable reason is that the skilled manual workers have shared in decentralization trends, particularly in the late 1960s. However, the outward movement of low status manual workers to peripheral council estates is not reflected in the indices of table 9.3 which are based on residential property ownership.

Zonal class changes[24]

Tables 9.4 and 9.5 present evidence on the changing socio-economic class composition of the zones as revealed in the occupational data obtained from the Register of Sasines. In view of the emphasis in the urban house

167

price determinants literature on the influence of neighbourhood status on house prices and on changing social class composition as a major influence on the dynamics of residential area change, these data need to be analyzed in the context of the conclusions derived from study of the zonal prices. Table 9.4 shows the number of buyers in the professional and managerial groups as a percentage of total buyers for whom occupations were known. [25] These statistics are shown separately for short intervals of approximately one decade and for the period 1905—71 as a whole.

Interpretation of table 9.4 requires an answer to four separate but interrelated questions. What happens to zonal class changes over time? How does class composition vary between rings (concentric zones)? How does class composition vary from one sector to another? What degree of correspondence exists between zonal class and the prevailing house price levels in the zone? In fact, generalization on any of these questions is very difficult. There seems to be a consistent tendency for high-class zones to be located in the west and low-class zones in the east, and this is compatible with the findings on sector price variations. On the other hand, there are some notable exceptions to this generalization, such as the low and declining class composition of 2WSW and 3WSW and the high and rising status of 2SSE and 3SSE.

Within each period, although some of the lowest class zones are located in the inner ring (Ring 1), very high-class zones are also found in that ring, again in the west (1WSW, 1WNW and 1NNW). Low to intermediate class zones predominate in Rings 2 and 3, but again there are some high-class zones particularly in the WNW and SSE sectors. [26] Even in the outer rings, intermediate class zones tend to dominate, though the WNW peak sector exhibits high and generally rising class composition over time. The evidence, therefore, fails to confirm the hypothesis that suburban zones have a significantly higher socio-economic class composition than closer-in zones. The tendency in that direction is slight, if it exists at all, and there are several notable exceptions.

On the other hand, sector class differentials, particularly the contrast between the west and the east, are much more firmly established. Even here, however, there are exceptions — particularly the rising social class of the southeast quadrant in the second and third rings. Also, there are low-class zones in the west usually in areas affected by industrial development and/or by council housing estates: these include Granton (3NNW), Saughtonhall—Gorgie (2WSW and 3WSW) and, towards the end of the study period, Sighthill (5WSW). Considering the period 1905—71 as a whole does little to alter these conclusions. There are four peak class areas: the inner city to the west (1WSW, 1WNW and 1NNW); the WNW

168

Table 9.4

Percentage of high-class buyers, by zones 1905–71

	1905–19	1920–29	1930–39	1945–54	1955–64	1965–71	1905–71
1 NNE	28·6	13·2	7·5	21·9	19·3	12·5	17·2
1 ENE	–	44·4	–	17·4	21·9	25·9	27·1
1 ESE	–	–	–	–	–	–	–
1 SSE	24·4	17·3	20·4	19·3	–	–	20·4
1 SSW	38·1	32·7	13·5	17·0	26·0	46·7	29·0
1 WSW	–	78·8	62·5	72·9	79·3	–	71·4
1 WNW	–	71·2	63·2	51·0	45·6	50·0	56·2
1 NNW	41·2	39·0	53·7	51·1	54·7	72·1	52·0
2 NNE	48·4	33·1	20·6	20·1	14·2	22·7	26·5
2 ENE	13·8	20·8	8·8	13·4	10·3	12·3	13·4
2 ESE	–	–	–	–	–	–	–
2 SSE	31·5	45·9	34·2	49·0	47·3	59·9	45·0
2 SSW	30·0	28·3	24·3	31·1	28·5	35·8	29·7
2 WSW	37·3	38·9	41·6	21·8	23·7	30·1	33·4
2 WNW	–	–	19·7	45·5	49·4	53·3	42·0
2 NNW	38·2	42·0	40·6	49·5	50·0	51·4	46·0
3 NNE	–	–	–	–	–	–	–
3 ENE	29·4	–	15·2	27·7	18·7	24·4	21·4
3 ESE	15·2	24·6	24·2	24·8	34·2	36·0	28·1
3 SSE	48·9	49·1	44·5	54·5	59·9	59·3	51·5
3 SSW	62·7	63·1	32·5	55·9	45·5	68·8	54·8
3 WSW	–	32·1	–	27·9	18·7	17·3	25·9
3 WNW	–	31·3	31·3	45·5	56·6	46·0	42·1
3 NNW	–	–	–	–	6·6	7·5	7·1
4 NNE	–	–	–	–	–	–	–
4 ENE	–	–	–	–	–	–	–
4 ESE	41·2	41·4	17·5	26·3	30·3	25·7	30·8
4 SSE	–	–	41·0	41·5	29·1	30·0	35·3
4 SSW	–	–	34·8	47·2	50·9	62·3	46·0
4 WSW	36·5	32·3	33·6	31·8	22·7	33·5	32·2
4 WNW	–	–	–	44·9	55·2	73·8	58·0
4 NNW	–	–	–	–	–	–	–
5 NNE	–	–	–	–	–	–	–
5 ENE	–	–	–	–	–	–	–
5 ESE	–	–	20·0	34·7	–	–	27·4
5 SSE	–	–	–	–	–	–	–
5 SSW	–	–	–	–	–	59·4	59·4
5 WSW	–	–	24·1	33·3	33·6	29·8	30·2
5 WNW	–	–	56·3	50·0	52·6	70·0	56·7
5 NNW	–	–	–	–	–	–	–

sector as a whole, the SSW sector between Rings 3 and 5; and the southeastern secondary price peak area (2SSE and 3SSE). The trough class areas tend to be rather smaller: the inner ring in the east; the ENE sector; the 3NNW zone and the 3WSW zone. These data tend to confirm the view that proximity to industry tends to repel high-class residents. Also, class composition improves with clockwise movement from the ESE, at least up to the WSW sector where a temporary regression sets in.

The most important feature of these results is their striking consistency with the findings on zonal prices. The degree of correspondence at the zonal level between price and socio-economic class composition is very close. High class and high property prices are mutually reinforcing, not only because high-class households can afford to spend more on housing but because high-class neighbourhoods attract competition for available housing and this tends to push up the prevailing house price levels. However, the association between high prices and high class cannot be explained in terms of some simple spatial theory such as that which emphasises the role of middle-class mobility in suburbanization and in differential inner city – suburban property price behaviour. Both high and low price zones and high and low-class neighbourhoods may be located next to each other. Once again, this confirms the argument that the concepts of a 'neighbourhood' or a private housing sub-market refer to a smaller area than implied in the urban structure literature that stresses the mutual repulsion between high and low-class residential areas. Thus, proximity to industry and to council housing tends to affect property price levels or area socio-economic class composition only over relatively short distances.

Table 9.5 offers more precise indicators of changing social class composition at the zonal level. The statistic shown in table 9.5 is obtained in the following way. First, social class 2 (self-employed non-professional workers) was excluded from the analysis since builders fell into this category and accounted for a high proportion of sellers (of new houses). Second, the percentages of purchases and sales of residential property made by social classes 0 and 1 were calculated for each zone with more than ten observations for both buyers and sellers in each of the six sub-periods. [27] Third, the buyers percentage was expressed as a ratio of the sellers percentage. These ratios provided an index of rising or falling social class ranking in each zone at different periods, according to whether the ratio exceeded or was less than unity. However, as shown in table 9.6, the ratio of high-class buyers to high-class sellers fluctuated at a city-wide level during the course of the century. Accordingly, a fourth step was necessary to adjust the index of rise or fall in the social class rank of zones

170

Table 9.5

Zonal class changes, 1905—71

	1905—19	1920—29	1930—39	1945—54	1955—64	1965—71
1 NNE	0·06	−0·37	−0·34	−0·18	−0·28	−0·59
1 ENE	0·09	0·32	0·34	−0·21	−0·15	−0·31
1 ESE	–	–	–	−0·44	−0·13	–
1 SSE	−0·27	−0·26	0·02	−0·32	−0·29	0·70
1 SSW	0·06	−0·05	−0·22	−0·17	−0·18	−0·08
1 WSW	0·25	0·22	0·22	0·09	0·24	0·05
1 WNW	0·30	0·20	0·19	0·01	−0·03	−0·12
1 NNW	0·01	−0·02	0·37	0·15	0·06	0·17
2 NNE	0·32	0·10	0·03	−0·25	−0·28	−0·25
2 ENE	−0·21	−0·20	−0·28	−0·40	−0·45	−0·63
2 ESE	–	–	−0·05	–	0·09	–
2 SSE	−0·29	0·22	0·47	−0·03	−0·02	0·13
2 SSW	−0·09	−0·12	0·07	−0·07	−0·09	−0·03
2 WSW	0·32	−0·03	0·36	−0·13	−0·06	0·30
2 WNW	–	−0·38	−0·04	0·37	0·32	−0·14
2 NNW	0·31	0·06	0·13	0·17	0·03	−0·04
3 NNE	–	–	–	–	–	–
3 ENE	−0·21	−0·15	−0·40	0·24	−0·23	−0·32
3 ESE	−0·51	−0·18	−0·23	0·25	0·19	−0·06
3 SSE	−0·10	0·11	0·17	0·31	0·09	−0·10
3 SSW	0·14	0·07	−0·19	0·30	0·21	0·23
3 WSW	–	−0·12	0·15	0·00	0·11	−0·47
3 WNW	–	−0·37	−0·08	0·46	0·19	−0·23
3 NNW	–	–	–	−0·80	0·46	−0·56
4 NNE	–	–	–	–	–	–
4 ENE	–	–	–	–	–	–
4 ESE	0·27	0·26	0·18	−0·06	−0·17	−0·31
4 SSE	–	–	0·39	0·27	0·06	0·41
4 SSW	–	–	−0·11	0·11	0·13	0·13
4 WSW	−0·08	−0·07	0·02	−0·11	−0·25	0·03
4 WNW	–	–	–	0·16	0·35	0·12
4 NNW	–	–	–	–	–	–
5 NNE	–	–	–	–	–	–
5 ENE	–	–	–	–	–	–
5 ESE	–	–	3·12	0·45	−0·15	1·40
5 SSE	–	–	–	–	–	–
5 SSW	–	0·24	–	0·38	–	0·23
5 WSW	–	–	–	0·04	0·14	−0·35
5 WNW	–	–	0·80	0·07	0·13	0·23
5 NNW	–	–	–	–	–	–

Table 9.6

Fluctuations in the proportion of high class buyers and sellers*

	Buyers			Sellers			Buyers/ sellers
	total in classes 0,1,3,4,5 & 7	total in classes 0 & 1	percentage in classes 0 & 1	total in classes 0,1,3,4,5 & 7	total in classes 0 & 1	percentage in classes 0 & 1	ratio of percentage of buyers in classes 0 & 1 to percentage of sellers
1905–19	822	393	47·8	628	357	56·8	0·84
1920–29	1,555	701	45·1	1,467	874	59·6	0·76
1930–39	1,968	684	34·8	1,417	813	57·4	0·61
1945–54	2,713	1,080	39·8	2,111	1,054	49·9	0·80
1955–64	3,554	1,269	35·7	2,719	1,172	43·1	0·83
1965–71	1,934	885	45·8	2,085	949	45·5	1·01

*In calculating the statistics for this table, zones with less than ten occupations of sellers or buyers 'available' in the classes under analysis for a particular period were excluded.

relatively to changes in the social class composition of property owners over time in the city as a whole, particularly since these aggregate changes frequently reflected nationally determined factors such as the liberalization of building society lending terms and conditions or changes in household preferences in favour of owner-occupation. This fourth step took the form of subtracting from the zonal buyer/seller ratio the city-wide ratio shown in table 9.6 for the corresponding period. The data in table 9.5 may consequently be interpreted in the following way. Positive values indicate rising social class ranking, while negative values suggest falling class status *relative* to changes in social class composition among property owners in the city as a whole. Moreover, the larger the figure the greater is the change (whether positive or negative) in social class ranking.[28]

The adjustments to the statistic used in table 9.5 were necessary to ensure meaningful interpretation of the longitudinal evidence. Otherwise, the analysis would be distorted by the fact that the average class level of property buyers (and sellers) has tended to decline over time, mainly as a consequence of the spread of home ownership. However, table 9.6 shows that this decline has by no means been continuous. The buyers/sellers ratio has been below unity over most of the period because of the entry of middle and lower income groups into the private property market and because of the secular fall in the privately rented sector (the transfer from landlord to owner-occupier usually involves a fall in the class level of the owner). But there have been marked fluctuations in the ratio. The major change was the decline in the average class level in the inter-war period, especially in the 1930s. The main reasons were the construction of low-cost private housing for speculative sale and a commensurate fall in public sector housebuilding, the reduction in mortgage repayments associated with declining interest rates and more liberal building society lending conditions, and a significant shift in household preferences in favour of owner-occupation. All these factors led to a spread of home ownership down the social class scale. On the other hand, since 1945 this trend has been reversed, after the mid-1960s dramatically. The fluctuation has been almost entirely due to variations in the social class composition of buyers since the average class level of sellers has been more or less consistently downwards. The major factor in the reversal has been the increasing cost of home ownership, partly a function of rising house prices, especially in an expensive housing market such as Edinburgh, partly due to higher mortgage rates. A subsidiary factor may have been a return to the city of out-of-town middle-class households in response to increasing arterial road traffic congestion and other influences making suburban living less attractive. A consequence of these trends is that many of the potential lower class housebuyers have been shut out from entry into the owner-occupied sector.

As a result of adjustment to reflect city-wide fluctuations in the class composition of property owners, the statistics of table 9.5 frequently exhibit considerable unevenness, with some zones presenting a complex picture of positive and negative values of widely different magnitude. Despite the increased difficulties in the way of interpretation, these relativity adjustments are nevertheless justified.

(i) The northeastern and eastern sectors

In the northeastern and eastern sectors of the city (NNE, ENE and ESE, sectors which absorb most of Leith) there has been a general decline in the average social class level of virtually all the zones. This is particularly true of the inner rings in the periods after World War II when many landlords have been selling old property to tenants or prospective owner-occupiers from lower social classes or seeing their properties coming under corporation demolition schemes. Ring 3 of these eastern sectors exhibits a continued decline in social class in the earlier periods, a rise in class rating after 1945 but a tendency to renewed decline in the most recent of the sub-periods. The policy of Edinburgh Corporation to use land in these sectors for low-cost council housing for families in need of rehousing from inner-city slums was described above (see p. 27). This policy stemmed from the facts that this land is adjacent to industrial workplaces at Leith and is level (apart from Holyrood Park). The level sites which encouraged the council to use the land for cheap public housing also attracted private speculators who built large areas of relatively low priced private housing in the inter-war period. Consequently, table 9.5 shows many negative statistics for these areas during this period as many lower middle-class families found housing in these zones. High-class families, on the other hand, looked for accommodation on higher, environmentally more attractive areas of the city. After 1945, however, the general housing shortage made for a temporary revival in social class composition of eastern sectors in the third ring.

(ii) The inner city

Examination of the eight zones in the inner ring reveals some variation in trends. Some zones correspond to *a priori* expectations of inner-city decline in social class. Progressive decline has occurred in 1NNE, 1ENE, 1ESE, 1SSW and 1WNW. On the other hand, 1WSW and 1NNW have

174

preserved their social class rating very well. This is due to the distinctive nature of Edinburgh's inner city with its unusual number of fine residences built during the Georgian period for the higher classes and the fact that in these sectors invasion by non-residential land use has not been so marked as in some of the other inner-city zones. Also, these two zones have gained disproportionately from gentrification. The zone 1SSE showed a general decline in social class until very recently. The reversal in its experience is due partly to gentrification, partly to the demolition of very cheap tenement flats in St. Leonard's.

(iii) Ring 2 (zones of transition?)

The fluctuations in the social class composition of zones in ring 2 are particularly interesting. Although the zones have geometrically regular boundaries they may still be treated as potential 'zones in transition' as described in urban sociological analyses,[29] since they cover the area of Edinburgh between one and two miles of Princes Street, immediately adjacent to the central business district and much of it still used for residential purposes.

The accepted hypothesis is that these relatively central residential areas will decline in social class rating with the outward expansion of cities during the twentieth century. Analysis of table 9.5 suggests that this general trend has not been followed in Edinburgh. As noted above there has been a decline in social class in the northeastern second ring, but this was primarily due to higher class people selling off cheap tenement flats which they had previously rented to the working class population of Leith. The 2SSE and 2SSW zones comprise the Victorian and Edwardian upper and middle-class areas of Merchiston, Morningside, Grange and Newington.[30] Although there has been some decline in social class in these zones since 1945,[31] this decline has not been of the magnitude or increasing momentum to justify the label of 'zones of transition'. Table 9.5 confirms the evidence of the social class map of Edinburgh (see fig. 9.1, p.161) that these areas have retained to a remarkable degree their early high social class composition.

There are several reasons for this. An economic factor has been the scarcity of alternative private building sites within the city boundary. Also, although it has declined, the privately rented sector has remained relatively large in Edinburgh. Many rented properties in the hands of high-class owners are located in the inner suburbs. In terms of fabric, the houses in these areas are different from those in many other cities. The main material used is stone, more elegant and durable than the brick used in cities such as Birmingham. Environmentally, Edinburgh is much more varied than cities on more level sites, and the open prospect of some of these inner suburbs is more attractive than many of the building sites in the outer suburbs.

In addition, several socio-economic and more purely social factors are important. Edinburgh has not experienced a large influx of Commonwealth or Irish immigrants to produce the pressure on the private housing sector which has occurred in many British industrial cities. Second, because of its function as a centre for education, the legal profession and the arts, Edinburgh has within the two highest social classes a larger proportion in the 'liberal professions' or in professions that are dependent upon the contacts which accrue from central living. To such people, living in more central suburbs in houses or flats of character may be preferable to living in newer properties in the outer suburbs. During the postwar period the growth of both Edinburgh and Heriot-Watt Universities, both very accessible from these districts, has probably helped to preserve their relatively high social class rating. Finally, areas such as Morningside have been the homes of many famous Scotsmen of the past, and this has given these districts a symbolic prestige of the kind attached to Beacon Hill in Boston (Firey, 1947). The residents of such districts may be expected to be sufficiently politically informed and articulate to defend their neighbourhood against unwelcome encroachment. The same argument may be applied to 2NNW which contains the similar district of Inverleith, and also shows little social class decline. This analysis does not apply to the 2WSW zone, where industrial development and tenement property has meant that this district has never held a high social class rating.

(iv) The outer suburbs

The tendency for a decline in social class rating of the suburbs in the northeastern and eastern sectors was noted above. The outer suburbs in the remaining sectors show considerable variation. The main factors explaining this variation are highly interrelated. Sectors in which there has been extensive council housebuilding are also areas of uninteresting topography, which have also attracted industry. In these sectors there is a tendency for the social class of private housing to decline. Thus, in the WSW and NNW sectors, where there has been most council housing activity and old privately rented housing is common, social class composition shows signs of decline in virtually every zone, certainly by the end of the study period. Conversely, in the environmentally more attractive areas of the SSW and WNW sectors where there has been less public housing development there has been in most zones substantial relative improvement in social class mix. Despite these inter-zonal differences, the general tendency in the outer suburbs is for the class composition of property owners to move in favour of the higher social classes.

(v) Summary

Even in the inner ring there was a variety of experience in zonal class composition changes. As expected, most of the zones experienced declines in class level over most of the period. However, there were notable exceptions, particularly in the west. For instance, the class composition of 1WNW changed favourably relative to the city as a whole in each period, and this was also true in 1NNW apart from in the 1920s. Looking at the inner ring as a whole, there were shifts in its class mix over time. Before 1920 all the zones except for 1SSE experienced rises in socio-economic mix; after World War II, on the other hand, most of the zones were declining in their class composition.

The variety in zonal performance carries over into the second ring. The most striking feature was the continuously deteriorating class composition of the 2ENE zone, and there was also a serious decline in the social class mix of the adjacent 2NNE zone. Very few zones consistently displayed improvement. The 2NNW zone came closest to an upward class change. In Ring 3, upward movements in class composition predominate, though again there are exceptions in the eastern sectors of the city (3ENE and 3ESE). The other striking feature is the variation within this ring over time. Before 1920, for instance, most zones in this ring were experiencing a deteriorating class mix. After 1945, on the other hand, there were drastic improvements in the socio-economic composition in almost all zones, but this has been completely reversed since 1965.

Interpretation of experience in the outer rings is handicapped, particularly in Ring 5, by the lack of observations. However, within the limitations of the data, the general picture is one of improving class composition. The exceptions are 4ESE since 1945 and, intermittently, 4WSW.

Conclusions

The general implications of table 9.5 are clear. Although experience varied widely over time, between zones within a particular ring and even within the generally low-class east and the high-class west, the most striking feature is the contrast between the three inner rings and the outer two. Suburbanization appears to be closely associated with rising class composition as reflected in property ownership changes. On the other hand, the improvement in some inner-city zones (1SSE and 2SSE, 1NNW, 1WSW and 2WSW) particularly in recent years is evidence of the heterogeneity of tastes among the wealthy and high-class occupational groups. Income enables households to exercise greater freedom of choice in residential site selection, and even if the suburban villa was the most typical choice there are many, probably an increasing number of, households which prefer a period house or a flat closer to the city centre. Second, referring back to the analysis of chapter 7 shows that there is a remarkably close correspondence between changes in zonal class composition and the relative rate of change in zonal house prices. This suggests that the social class composition of residential neighbourhoods has a marked impact upon house prices.

Third, the evidence in table 9.5 illustrates very strongly that the pace of zonal class changes may vary markedly over time, and that there are several clear-cut examples of a change in the direction of social class composition at the zonal level. These shifts reflect forces usually specific to the individual zone. For instance, in some cases the corporation's housing policy had a marked impact by reducing the attractiveness of a zone to middle-class residents by building large council housing estates; in other cases, e.g. the southwest, the development of industrial sites had a similar effect.

It is not inappropriate to stress once again the variety of experience even between adjacent zones or in the same zone over a long period of time. The interaction of general social trends (e.g. middle-class suburbanization, filtering down of home ownership) and purely local influences (industrial growth, the development of council housing, conversions to non-residential use, inner-city redevelopment, etc.) may work itself out in very complex ways. The greater the degree of spatial disaggregation, the more obvious it becomes that it is dangerous to make glib generalizations about changes in the social class composition of residential neighbourhoods.

This analysis suggests that understanding the dynamics of the social class composition of urban sub-areas requires considerable emphasis upon the role of *local factors*. In the case of Edinburgh these factors include:

(a)   strong links between public housing policy and social class movements in the private housing market;
(b)   the role of local topography and environmental amenity in influencing how the higher social classes exert their ability to select residential sites;

178

(c)   the importance of the local socio-economic employment structure in determining the spatial distribution of social classes. This is reflected particularly in the continuing high social class of some of Edinburgh's inner suburbs;

(d)   the local availability of private building land.

General models of urban spatial structure may be re-examined in the light of table 9.5. Superficially, Hoyt's sectoral model appears more applicable than Burgess's concentric ring model. However, the sectoral model is assisted by the topography of Edinburgh. The concentric model would be more applicable in a more 'featureless' city. It might have been more justifiably applied to Edinburgh if the area surrounding the city had been included. The shortage of building land in the city has pushed Burgess's commuter zone with its high-class residents out beyond the city boundary. Nevertheless, a firmer conclusion is that these very general aggregate models run into considerable difficulty when tested against more spatially disaggregated data.

Notes

[1]   For example, see Duncan and Duncan (1955a).

[2]   See the discussion by Timms (1971), pp. 86–91.

[3]   The similarity between the ideas of the Chicago school and functionalist theory is discussed in Pahl (1972). A classical exposition of functionalist theory is contained in Davis and Moore (1945).

[4]   For Weber, class was defined in terms of people sharing a similar position in relation to commodity and labour markets in which they might use their power to supply goods or skills in return for income. Status was treated as analytically, and to a significant degree empirically, distinct from class. Status groups are based upon the differential honour which men assign to various groups in society, are more self-conscious of their existence as a group or 'community', and share distinct life styles (Gerth and Mills, 1948, 180–95). Weber suggested that class and status may be more or less incongruent at different points in history but Parkin (1971, p.39) argues that the two dimensions coalesce in the occupational order of modern industrial societies.

[5]   See for example Beshers (1962), ch.5.

[6]   One of the authors (Furbey) is engaged in collecting additional information concerning social class relations and political processes in twentieth-century Edinburgh to develop further the interpretation of the statistics presented in this chapter.

[7] The records in the Register of Sasines for 1971 were incomplete at the time of sampling.

[8] The 1966 census enumeration districts were based upon a 10 per cent sample.

[9] We are most grateful to Mr. P.S. Taylor of the University of Kent at Canterbury for making available his collation of the results of these studies for this chapter.

[10] The reader may find it useful here to refer back to the descriptive analysis of pp.21–31.

[11] The concentric zone model bears up rather better in terms of house price behaviour. See pp.122–5.

[12] However, their class mix, is more accurately described as intermediate rather than very high. See tables 9.4 and 9.5, pp.169 and 171.

[13] For a more precise spatial analysis see pp.167–77.

[14] This examination included occupational data checks on a companion research project for the whole of Scotland.

[15] The quality of the Sasines occupational data was examined earlier in a comparative context via a study of social class and property ownership in Glasgow, Aberdeen and Dundee. See Furbey (1974). This analysis explored the relationship between social class and property ownership in relation to both national and local trends, and suggested that the Sasines data and the tenfold classificatory scheme adopted were adequate for spatial class distribution analysis.

[16] Among buyers the 'not available' share rose from 45 per cent in 1905–19 to almost 72 per cent in 1965–71; among sellers the proportions were 41 and 65 per cent respectively.

[17] The analysis of social class and property ownership in Glasgow, Aberdeen and Dundee referred to above also provided evidence that the 'not available' share was unbiased.

[18] See p.57. The relatively high proportion of occupations 'not available' was a major factor demanding a higher level of aggregation.

[19] The average number of buyers to whom occupations could be assigned in areas with more than thirty observations for all periods was calculated as ninety-nine.

[20] In the case of the unskilled manual group in particular, the largest number of recorded buyers in any period for the whole city was forty-nine (1955–64).

[21] Because of the progressive decline in the privately rented sector buyers are more likely to be owner-occupiers than sellers.

[22] This is supported by the earlier descriptive analysis of Edinburgh's growth. See pp.23–31.

[23] This is the phenomenon known as 'gentrification'.

[24] In this analysis we prefer the use of the term 'class' to 'status' in the measurement of changes in the socio-economic position of households. There are several reasons justifying this preference. Status is the more common term in the American literature, but American society is divided up into a much more numerous set of categories according to criteria other than the work situation (e.g. incomes, job conditions). In Britain the stratification system is not so cross-cut by racial, religious and cultural differences which result in different life styles and prestige (i.e. status). Instead, according to the findings of Parkin (1971) and Goldthorpe and Lockwood (1969), the economic and status dimensions of stratification tend to fuse together much more closely in the occupational structure. Class is usually regarded as being determined by what a person has to sell in the market (e.g. skills), and hence it appears to embrace the idea of stratification arising from the occupational structure much better than status which refers more specifically to prestige and life-style. Also, the meaning of class incorporates economic as well as social elements, and given the direct relationship between house price levels and the occupation of buyers this economic dimension to class makes it the more appropriate concept to use here.

[25] For a description of the occupational groups see pp.162—3.

[26] The SSE sector is rather different from the other eastern sectors. It does not border on the sea, and the land in the area is more undulating, and hence more environmentally attractive, than the 'raised beaches' of the coastal sectors.

[27] Thus, the percentage is number of buyers (sellers) in classes 0 and 1 divided by number of buyers (sellers) in classes 0, 1, 3, 4, 5 and 7.

[28] The figures for the 5ESE zone in 1930—39 and 1965—71 are unrealisitically high, and are probably to some degree freak results due to the small number of observations.

[29] See Burgess's diagram in Park et al. (1925). The term 'zone in transition' is also used by Rex and Moore (1967), pp. 272—85.

[30] The development and character of these districts was described on p.25.

[31] In 2SSE there was, in fact, an improvement in its social class rating in 1965—71.

10   Conclusions

The availability of a vast amount of data, especially on prices, in the Register of Sasines relating to both land and properties and stretching back over a long period of time permits the analysis of the dynamics of urban spatial structure on a scale hitherto impossible. However, this analysis refers to a case study of one city. Although the data permit tests to be made of classical models of urban spatial structure and shed some light on the validity of alternative theories of residential location, the case study characteristics of the research should not be forgotten. It would be dangerous to generalize these results to apply to other cities, particularly to American cities which have been the laboratory for a high proportion of urban spatial structure research. The age of the city, its ethnic, social and institutional structure, its predominant transportation technologies, its economic characteristics, the life-style of its citizens, the form of its political control, these and many other features are vastly different. Even within the context of the United Kingdom, Edinburgh is by no means typical of other large cities.[1] Its location in Scotland, with its singular land tenure system, its tradition of tenement buildings and its more recent tradition of a large council housing sector, sets it apart from other *large* British cities with the exception of Glasgow. The latter feature has, of course, major impacts on residential and social spatial structures. Its location on the coast with absolute physical constraints to spatial expansion implies a structure rather different from that of inland cities, with distortions and irregularities not only in the directly affected northern and eastern sectors but rippling out over the rest of the city. As suggested at the beginning of the book, the historical development of the city has had lasting effects on its modern spatial structure. Its topography is unusual, particularly in the centre and the southeast. Its functions as a capital city have had important repercussions on the city's employment structure and hence on its social structure.

In spite of these qualifications, the value of this research is not solely based upon the case study approach. While it is true that a complex intermesh of historical, physical, economic and social factors mould the individual character and superficial structure of a city, a more universal set of influences and forces is at work underneath. These influences tend to operate everywhere in cities in developed countries, though in a differential manner. They include *inter alia:* a desire by households and firms to be accessible to the services they require; locational interaction between different kinds of locators (households, manufacturing plants, offices, shops, public buildings, etc.); certain efficiency characteristics of the urban transportation network, such as its radial structure; determinants of the spatial relations between social classes in residential neighbourhoods; the existence of an urban land value gradient; and the influence of time on urban spatial structure.

From the point of view of urban theory, the most interesting results of this study are those that shed light on the validity of alternative residential location models. In particular, the classical accessibility and 'trade-off' theories were shown to be incomplete. Accessibility to environmental amenities, e.g. pleasant residential neighbourhoods, was found to be as important as accessibility to the CBD. Area preference variables such as the absence of industry were important influences on house price. The 'best fit' house price determinant model, in fact, included a mix of accessibility variables, environmental considerations, neighbourhood characteristics and dwelling attributes. On the other hand, all the tests undertaken in this study were of an indirect nature, i.e. attempting to explain the overall spatial pattern of urban house prices, and would need support from micro-behavioural analysis focusing on the individual residential locator, i.e. the household, before we could be sure about the need for a drastic revision in residential location theory. Nevertheless, this study suggests that the residential site choice and the determinants of spatial house prices are much more complicated phenomena than the conventional 'trade-off' theories suggest.

Some of the other results of the study reinforce rather than contradict currently accepted theory. For instance, Hoyt's radial sector model, both in its static and dynamic versions, stood up to empirical testing very well, especially once Edinburgh's topography and its large council housing stock are taken into account. The high price sector (WNW) retained its status over long periods of time; intermediate price sectors were found both next to the high price sector (i.e. NNW) or in other parts of the city (SSE); exogenous forces can alter the status of sectors quite dramatically (e.g. in the WSW); and the low price sectors tend to be located at the opposite end of the city to the high price sector (in the east rather in the west). On the other hand, stability in sector ranks was not associated with stability in either absolute or relative price variations between sectors. Comparing the post-World War II period with before 1939, sector price differentials have narrowed, and this sector price convergence has manifested itself primarily as a relative loss in status for the high price

184

sector rather than an upward change in status for the low price sector. However, this is also consistent with Hoyt since he argued that neighbourhood status tends to decline over time.

However, it may be argued that the radial sector approach is too aggregative, and Hoyt himself noted a tendency for much greater residential differentiation at the small area level, with the highest class residential areas becoming much smaller spatial clusters, more homogeneous internally in dwelling quality and clearly separated from the lower (though still high) class neighbourhoods around them. Focusing on smaller neighbourhoods requires a much greater level of spatial disaggregation, and this explains why this study includes zonal analysis. The size of the zones reflected a compromise between the need for finer spatial detail and representativeness of the sample considerations, especially for the sparser social class data. This zonal analysis could be regarded as an extension of Hoyt's work, and as an exploration beyond the spatial price variations to the social class differences that − in Hoyt's model − underpin them. Moreover, the data available permitted a dynamic analysis over a sixty-year period.

Although property prices tended to be higher with outward movement from the CBD as revealed by ring analysis, there was no marked trend for the rate of change in house prices to be positively associated with distance. The more disaggregated zonal analysis reveals increasing residential segregation with, for example, the polarization of inner-city housing into a cluster of low price zones. On the other hand, although suburban neighbourhoods tended to contain higher-price properties there were notable exceptions with trough suburban zones in areas of industrial development or extensive council housing. Moreover, rather surprisingly, peak and trough zones were frequently located adjacent to each other. This finding suggests that residential neighbourhoods are smaller in area than implied in Hoyt's hypothesis of mutual repulsion between high and low-class radial sectors. As for the dynamics of zonal price changes, there is no clear relationship between price behaviour and the location of a zone in space. Overall housing conditions and the specific characteristic of each zone are also important. Thus, the dynamics of intra-urban house prices reflect more complex phenomena than the standard hypotheses, based on static studies, imply.

The hypothesis of a high degree of residential segregation in Edinburgh supported by the zonal house price data is further reinforced by indices of residential segregation derived from both census and Sasines occupational data and by social class maps. The sectoral pattern is much stronger than the concentric zone pattern. One reason is that the concentric ring model assumes a featureless plain, whereas the spatial segregation of social classes in Edinburgh has been influenced heavily by its physical geography, the corporation's housing policies and the feuing system. The Sasines data also show increasing residential segregation over time. The main reasons have been: the decline in the privately rented sector in low quality housing areas has been associated with a fall in the average class of *owners;* suburbanization has led to a decline in the social status of inner-city residential neighbourhoods; and suburbs have become more homogeneous internally. The evidence also suggests that the spatial distance between social classes is an increasingly reliable indicator of the social distance between them.

The social class zonal data point to the following conclusions: the location of high-class zones in the west and low-class zones in the east; the presence of high-class zones even in the inner ring and the failure of suburban zones to exhibit significantly higher socio-economic class composition; a striking consistency between price level and social class at the zonal level; the declining status of inner-city areas has been much more modest in recent years than earlier in the century; and, not only can the pace of change in status vary over time, there may be shifts in direction. Such shifts may be due to local conditions such as the development of industry or council housing or, more probably, to aggregate housing conditions such as the connection between low cost private housebuilding in the 1930s and the emergence of low-class owner-occupiers or the influence of rapid house price inflation in the 1960s on barriers to entry of low income groups into the private housing market. However, the most general and most important implication from analysis of the zonal data is that further disaggregation and the injection of a truly dynamic aspect distort the simplistic hypotheses associated with Hoyt and others. Understanding the determinants of residential spatial structure in a modern city requires a combination of deductive analysis based on urban spatial theory *and* inductive generalizations derived from the specific characteristics of the city in question.

The analysis of the determinants of land values in this study generated results more consistent with standard theory. It pointed to the importance of the degree of urbanization and increased competition in the urban land market (both reflected in the time variable), of distance and other locational characteristics, and of the nature of the urban land market itself – particularly the expertise and behaviour of the different actors, including Edinburgh City Corporation, engaged in this market. Although the same key forces, time and distance, were operative in both the public and private land market, their relative importance was not the same.

Distance is less important for private housing because the journey to work constraint is not as restrictive as with working-class housing. Time was more dominant in the private land market because this market was more competitive especially since most private land purchases have been made more recently than the corporation's purchases in a period when land shortages have been more acute. Moreover, the evidence for other variables (plot size, direction and seller type) all point to a very imperfect substitutability between land for public and for private housing. For instance, small plots are more useful for the private sector, environmental quality and neighbourhood amenities put a premium on certain sites in the private land market, and non-economic factors were much more likely to influence the prices paid when the city corporation rather than a private builder was the purchaser.

Note

[1] Indeed, finding a typical city might be difficult since British cities and towns are so varied in both structural form and visual appearance.

Bibliography

Abercrombie P. and Plumstead D., *A Civic Survey and Plan for Edinburgh*, Oliver and Boyd, 1949.

Adams T., 'Town planning and housing' supplement to *Architectural Review*, May 1910, pp. 311–16.

Alonso W., *Location and Land Use*, Harvard UP, 1964.

Anderson R.J., Jr. and Crocker T.D., 'Air pollution and residential property values' *Urban Studies*, no. 8, 1971, pp. 171–80.

Apps P., 'An approach to modelling residential demand', mimeo, 1971.

Ball M.J., 'Recent empirical work on the determinants of relative house prices' *Urban Studies*, no. 10, 1973, pp. 213–33.

Beckmann M.J., 'On the distribution of urban rent and residential density' *Journal of Economic Theory*, no. 1, 1969, pp. 60–7.

Beshers J.M., *Urban Social Structure*, Free Press, 1962.

Blumenfeld H., 'The tidal wave of metropolitan expansion' *Journal of American Institute of Planners*, no. 20, 1954, pp. 3–14.

Briggs A., *Victorian Cities*, Penguin Books, 1968.

Brigham E.F., 'The determinants of residential land values' *Land Economics*, no. 41, 1965, pp. 325–34.

Burgess E.W., 'The growth of the city' in Park R.E., Burgess E.W. and McKenzie R.D., *The City*, Chicago UP, 1925, pp. 47–62.

Collison P. and Mogey J., 'Residence and social class in Oxford' *American Journal of Sociology*, no. 64, 1959, pp. 599–605.

Committee on the Registration of Title to Land in Scotland, Report of the, 1963, Cmnd. 2032.

Company of Merchants of the City of Edinburgh, *The Development of Edinburgh: Report of a Special Committee of the Company*, 1919.

Cramond R.D., *Housing Policy in Scotland, 1919–64: A Study in State Assistance*, University of Glasgow Social and Economic Studies: Research Paper No. 1, Oliver and Boyd, 1965.

Cubbin J.S., 'A hedonic approach to some aspects of the Coventry housing market', Warwick Economic Research Papers 14, 1970.

Davies J.G. and Taylor J., 'Race, community and no conflict' *New Society*, vol. 16, no. 406, 1970, pp. 67–9.

Davis K. and Moore W.E., 'Some principles of stratification' *American Sociological Review*, no. 10, 1945, pp. 242–9.

189

Devletoglou N.E., *Consumer Behaviour: An Experiment in Analytical Economics,* Harper and Row, 1971.

Duncan O.D. and Duncan B., 'A methodological analysis of segregation indices' *American Sociological Review,* no. 20, 1955a, pp. 210–17.

Duncan O.D. and Duncan B., 'Residential distribution and occupational stratification' *American Journal of Sociology,* no. 60, 1955b, pp. 493–503.

Edinburgh District Trades and Labour Council, *Report by the Executive Committee on the Condition of Housing in Edinburgh,* 1921.

Edinburgh Public Libraries, *Edinburgh Tramways (with Connections in Leith),* 1906.

Ellis R.H., 'Modelling of household location' *Highway Research Record,* no. 207, 1967, pp. 42–51.

Evans A.W., *The Economics of Residential Location,* Macmillan, 1974.

Firey W., *Land Use in Central Boston,* Harvard UP, 1947.

Fisher W.D., 'Econometric estimation with spatial dependence' *Regional and Urban Economics,* no. 1, 1971, pp. 19–40.

Foster J., 'Nineteenth century towns: a class dimension' in Dyos H.J. (ed.), *The Study of Urban History,* Edward Arnold, 1968, pp. 281–299.

Frieden B.J., 'Locational preferences in the urban housing market' *Journal of American Institute of Planners,* no. 27, 1951.

Furbey Robert, 'National and local in social class relations: some evidence from three Scottish cities' *Social and Economic Administration,* vol. 8, no. 3, 1974, pp. 192–219.

Gerth H.H. and Mills C.W. (eds), *From Max Weber: Essays in Sociology,* Routledge and Kegan Paul, 1948.

Gilbert W.M. (ed.), *Edinburgh in the Nineteenth Century,* J. and R. Allan, 1901.

Goldthorpe J.H., Lockwood D., et al. *The Affluent Worker,* Cambridge UP, 1969.

Goodwin E., Macdonald C. and Seale S., 'Land prices in Scotland: a study of building land purchases, 1959–72', Scottish Development Department, CPRU Paper No. 9, 1974.

Gordon G., 'The evolution of status areas in Edinburgh' in Institute of British Geographers, study group in urban geography, *The Social Structure of Cities,* IBG, Liverpool, 1966, pp. 27–37.

Gordon G., 'Status areas in Edinburgh', Ph.D. dissertation, University of Edinburgh, 1971.

Haddon R.F., 'A minority in a welfare state society: the location of West Indians in the London housing market' *New Atlantis,* no. 2, 1970, pp. 80–133.

190

Haig R.M., 'Toward an understanding of the metropolis' *Quarterly Journal of Economics,* no. 40, 1926, pp. 179–208.

Harvey D., *Social Justice in the City,* Edward Arnold, 1973.

Hoinville G. and Jowell R., *Classification Manual for Household Interview Surveys in Great Britain,* Social and Community Planning Research, 1969.

Hoyt H., *Structure and Growth of Residential Neighbourhoods in American Cities,* Federal Housing Administration, Washington 1939.

Hunter D.L.G., *Edinburgh's Transport,* Advertiser Press, Huddersfield 1964.

Ingram G.K., Kain J.F., Ginn J.R. et al., *The Detroit Prototype of the NBER Urban Simulation Model,* NBER, 1972.

Johnston R.J., *Urban Residential Patterns,* Bell, 1971.

Kain J.F., 'The journey to work as a determinant of residential location' *Papers and Proceedings, Regional Science Association,* no. 9, 1962, pp. 137–60.

Kain J.F. and Quigley J.M., 'Evaluating the quality of the residential environment' *Environment and Planning,* no. 2, 1970a, pp. 23–32.

Kain J.F. and Quigley J.M., 'Measuring the value of housing quality' *Journal of the American Statistical Association,* no. 65, 1970b, pp. 532–48.

Keir D. (ed.), *The City of Edinburgh,* vol. 15, *Third Statistical Account of Scotland,* Collins, 1966.

Lane R., 'Some findings on residential location, house prices and accessibility', mimeo, 1970.

Laumann E.O., *Prestige and Association in an Urban Community,* Bobbs-Merrill, 1966.

Lösch A., *The Economics of Location,* Yale UP, 1954.

Lowry I.S., *A Model of Metropolis,* RAND Corporation, 1964.

McCrone D. and Elliot B., 'Analysis of landlords and their holdings in the City of Edinburgh, 1971–2', mimeo, 1973.

Macrae E.J., 'Historical review' in Abercrombie and Plumstead, op. cit., 1949, pp. 5–16.

Massell B.F. and Stewart J.M., 'The determinants of residential property values', Program in Urban Studies DP6, Institute for Public Policy Analysis, Stanford 1971.

Mills E.S., 'The value of land' in Perloff H.S. (ed.), *The Quality of the Urban Environment,* Johns Hopkins Press, 1969, pp. 231–53.

Milnes N., *A Study of Industrial Edinburgh and the Surrounding Area, 1923–34,* P. S. King and Son, 1936.

Mohr E.A., 'Constructive mileage' *Traffic Quarterly,* July 1964.

Moser C.A. and Scott W., *British Towns: A Statistical Study of Their*

Economic and Social Differences, Oliver and Boyd, 1961.

Muth R.F., *Cities and Housing,* Chicago UP, 1969.

Nourse H.O., 'The effect of air pollution on house values' *Land Economics,* no. 43, 1967, pp. 181–9.

Pahl R.E., 'Urban processes and social structure', mimeo, 1972.

Park R.E., 'The urban community as a spatial pattern and a moral order' in Burgess E.W. (ed.), *The Urban Community,* Chicago UP, 1926, pp. 3–20.

Parkin F., *Class Inequality and Political Order,* MacGibbon and Kee, 1971.

Plowman D.E.G., Minchinton W.E. and Stacey M., 'Local social status in England and Wales' *Sociological Review,* no. 10, 1962, pp. 161–202.

Ramsøy N.R., 'Assortive mating and the structure of cities' *American Sociological Review,* no. 31, 1966, pp. 773–86.

Registrar General of Scotland, *Census of Scotland,* HMSO, 1901, 1911, 1921, 1931, 1951, 1961, 1966, and 1971.

Rex J. and Moore R., *Race, Community and Conflict: A Study of Sparkbrook,* Institute of Race Relations, Oxford UP, 1967.

Richardson H.W., *Urban Economics,* Penguin Books, 1971.

Richardson H.W., 'A comment on some uses of mathematical models in urban economics' *Urban Studies,* no. 10, 1973, pp. 259–66.

Richardson R., 'The physiography of Edinburgh' *Scottish Geographical Magazine,* no. 18, 1902, pp. 337–57.

Ridker R. and Henning J., 'The determinants of residential property values with special reference to air pollution' *Review of Economics and Statistics,* no. 50, 1968, pp. 246–57.

Rodwin L., *Housing and Economic Progress: A Study of the Housing Experiences of Boston's Middle-Income Families,* Harvard UP and the Technology Press, 1961.

Russell J., *The Story of Leith,* Nelson, 1922.

Saul S.B., 'House building in England, 1890–1914' *Economic History Review,* 2nd series, no. 15, 1962, pp. 119–37.

Schnore L.F., *The Urban Scene,* Free Press, 1965.

Scottish Home and Health Department, *Land Tenure Reform in Scotland,* HMSO, 1972.

Senior M.L. and Wilson A.G., 'Disaggregated residential location models: some tests and further theoretical developments', Department of Geography, University of Leeds, WP22, 1972.

Smith P.J., 'Site selection in the Forth Basin', Ph.D. dissertation, University of Edinburgh, 1964.

Solow R.M., 'Congestion, density and the use of land in transportation' *Swedish Journal of Economics,* no. 74, 1972, pp. 161–73.

Stegman M.A., 'Accessibility models and residential location' *Journal of American Institute of Planners,* no. 35, 1969, pp. 22–9.

Taylor P.S. and Taylor R.C., 'Socio-economic status and residential differentiation', mimeo, Centre for Research in the Social Sciences, University of Kent at Canterbury, 1971.

Timms D.W.G., *The Urban Mosaic: Towards a Theory of Residential Differentiation,* Cambridge UP, 1971.

Wabe J.S., 'A study of house prices as a means of establishing the value of journey time, the rate of time preference and the valuation of some aspects of environment in the London metropolitan region' *Applied Economics,* no. 3, 1971, pp. 247–56.

Watson J. Wreford, 'The rise and growth of Edinburgh' *An Atlas of Edinburgh,* Geographical Association, Edinburgh Branch, 1967.

Wendt P.F. and Goldner W., 'Land values and the dynamics of residential location' in Gillies J. (ed.), *Essays in Urban Land Economics,* Real Estate Research Program, UCLA, Los Angeles 1966, pp. 188–213.

Wilkinson R.K., 'The determinants of relative house prices', paper presented to the CES Urban Economics Conference, Keele 1971.

Wilkinson R.K., 'House prices and the measurement of externalities' *Economic Journal,* no. 83, 1973, pp. 72–86.

Wilkinson R.K. and Archer C.A., 'Measuring the determinants of relative house prices' *Environment and Planning,* no. 5, 1973, pp. 357–67.

Willmott P. and Young M., 'Social class and geography' in Donnison D.V. and Eversley D.E.C. (eds.), *London: Urban Patterns, Problems and Policies,* Heinemann, 1973, pp. 190–214.

Wingo L., Jr, *Transportation and Urban Land,* Resources for the Future, Johns Hopkins Press, 1961.

Yeates M.H., 'Some factors affecting the spatial distribution of Chicago land values, 1910–60' *Economic Geography,* no. 41, 1965, pp. 57–70.

Young D. et al., *Edinburgh in the Age of Reason: A Commemoration,* Edinburgh UP, 1967.

Youngson A.J., *The Making of Classical Edinburgh,* Edinburgh UP, 1966.

Name Index

Quigley, J.M.   73, 76–8, 96

Ramsøy, N.R.   158
Rex, J.   154, 155, 181
Richardson, H.W.   100, 105
Richardson, R.   2, 3
Ridker, R.G.   78, 79
Rodwin, L.   109
Russell, J.   4, 5

Saul, S.B.   69
Schnore, L.F.   97
Scott, W.   160
Seale, S.   152
Senior, M.L.   105
Smith, P.J.   3, 24, 26–9, 152
Solow, R.M.   78, 105
Stacey, M.   1
Stegman, M.A.   99, 100
Stewart, J.M.   78, 96

Taylor, J.   155
Taylor, P.S.   158
Taylor, R.   158
Timms, D.W.G.   179

Wabe, J.S.   79
Watson, J.W.   2, 3
Weber, M.   154, 155
Wendt, P.F.   75, 78, 79
Wilkinson, R.K.   73, 76–8, 96, 99
Willmott, P.   160, 162
Wilson, A.G.   105
Wingo, L. Jr.   97

Yeates, M.H.   75
Young, D.   7
Young, M.   160, 162
Youngson, A.J.   4, 6, 7, 8, 11

Subject Index

The Authors

All three authors were previously associated with the Centre for Research in the Social Sciences, University of Kent at Canterbury where the research for this book was undertaken.

Harry W. Richardson has acted as consultant to the United Nations and the OECD amongst others. He was appointed Professor of Regional and Urban Economics at the University of Pittsburg in 1974. In the summer of 1975 he became Professor of Economics and of Planning and Urban Studies at the University of Southern California, Los Angeles.

Joan Vipond has held research and lecturing posts at the Universities of Durham, Aberdeen and Kent. Between 1973 and 1975 she was employed by the Department of Urban and Regional Development of the Australian Government. She is at present lecturer in Economics at the University of New South Wales.

Robert Furbey took a first degree in Sociology at the University of Sheffield and an MA at East Anglia. He lectures in the Department of Urban and Regional Studies at Sheffield Polytechnic, teaching on the BA Housing Studies degree course.